BLACK LEADERSHIP IN AMERICA 1895–1968

STUDIES IN MODERN HISTORY

General editors: *John Morrill and David Cannadine*

Titles already published

FRANCE IN THE AGE OF HENRI IV
  Mark Greengrass
VICTORIAN RADICALISM
  Paul Adelman
WHITE SOCIETY IN THE ANTEBELLUM SOUTH
  Bruce Collins
BLACK LEADERSHIP IN AMERICA 1895–1968
  John White

BLACK LEADERSHIP IN AMERICA 1895–1968

John White

LONGMAN
London and New York

LONGMAN GROUP LIMITED
Longman House, Burnt Mill, Harlow
Essex CM20 2JE, England
Associated companies throughout the world

*Published in the United States of America
by Longman Inc., New York*

First published 1985

BRITISH LIBRARY CATALOGUING IN PUBLICATION DATA

White, John, *19— -*
  Black leadership in America 1895–1968.——
  (Studies in modern history)
  1. Afro-American leadership
  I. Title   II. Series
305.8′96073   E185.615

ISBN 0-582-49244-0

LIBRARY OF CONGRESS CATALOGING IN PUBLICATION DATA

White, John, 1939–
  Black leadership in America, 1895–1968.

  (Studies in modern history)
  Bibliography: p.
  Includes index.
  1. Afro-American leadership – History.   2. Afro-
Americans – Politics and government.   3. Afro-Americans –
Biography.   4. Black nationalism – United States – History.
5. United States – Race relations.   I. Title.   II. Series:
Studies in modern history (Longman (Firm))
E185.61.W59 1985   973′.0496022   [B]   84-20078
ISBN 0-582-49244-0 (pbk.)

Set in 10/11pt AM Times
Printed in Hong Kong by
Commonwealth Printing Press Ltd

CONTENTS

Preface   vii
Acknowledgements   ix

1. Prologue: Limited options   1
    The styles of black leadership   1
    Strategies and tactics   3

2. Introduction: black protest and accommodation,
    1800–1877   10
    Perspectives   10
    Slave resistance: leaders and followers   11
    Free blacks in the slave South: the origins of
        conservative leadership   13
    Northern blacks before the Civil War:
        the origins of radical leadership   14
    Frederick Douglass (1817–1895): from militancy to
        conservatism   18
    Frederick Douglass and Booker T. Washington   20

3. Booker T. Washington (1856–1915): black enigma   23
    Separate but unequal: Southern race relations, 1865–1915.   23
    Booker T. Washington: early life   27
    Tuskegee   29
    The Atlanta Compromise Address   32
    Up From Slavery   34
    Black leader   35
    Washington and the wider world   37
    Washington and his black critics   38

4. W. E. B. Du Bois (1868–1963): talented propagandist   44
    Northern blacks organize for protest, 1890–1910   44
    The rise of the NAACP   46
    W. E. B. Du Bois: curriculum vitae   48
    The education of W. E. B. Du Bois   49

Crisis editor   56
'A Negro Nation Within a Nation'   57
Du Bois and pan-Africanism   58
'A Leader Without Followers': W. E. B. Du Bois,
   1934–1963'   61

5. Marcus Garvey (1880–1940): ghetto messiah   68
Waiting for Garvey? The northern ghetto, 1900–1920   68
Harlem   69
The National Urban League   70
Marcus Garvey: black Jamaican   72
Garveyism   80
Garvey and his black critics   83
Du Bois and Garvey   89

6. Malcolm X (1925–1965): sinner and convert   98
Black nationalism after Garvey: the separatist impulse,
   1930–1966   98
Malcolm Little and Malcolm X   103
The Nation of Islam   104
Malcolm X: Black Muslim   107
Malcolm X: Muslim   110
The Autobiography of Malcolm X   114
Malcolm X and his black critics   118

7. Martin Luther King, Jr (1929–1968): apostle for
non-violence   121

A New Deal for blacks? Civil rights and Negro protest,
   1932–1954   121
The Second World War   123
CORE   124
Martin Luther King, Jr: militant clergyman   126
MLK and JFK   133
SCLC in action   134
Chicago and Vietnam   139
King's reflections on four black leaders   143

8. Conclusion: the limits of black leadership since 1968   149

9. Epilogue: black leadership: continuities and contrasts   153

Booker T. Washington   156
W. E. B. Du Bois   159
Marcus Garvey   161
Malcolm X   163
Martin Luther King, Jr   165

Bibliographical essay   165

Index   179

PREFACE

For the past fifteen years, I have been teaching courses in Afro-American history to British and American undergraduates. This period saw a growing scholarly interest in all phases of the black experience in the United States: the origins of racism, the character of Negro slavery, black responses to servitude and freedom, the evolution of a distinctive Afro-American culture, the aims and achievements of the civil rights movement after 1945, and the emergence, by the 1960s, of more militant black protest. No student of the United States can any longer be unaware of the broad outlines of this scholarship, or of the contemporary significance of the unresolved issues of race and class in America, and the world at large.

This book reflects my belief that a study of those pre-eminent Negro leaders who commanded national and international attention in the century following the American Civil War, will reveal some of the continuities and contrasts in black reactions to unremitting white racism. A work of synthesis and explication it will, I hope, encourage readers to consult more specialized articles and monographs. Inevitably, it draws upon a large body of Afro-American historiography, the main contributions of which are cited in the Bibliographical essay. But it is also drawn from my experiences as a teacher, and the suggestions of students and colleagues on both sides of the Atlantic.

Although not intended as a survey of black American history in the twentieth century, I have tried to set these leaders against the economic, intellectual, political and social climate of the periods during which they achieved prominence. Throughout, I have tried to keep in mind the cautionary observation of H. Cruse that:

> Individual leaders can project ideologies of many different kinds and colour them with the hues of their own personal aspirations which very often obscure the very fundamental issues which are of crucial interest to the people for whom the leaders speak. Then the historians come along

and completely overlook or forget what the basic issues were for the people in the mass, and centre their attention on the personal characteristics of these leaders.[1]

JOHN WHITE
University of Hull
March, 1984

1. Harold Cruse, *Rebellion or Revolution* (New York, 1968), p. 157.

ACKNOWLEDGEMENTS

We are grateful to the following for permission to reproduce copyright material:

Hutchinson Publishing Group Ltd & Paul R. Reynolds Inc for extracts from *Malcolm X: Autobiography 1968–80* by Alex Haley; author's agents (Joan Daves) for extracts from speeches 1957, 1968 and 'I Have a Dream' by Martin Luther King Jr. Copyright © 1957, 1963 by Martin Luther King Jr. 1968 Estate of Martin Luther King Jr; Bobbs Merrill Co Inc for an extract from p xxxvii *Black Protest Thought in the 20th Century* (1971), by Meier, Rudwick & Broderick.

To the memories of my father, Norman White (1910–1978) and
Carol Kaplan White (1939–1978)

Chapter one

PROLOGUE: LIMITED OPTIONS

Since power and prestige are scarce commodities in the Negro
community, the struggle for leadership often becomes ruthless.
(Gunnar Myrdal, *An American Dilemma*)[1]

American Negro history is basically a history of the conflict between
integrationist and nationalist forces in politics, economics, and culture,
no matter what leaders are involved and what slogans are used.
(Harold Cruse, *The Crisis of the Negro Intellectual*)[2]

... the problem of Negro leadership ... has always been extremely
delicate, dangerous, and complex. The term itself becomes remarkably
difficult to define, the moment one realizes that the real role of the
Negro leader, in the eyes of the American Republic, was not to make the
Negro a first-class citizen but to keep him content as a second-class one.
(James Baldwin, 'The dangerous road before Martin Luther King')[3]

THE STYLES OF BLACK LEADERSHIP

In the quest for racial equality, civil and political rights, economic and
educational advancement, black Americans, both during and after
slavery, responded to the proposals and rhetoric of leaders drawn from
their own ranks. Yet one of the anomalies of Afro-American history is
that as an ethnic group, blacks have had only limited opportunities to
select their own leaders. Frederick Douglass, an ex-slave and the most
famous black abolitionist, was initially thrust into public gaze by his
white supporters. Booker T. Washington, also an ex-slave, owed his
elevation to such influential patrons as Theodore Roosevelt and the
industrialist-turned-philanthropist, Andrew Carnegie. W. E. B. Du Bois
became a key figure in the National Association for the Advancement of
Coloured People (NAACP) only with the approval of upper-class white

reformers of the Progressive era. Of the black leaders under consideration, only Marcus Garvey and Martin Luther King, Jr, owed their rise to the reception accorded them by blacks. But both were also perceived, if not sanctioned, by whites as the leaders of their respective movements. Malcolm X, it can be argued, gained his reputation as much from the publicity he received from the white-controlled media as from the approval of his black followers. Whatever their ideological complexion, black leaders in the United States historically have depended on white as well as on Negro recognition of their claims to speak for their race.

> All leaders have had to contend with a caste-like arrangement separating the races, defying all strategies. ... In practice ... blacks were not accepted as part of the political process; even where they were allowed to vote they were not given entree to the political machinery. ... Caste is the principal determinant of any discussion of historical Afro-American leadership. ... There was no expectation that a black leadership would arise from the people and be selected and sustained by them. ... Three characteristics marked the black leader: he did not derive his power from a democratic source, he was a self-styled exemplar, and his position was tenuous and vulnerable.[4]

Writing in 1944, the Swedish sociologist, Gunnar Myrdal, suggested that the extreme positions of Negro leadership behaviour on behalf of blacks as a subordinate caste were those of *accommodation* and *protest*.

> Accommodation is undoubtedly stronger than protest, especially in the South, where the structure of caste is most pervasive and unyielding. ... The white caste has an obvious interest in trying to have accommodating leaders to help them control the Negro group. ... On the other side of the caste gulf, the Negroes need persons to establish contact with the influential people in the white group. ... The Negroes in the South are dependent upon the whites not only for a share in the public services, but individually for small favours and personal protection in a social order determined almost exclusively by the whites ... the individual Negro who becomes known to have contact with substantial white people gains prestige and influence among Negroes for this reason. ... The Negro leader in this setting serves a 'function' to both castes and his influence in both groups is cumulative – prestige in the Negro community being an effect as well as a cause of prestige among the whites.[5]

Similarly, in the Northern states, government agencies, political parties and philanthropic organizations made 'contact' with the Negro community through white-appointed (or approved) black 'leaders' or observers. And:

> Leadership conferred upon a Negro by whites raises his class status in the Negro community. Correspondingly ... an upper-class position in the Negro community nearly automatically gives a Negro the role of Negro

leader. He is expected to act according to this role by both whites and Negroes.[6]

Much of the competitiveness and opportunism of Negro leadership has derived from this need to satisfy the demands of both white supporters and black constituents. Again, the agitation of black 'radicals' has often served to legitimate the claims of more 'moderate' Negro leaders in the eyes of white Americans. Thus personal as well as ideological rivalries have had positive effects in the struggle for racial equality. Yet 'leadership' has not been confined to individuals – however exceptional. In the twentieth century, the rise of national protest organizations like the NAACP, the National Urban League, the Congress of Racial Equality, the Southern Christian Leadership Conference, and the Student Nonviolent Coordinating Committee have provided a collective – and élitist – leadership for black Americans. Again, however, prominent members of these organizations have been designated as 'leaders' simply 'by virtue of their places in the organizations, ignoring the question of the base of their support in the Afro-American population'.[7] But whatever their measure of popular support, black leaders, despite variations in behaviour in different times and in different places, have all necessarily operated within what one historian has called 'a politics of limited options'.[8]

STRATEGIES AND TACTICS

Before the American Civil War, free blacks in the Northern states, although subject to widespread discrimination and a variety of proscriptions, agitated for the destruction of slavery, and the granting of civil liberties to the black population residing in those states where slavery had been abolished. Black spokesmen like David Walker, who issued his inflammatory *Appeal* from Boston in 1829, called on Southern slaves to strike for their freedom by violent insurrection. In 1843, Henry Highland Garnet, a former slave, urged his fellow black delegates at the National Convention of Coloured Citizens, held in Buffalo, New York, to endorse the violent overthrow of slavery. Frederick Douglass, by common assent the outstanding black leader of the nineteenth century, and also an ex-slave, became disenchanted with the paternalism and pacifism of that wing of the abolitionist movement led by William Lloyd Garrison, and supported the Union cause in the Civil War which, he hoped, would destroy slavery. During the war, he urged blacks to volunteer for the armed forces, despite the existence of racial discrimination and segregation. Such a course of action, Douglass hoped, would demonstrate the loyalty of Negroes to the Union, and

3

accelerate their achievement of civil equality. Other Northern black leaders, however, viewed racial equality as a dream impossible of realization, and advocated the emigration of Negroes to Africa, Central or South America as the only solution to implacable white racism.

Within the slave South, black resistance to servitude took many forms, ranging from open rebellion and secret conspiracy, malingering, feigned illness, running away and sabotage, to the more metaphysical forms of 'resistance' offered by black religion and the culture of the slave quarters. The free black caste within the South, although never providing overall leadership for slave resistance, succeeded in gaining a strong sense of collective worth and identity through the founding of religious, fraternal and educational institutions. Denied political rights, including the right to agitate, free blacks in the Old South developed an accommodating and conservative ideology of racial advancement. These patterns continued into the post-Civil War period to a remarkable extent. Militant proposals (within the context of their times) for combating persistent white prejudice and discrimination came out of the Northern states. More cautious, conciliatory and diplomatic proposals for effecting racial improvement continued to impress Southern blacks, aware of the dangers posed by virulent white racism, as well as the continued existence of various forms of involuntary servitude. Moreover, as recent studies indicate, black political leaders in the former Confederate states – both during and after Reconstruction – comprised disproportionate numbers of those who had been antebellum free persons of colour, or former slaves who had occupied relatively privileged positions. Again, such leaders, whatever their degree of black support, needed the goodwill of white leaders or political factions.

> Overall, the typical late nineteenth century black political leader in the South was a moderate. All were practical men who saw the necessity of compromise. They were also ambitious men who needed white support to advance themselves and the interests of their black constituents. Even the most militant spokesmen ... found astute compromise essential to obtain the benefits desired either personally or for the race.[9]

Myrdal observed the strategies and tactics employed by black leaders in general, and their variants as utilized by those living above the Mason-Dixon line sixty years after the end of Reconstruction. He concluded that the successful black leader necessarily became 'a consummate manipulator. Getting the white man to do what he wants becomes a fine art. ... The Negro leader gets a satisfaction out of his performance and feels pride in his skill in flattering, beguiling, and outwitting the white man.' But there was also a real danger that the Southern black leader would become simply a self-seeker and an opportunist, 'having constantly to compromise with his pride and dignity'. Northern black leaders, in contrast, beneficiaries of a long tradition of sanctioned protest, were both able and expected to produce displays of 'actual opposition' to white racism, and with less fear of retaliation from angered whites. But whether they operated in a repressive or more relaxed environment, black leaders, Myrdal noted, had often been engaged in a similar 'keen and destructive personal rivalry'.[10] (He was, however, quick to add that 'national Negro leadership is no more corrupt nor more ridden with personal envy and rivalry than any other national leadership'.)[11]

In the twentieth century, five black spokesmen have gained recognition as the outstanding advocates and ideologues of competing forms of racial advancement. After the death of Frederick Douglass in 1895, Booker T. Washington (1856–1915), as even his most bitter critics conceded, was the nationally acknowledged leader of American Negroes. The most powerful and influential black leader of his day, Washington remains a complex and ambiguous figure. 'No other leader in black history has been so closely identified with doctrines that weakened his people's aspiration for freedom, that urged them instead to make a virtue of their disadvantage.'[12] Born a slave, Washington urged the building of black character and responsibility, and was well versed in the racial mores and etiquette of the South, able to turn white patronage and paternalism to his advantage.

> As principal and founder of Tuskegee Institute, he was clearly working for the uplift of the freedman; he was a demonstrated builder, leader and administrator. ... Tuskegee was a black institution (although supported by white funds) and its principles and goals seemed to accept and validate the de facto system of racial castes. ... while Washington did not have a power base in a political sense, he had in Tuskegee an institutional base which freed him from primary dependency on anyone's political fortunes.[13]

Any assessment of the black experience after slavery must reckon with this enigmatic and controversial educator, activist and interracial diplomat.

During the last twelve years of his life, Washington encountered in William Edward Burghardt Du Bois (1868–1963), his most articulate and distinguished black opponent. A New Englander by birth, Du Bois gained a Harvard Ph.D., and became a prototypical member of and spokesman for the 'Talented Tenth' – the intellectual black élite which, he believed, would provide leadership for the race. Dedicated to the acquisition of civil rights for blacks and initially favouring racial integration, Du Bois joined with Northern black militants like Monroe Trotter and with liberal whites to challenge Washington's hegemony. As poet, novelist, sociologist, historian and a founding member of the NAACP (and editor of its publication, *Crisis*), Du Bois emerged from his public indictment of Washington as the propagandist of the Negro protest movement.

When Du Bois criticized Booker T. Washington, it was in part for his tendency to stand mute before the great indignities against black people. But, more pointedly, Du Bois attacked Washington's programme of education because it lacked any sense of a need to train a black leadership. .... As a reformist, antagonistic to caste arrangements, Du Bois wanted a cadre of college- and university-trained men and women who would challenge customary racial attitudes. It may have been unfortunate that Du Bois used the term 'talented tenth' to describe this group of leaders, because he has since been accused of élitism as against the assumed humility of Washington. Certainly, Du Bois was élitist in that he expected that only highly intelligent and educated black leaders could design and bring about effective reform. But Booker T. Washington was élitist in his own way, believing that blacks needed to be lifted up and that men like himself would be their models.[14]

While neither Washington nor Du Bois ever commanded a mass following among blacks, Marcus Garvey (1880–1940), achieved that distinction in the course of his short but spectacular American career. A declared disciple of Booker T. Washington, Garvey, a Jamaican, was the leading black nationalist in America in the period during and immediately after the First World War. Pledged to the liberation of Africa from white colonial rule, the inculcation of racial pride in Afro-Americans and the separation of the races in America, Garvey's racial philosophy, his successes and failures, attracted the scorn and ridicule of Du Bois to an extent that made his earlier differences with Washington appear comparatively innocuous. Garvey returned Du Bois' enmity (and that of other American black leaders) with interest and enthusiasm. Where Washington had spoken for a Southern black peasantry, and Du Bois for a growing Northern black urban bourgeoisie, Garvey capitalized on the depressed condition of the urban black population, confined to the physical and psychological constraints of the ghetto. Although Garvey's American career was brief, it reflected the rise of a black ghetto, Harlem, as the most important Negro settlement in the United States. Moreover, his influence persisted into the 1960s, with the re-emergence of militant black nationalism, symbolized by the slogan 'Black Power', with its connotations of racial assertiveness, separatism and pride in the alleged African cultural heritage of Afro-Americans.

Although the black socialist A. Philip Randolph's March on Washington Movement during the Second World War signalled the shift of black leadership towards direct action protest, not until the dramatic appearance of the Negro clergyman Martin Luther King, Jr (1929–68), during the Montgomery, Alabama, bus boycott of 1955, did another black American leader command national (and international) attention. The exponent and practitioner of non-violent direct action in the cause of racial integration, King (like Booker T. Washington, a Southerner) became, by common consent, the personification and symbol of the civil rights movement which had as its goal the realization of racial democracy in America.

> Although King had a mass following, his non-violent strategy had clear class implications. In his efforts to abolish segregationist laws and practices, King organized demonstrations that emphasized the respectability of the demonstrators. ... Indeed, King's middle-class respectability made him the choice of black leaders in Montgomery to be spokesman for the bus boycott. His credentials were impeccable. With his prominent family background, good education, and doctoral degree, King was an intellectual who spoke with an elegance certain to impress even the southern aristocracy. King's leadership was symbolic of the middle-class character of the early civil rights movement.[15]

But, towards the end of his life, King (like Du Bois) expanded his vision to project a coalition of the underprivileged, black and white. He also became a notable critic of growing American involvement in Vietnam. Ironically, King delivered his famous 'I have a dream' oration, the climax of the 1963 civil rights March on Washington, as Du Bois died in self-imposed exile in Ghana.

Like all other black leaders, King had his rivals and detractors. Malcolm X (1925–65), born Malcolm Little, was, like Martin Luther King, a preacher – for a significant period of his life, the leading spokesman for the separatist Nation of Islam (the Black Muslims). After his break with the Nation, on doctrinal and personal grounds, Malcolm X became the best-known (and certainly the most notorious) ideologue for black militancy and racial separatism. He was also an admirer of Marcus Garvey. Where King espoused non-violence and the redemptive value of love and suffering, Malcolm X appeared to condone, if not actively promote, racial warfare. The Black Power slogan and the subsequent rise of such extremist groups as the Black Panther Party were offshoots of Malcolm X's black nationalism. Like Garvey, Malcolm X struck a responsive chord among the black population of the urban ghettos; like Martin Luther King, he was to die a violent death, with his attitudes undergoing significant change.

> By the time of his assassination in 1965, he had become convinced that American capitalism was dying. Having reconsidered his earlier views that all whites were devils, he remained only a few steps from an awareness of the common oppression of the poor, white as well as black.[16]

After the deaths of King and Malcolm X, no black leader attained their stature or influence, as perceived either by whites or blacks. In 1980, the magazine *Black Enterprise* reported after a poll of 5,000 readers that 'over the last ten years, the absence of clear-cut leadership has been the single most noticeable handicap of the black struggle for equality'. The death in 1981 of Roy Wilkins, who had served as executive director of the NAACP for twenty-two years, and the resignation of Vernon Jordan, president of the National Urban League for the previous ten years, came at a time of increasing demoralization and frustration within the already fragmented civil rights movement. After its successful campaigns to end segregation in public accommodations and transportation, and the gaining of legal guarantees of civil and voting rights, the civil rights movement (fundamentally concerned with economic issues) saw a sharp decline in political influence after the conservative Reagan administration took office. (In 1980, the average black family income was $15,806, as against $24,939 for whites; unemployment rates for blacks were three times as great as those for whites.)

But some Negroes view the absence of one or two dominant national leaders as a sign of racial progress. With nearly 200 black mayors of American cities, and rapid increases in the numbers of blacks within the professions and business corporations, black leadership, they assert, has taken a more collective form. As Willie Dennis, the Negro speaker of California's state assembly remarked in 1981:

> Now the politicians who are black are providing one aspect of black leadership, the religious community another, the professional organizations another. This adds up to even greater institutional change than could ever have been brought about by a Martin Luther King rally.[17]

In 1984, black Americans, for the first time, were able to vote for a serious black contender for the Democratic Party's presidential nomination. The Reverend Jesse Jackson, a Baptist minister, was a member of the Southern Christian Leadership Conference, and a follower of Martin Luther King.

The following chapters attempt to summarize and evaluate the contributions of Frederick Douglass, Booker T. Washington, Marcus Garvey, Malcolm X and Martin Luther King to the black protest in America, as perceived by themselves, their contemporaries and historians. None of these black leaders ever held (or aspired to) high political office, but as one black historian has observed:

> Those leaders who lacked political clout – Booker T. Washington, W. E. B. Du Bois, A. Philip Randolph, Martin Luther King, Malcolm X – embodied a vision, passion, and integrity that are generally lacking in the political mechanic.[18]

By placing their racial philosophies and leadership strategies in historical context, this study should illustrate the themes of continuity and change in black leadership proposals and demands from the late nineteenth century to the split within the civil rights coalition of the 1960s. In effect, the continuity will be seen to lie in persistent black protest against the inequities of a caste system in a democratic society. Change will be evident in the varying connotations of such seminal concepts as 'integration', 'separatism', 'accommodation' and 'protest'. In brief, the intention is to provide, within short compass, both individual and interrelated biographies of these major figures in the American and Afro-American experience.

REFERENCES

1. Myrdal, G., *An American Dilemma* (New York, 1944), p. 775.
2. Cruse H., *The Crisis of the Negro Intellectual: from its origins to the present* (New York, 1967), p. 564.
3. Baldwin J., 'The dangerous road before Martin Luther King', in C. E. Lincoln (ed.) *Martin Luther King, Jr: a profile* (New York, 1970), pp. 106–7.
4. Huggins, N., 'Afro-Americans', in J. Higham (ed.) *Ethnic Leadership in America* (The Johns Hopkins U.P., 1978), pp. 95–8.
5. Myrdal, op. cit., p. 722.
6. Myrdal, op. cit., p. 727.
7. Huggins, op. cit., p. 94.
8. Gerber, D. A., 'A politics of limited options: Northern black politics and the problem of change and continuity in race relations historiography', *Journal of Social History,* 14(1980–81), 235–55.
9. Meier, A., 'Afterword: new perspectives on the nature of black political leadership during Reconstruction', in H. N. Rabinowitz (ed.) *Southern Black Leaders of the Reconstruction Era* (University of Illinois Press, 1982), p. 402.
10. Myrdal, op. cit., pp. 773, 778.
11. Myrdal, op. cit., p. 779.
12. Anderson, J., 'The shadow of Booker T. Washington', *New York Review of Books,* 9 Aug. 1973, p. 34.
13. Huggins, op. cit., p. 98
14. Huggins, op. cit., pp. 102–3.
15. Horton, J. O. and Horton, L. E., 'Race and class', *American Quarterly,* 35(1983), 156.
16. Horton and Horton, op. cit., p. 157.
17. *Time,* 21 Sept. 1981, p. 31.
18. Huggins, op. cit., p. 114.

Chapter two

INTRODUCTION: BLACK PROTEST AND ACCOMMODATION, 1800–1877

Get the blacks started, and if you do not have a gang of tigers and lions to deal with, I am a deceiver of the blacks and of the whites. If you commence, make sure work – do not trifle, for they will not trifle with you – they want us for their slaves, and they think nothing of murdering us in order to subject us to that wretched condition – therefore, if there is an attempt made by us, kill or be killed.

(David Walker's *Appeal*)[1]

Many free Negroes, especially the élite, depended on white protectors to reduce the risks of living in a slave society and to improve their chances for material prosperity. They strengthened their relationships with whites by patronizing white merchants and tradesmen – and thereby retarding the development of Negro-owned businesses – by keeping whites informed of the activities of the more rebellious blacks, and by deferring to whites on all occasions. In doing so, they satisfied the paternalistic pretensions of upper-class whites. ... In seeking security from whites, free Negroes implicitly renounced their objections to the Southern caste system.

(Ira Berlin, *Slaves Without Masters: the free Negro in the antebellum South*)[2]

PERSPECTIVES

The varied responses of black Americans to their subordinate position in American society extend back to the establishment of racial slavery in the colonial period. In the era following the American Revolution – which both strengthened the institution of slavery and heightened black aspirations for freedom and equality – these responses continued and multiplied. Negro slaves and 'free people of colour', North and South, resisted or made some kind of accommodation to enslavement, supported or dismissed proposals for black repatriation or colonization overseas, challenged or adapted to emerging patterns of racial segregation, embraced or rejected notions of their African cultural heritage, favoured or discounted alliances with whites and, from the 1830s, in the Negro Convention and abolitionist movements, attacked all forms of racial discrimination. In the century after the Emancipation Proclamation of 1863, black leaders and organizations, with or without white approval and support, continued the struggle against the inequities of the caste system which had replaced slavery. Their differing ideological premises also continued to reflect those of earlier black leaders. The career of Frederick Douglass, which spanned the events and issues of the Civil War and its aftermath, will serve to illustrate the possibilities and pitfalls of black leadership in an American Republic devoted to the principles of white supremacy, and one which effectively denied to blacks the rights to life, liberty and the pursuit of happiness.

SLAVE RESISTANCE: LEADERS AND FOLLOWERS

Slaves in the antebellum South protested against their condition by acts of outright physical resistance and more subtle forms of non-cooperation – feigned illness and stupidity, arson, neglect of crops and livestock – with their owners. Recent scholarship suggests that slaves also 'resisted' the damaging psychological effects of servitude through their creation of a distinctive and dynamic folk culture, which drew part of its form and much of its content and function from Africa. Folk-tales, music, dance and, above all, the religious songs of the slaves – the spirituals – with their selective adaptation of the symbols and texts of Christianity, offered slaves some protection against the dehumanizing effects of their situation. Again, it is now generally agreed, the master–slave relationship was more complex, many-sided and open to adjustment and compromise than was once imagined. To a surprising extent, slaves controlled their masters, and asserted their claims to be given fair treatment. American slaves also enjoyed a better material standard of living than their counterparts in other New World slave societies, and succeeded in maintaining a community spirit, marked by a sense of obligation to fellow bondsmen, a strong sense of family and kinship ties, and a pride in ancestry. For these reasons, in addition to a realistic awareness of the superior strength of the surrounding white population, slaves in the American South (unlike their Latin American and Caribbean counterparts) did not engage in full-scale or frequent revolts. Slave 'leaders' – parents, preachers, those thought to possess special powers – generally encouraged more passive forms of 'resistance': the strengthening of community and family bonds, the comforts offered by a partially autonomous religion, and the cultivation of internal constraints against external white pressures. In at least three notable instances, however, black leaders in the slave South demonstrated their capacity to plan uprisings against a system designed for their permanent exploitation and subjugation.

In 1800, Gabriel Prosser, a slave in Henrico County, Virginia, organized a conspiracy among his fellow slaves, aimed at overthrowing slavery and establishing a black state. A small guerilla force of about 200 men was to enter Richmond, capture arms, overcome the white population and take the governor hostage. Prosser, a skilled blacksmith who was probably literate, was familiar with the Scriptures, and with the ideals inspired by the French Revolution. His plan involved the systematic allocation of tasks to various individuals, the calculation of the number of slaves likely to support the rebellion, and clandestine meetings to formulate strategy and tactics. The conspiracy was betrayed to the Virginia authorities by two of Prosser's slave followers, the incipient revolt was crushed, and Prosser, along with thirty of his followers, was executed. Despite its failure, Prosser's conspiracy helped to fasten the fear of slave revolt on the mind of the white South.

The second significant nineteenth-century slave conspiracy was that inspired and organized by Denmark Vesey, in and around Charleston, South Carolina, in 1822. Vesey, a former slave who had managed to purchase his freedom, was a deeply religious man, and a leading member of the African Methodist Episcopal Church. Inspired by the Old Testament accounts of Jewish enslavement and persecution, Vesey saw himself as a black Moses, destined to lead his people out of bondage. He also hoped to secure external aid from the West Indies and Africa to maintain an independent black state. Again, the conspiracy was betrayed, over 130 of the alleged participants were arrested, and 35, including Vesey, were executed. Although Vesey does not appear to have had any clear idea as to the form and structure of the state that he wished to establish with the overthrow of slavery, his conspiracy, like that of Prosser, demonstrated that slaves and former slaves in the Old South possessed the capacities for leadership, and the ability to attract followers.

Nat Turner, a Virginia slave, was to lead the most dramatic nineteenth-century slave revolt in Southampton County, Virginia, in 1831. The son of an African-born slave mother, Turner was moved to violence by the events and mystical experiences of his childhood and youth. Like Vesey, Turner drew upon an apocalyptic version of Christian doctrine, together with revelations and prophetic visions, to justify his actions. Notwithstanding the fact that he had been kindly treated by his master, Joseph Travis, Turner and his slave followers murdered the Travis family and about fifty other whites before the state militia put down the insurrection. Turner, after eluding capture for several weeks, was tried and hanged in November 1831. His revolt terrified the white South, prompted the Virginia legislature to discuss the possibility of ending slavery (the motion was defeated), and, largely due to the fictional portrayal of the episode by the Southern white novelist William Styron in *The Confessions of Nat Turner* (1967) provided a generation of black militants (despite their rejection of Styron's depiction of Turner himself) with an authentic hero and slave leader.

FREE BLACKS IN THE SLAVE SOUTH: THE ORIGINS OF CONSERVATIVE LEADERSHIP

Free negroes occupied ambiguous, complex and precarious positions in New World slave societies. The very existence of 'free people of colour' seemed to invalidate the equation between bondage and blackness, and profoundly affected the nature of slavery and the pattern of race relations – before and after general emancipation – in particular countries. At one remove from slavery, free blacks in the South (by 1860 there were nearly half a million free blacks in the United States, approximately half of them in the slave states) exhibited class, colour and denominational divisions, tended to avoid alliances with slaves, and were generally dependent on white patronage and goodwill for their survival and advancement. In dealing with free Negroes, Southern whites demonstrated their ambivalent attitudes towards an anomalous group, and in attempting to control the free black population, rehearsed many of the laws and practices which would be applied to all Southern blacks after the Civil War. In turn, free blacks created their own distinctive institutions and, by their very existence, offered an alternative life-style and condition to which slaves could aspire.

Largely the creation of the American Revolution (when both the British and the colonists offered blacks freedom as a reward for military service), self-purchase and manumission by masters, Southern free blacks throughout the antebellum period faced increasing repression and discrimination in a society pledged to the continuance of its 'peculiar institution' of Negro slavery. Manumission became progressively more difficult from the Upper to the Lower South, and free blacks also faced the danger of being kidnapped and sold into slavery. Usually more skilled, better educated and lighter skinned than the mass of slaves, free blacks who worked as farmhands, craftsmen, artisans and small tradesmen, also faced economic competition from slaves and white immigrants. While free blacks and slaves had much in common – colour, family ties, work experiences and church membership – there were also conflicting pressures which effectively weakened any strong sense of racial unity and precluded a slave-free black alliance for the overthrow of white hegemony. However degraded or uncertain their position in Southern society, free blacks could not help but be aware that their prospects for survival, as well as for economic advancement, depended on their ability and willingness to distinguish themselves, in the eyes of whites, from the mass of slaves. Again, wealthy and light-skinned free Negroes shunned the African churches, benevolent and fraternal organizations favoured by darker and poorer free blacks, and formed their own exclusive clubs and organizations. With the general emancipation which followed Confederate defeat in 1865, prominent free blacks of the pre-war period maintained their position as an élite, and served as congressmen and state legislators during Reconstruction. They also continued to favour the cautious and conciliatory racial policies which they had practised and perfected during slavery. Despite the fact that Denmark Vesey had been a free black, Southern free blacks, as a caste, displayed conservative rather than radical tendencies. 'When free Negroes assumed leadership after the war, they often continued this same cautious strategy of race improvement.'[3]

NORTHERN BLACKS BEFORE THE CIVIL WAR: THE ORIGINS OF RADICAL LEADERSHIP

As in the South, the free black population of the Northern states was greatly enlarged by the events and ideology of the American Revolution. The Northern colonies had used slaves, in a variety of occupations, but had never constituted a slave society, and the intellectual ferment of the Revolutionary era, grounded in natural rights philosophy, was seen as inimical to the perpetuation of racial slavery. Northern white workers protested against the slaves' competitive position in the labour market, and the rise of early and effective abolitionist agitation in the Northern colonies and states furnished other reasons for the emancipation of the slave population. As a consequence of these disparate factors, by 1804 every Northern state had provided for the eventual abolition of slavery. By the mid 1820s, the Northern and Southern states of the Union were clearly distinguishable in their attitudes to slavery, but not in their attitudes towards blacks. Alexis de Tocqueville, visiting America in the 1830s, observed:

> The prejudice of race appears to be stronger in the states which have abolished slavery than in those where it still exists; and nowhere is it so important as in those states where servitude has never been known.

Recent studies have confirmed the accuracy of Tocqueville's impressions. Anti-Negro sentiment and legislation in the states of the

North-east and the territories of the West, marked the period from the early 1800s down to the Civil War. In many respects, the condition of the free black population of the North was similar to that of the South. Nearly every Northern state barred blacks from voting, serving in the militia or receiving more than a rudimentary education. Racial segregation was evident in all forms of transportation, and in hotels, restaurants, prisons, hospitals and cemeteries. Minstrel shows – the most popular form of entertainment in nineteenth-century America – conveyed romanticized images of plantation slavery and crude caricatures of the alleged stupidity, fecklessness and gullibility of Northern free blacks. Ironically, free blacks in the North now became frozen on the bottom rungs of the economic ladder as they faced increasing competition from white immigrants. But in one respect at least, Northern blacks possessed – and utilized – an advantage not shared by their Southern counterparts. The expansion of the North's white population, which increased at a faster rate than its black population, provided whites with a sense of security unknown to white Southerners. Northern blacks, were, therefore, allowed to retain certain basic civil liberties – the right to petition for redress of grievances, to publish their own journals and newspapers, and to engage in political protest and activities.

In 1827, a group of black New Yorkers founded *Freedom's Journal,* the first black newspaper, edited by John Russwurm and Samuel Cornish. Their paper attacked the American Colonization Society, established in 1816, asserting that its real aim was the strengthening of slavery by the removal of the free black population from the United States. Similarly, Richard Allen, a Philadelphia-born slave who had purchased his freedom in 1777, the year of his conversion to Methodism, quickly rejected the church's discriminatory treatment of its black members. From his base in Philadelphia, and in the face of white hostility, Allen concluded that only a separate church, served by black clergy, could meet the spiritual and temporal needs of the free Negro. He began to organize and implement a black version of Wesleyanism, became the first black bishop of the African Methodist Episcopal Church and organized the first meeting of the National Negro Convention movement in 1830. Unable to condone slave violence, Allen provided the organizational structure for black abolitionism, and inspired free blacks in other parts of the North to establish their own churches. Important in their own right, Allen's career and achievements also provided a notable nineteenth-century precedent for black clerical leadership in the struggle for racial justice.

After 1830, and the rise of militant moral abolitionism, represented most notably by William Lloyd Garrison, Northern blacks (who subscribed to the first issues of Garrison's newspaper, *The Liberator*) supported the aims of the movement: the ending of slavery and the eradication of racial prejudice in the nation at large. This involvement in the abolitionist movement brought black leaders to national attention, and added a sense of urgency to the cause which it had previously lacked. David Walker, Boston agent for *Freedom's Journal,* issued his *Appeal* in 1829 – a nineteenth-century Black Power manifesto, urging Southern slaves to strike for their freedom, as it laid bare the cruelties inflicted on blacks 'by the enlightened Christians of America'. In 1843, Henry Highland Garnet, a former slave, informed delegates to the National Convention of Coloured Citizens at Buffalo, New York, that slaves would be justified in using violence to gain their freedom. Echoing Walker, Garnet, in his 'Address to the Slaves of the United States of America' exhorted them:

> Brethren, arise, arise! Strike for your lives and liberties. You cannot be more oppressed than you have been – you cannot suffer greater cruelties than you have already. Rather die free men than live to be slaves. Remember that you are FOUR MILLIONS. Let your motto be resistance! resistance! RESISTANCE!

Such aggressive and uncompromising sentiments effectively separated black from white abolitionists, most of whom, following Garrison's lead, declared themselves pacifists, and saw their call for emancipation as an appeal to reason, an exercise in moral suasion. Although blacks came to form separate abolitionist organizations, their earlier alliance with white reformers set significant precedents for interracial cooperation in the cause of civil rights, which were to be revived by the formation of the NAACP and the National Urban League, in the early twentieth century (see Ch. 4 and 5).

Increasingly, after 1830, Northern blacks denounced segregated schools as unequal and inferior, and demanded educational integration. The Negro Convention Movement – a Northern phenomenon until after the Civil War – also operated sporadically from 1830 to 1860. Early conventions, attended by Negro ministers, lawyers, businessmen and physicians, lodged protests against slavery and the proscriptions which faced free blacks. Delegates to these conventions, with the support of participating white abolitionists, supported the creation of manual labour schools for both blacks and whites. As the white-dominated abolitionist movement became split between its moral suasionist and political activist wings, while continuing to display racist assumptions and attitudes, the Negro Convention Movement became more militant, and endorsed independent black protest against disfranchisement and segregation. Although the convention movement failed to secure mass support for any one strategy – cooperation with whites, independent action or emigrationism – or to achieve black political, social or economic equality, it provided forums, at the state and national levels, for a developing free black leadership class. Again, earlier than white abolitionists, blacks denounced the thinly veiled racism of the American Colonization Society, and supported two basic elements of the dominant racial ideology of the nineteenth century: racial equality and integration within the United States.

Yet there were also dissenting black voices. During the 1850s, Alexander Crummel, Samuel Ringgold Ward, Henry Highland Garnet and Martin R. Delany rejected their earlier support for continuing the fight for racial justice in America, and advocated emigration and colonization for blacks. Of this group, Martin R. Delany became the leading spokesman for black nationalism and black emigrationism in the two decades preceding the Civil War. Born in Charleston, Virginia, in 1812, the grandson of slaves, Delany was proud of his African ancestry. By the age of forty, Delany had embarked on successful careers in medicine and journalism. In 1852, he published his best-known work, *The Condition, Elevation, Emigration, and Destiny of the Coloured People of the United States,* in which he declared of American Negroes: 'We are a nation within a nation: as the Poles in Russia, the Hungarians in Austria, the Welsh, Irish and Scotch in the British dominions.' Opposed to black emigration to Liberia, as proposed by the American Colonization Society, Delany advocated the establishment of an autonomous black state in East Africa to which black Americans could emigrate. (He later declared his preference for the West Indies, Central and South America as offering better prospects.) In his speeches and writings, Delany stressed the racist nature of American society. After travelling widely in West Africa, Delany, on the eve of the Civil War, was converted to the idea of black emigration to Africa, but was unable to arouse mass support for the proposal. With the outbreak of the Civil War, Delany abandoned emigrationism in favour of working for racial equality in America, and was active in the Freedmen's Bureau, the one federal agency created to protect the rights of blacks freed by the Emancipation Proclamation and Confederate defeat.

In the antebellum period, few blacks responded to calls for mass emigration, lacking sufficient funds and, more significantly, regarding themselves as more American than African. But in articulating concepts of black separatism, voluntary repatriation and identification with Africa, mid nineteenth-century black spokesmen made apparent their conviction that racial integration and equality were chimeras. In the twentieth century, W. E. B. Du Bois, Marcus Garvey and Malcolm X were to draw on such sentiments and convictions in their own formulations of black nationalist ideology.

Northern blacks, then, whatever their proposed solutions to the racial issue in the thirty years before the Civil War, displayed an increasing assertiveness and sense of identity. They also turned their own enforced segregation to good advantage with the creation of black schools, churches and conventions. Among black leaders, North and South, in the nineteenth century, one achieved an international reputation, spoke directly of slavery, the Civil War and Reconstruction, and had multiple careers as an abolitionist, reformer, adviser to American presidents, political activist and autobiographer. A brief survey of the experiences of Frederick Douglass (1817–95) will illustrate the successes and failures of an exceptional black leader as he confronted the dangers and dilemmas of the Afro-American in the nineteenth century.

FREDERICK DOUGLASS (1817–1895): FROM MILITANCY TO CONSERVATISM

Born in Maryland, Frederick Douglass was for several years a house slave in Baltimore, where he learned to read and write. In 1838, when he could no longer tolerate his condition and treatment, Douglass escaped from slavery, married Anna Murray, a free black, and settled in New Bedford, Massachusetts. After seeing a copy of Garrison's *The Liberator,* Douglass became an ardent and enthusiastic abolitionist and, in 1841, became a lecturer for the Massachusetts Anti-Slavery Society, and an avowed Garrisonian. An eloquent orator, Douglass soon became the leading black spokesman for abolition. When doubts were expressed that he had ever been a slave, Douglass produced, in 1845, his *Narrative of the Life of Frederick Douglass,* a graphic and utterly convincing depiction of his slave experiences, and a landmark in abolitionist (and black American) literature. Fearful for his safety after the publication of the *Narrative,* Douglass's friends sent him on a two-year visit to Britain, where he impressed audiences with his high intelligence and withering condemnations of slavery. After his British supporters purchased his freedom, Douglass returned to America, and moved to Rochester, New York, where he established his own weekly newspaper, *The North Star,* in 1847. As a journalist, essayist and public speaker, Douglass inveighed against the twin evils of slavery and racial discrimination. In addition to his support for abolition, Douglass was active in espousing a variety of reforms – women's rights, temperance and world peace, and opposed capital punishment, lynching and the convict lease system. He was also an advocate of 'industrial education' for blacks, self-help, capital accumulation and strict morality.

> His belief in racial pride, constant agitation against racial discrimination, vocational education for blacks, non-violent passive resistance, recognition of a separate black 'nation within a nation', and integration of blacks in American society, antedated twentieth century black nationalists, Booker T. Washington's emphasis on vocational education and self-help, and Martin Luther King's non-violent direct action.[4]

A supporter of the Liberty and Republican parties, Douglass was also active in the Negro Convention Movement of the 1840s and 1850s.

Personal rivalries and ideological differences led him to split with the Garrisonians in 1851. Douglass rejected the Garrisonian slogan of 'No Union With Slaveholders' as an abandonment of the slave to the not-so-tender mercies of Southern slaveholders, disagreed with Garrison's view that the federal Constitution was a pro-slavery document, and resented Garrison's attacks on the Northern churches, citing the existence of anti-slavery sympathizers in some denominations. Moreover, Douglass resented the patronizing attitudes of many white abolitionists, and believed that to be successful, abolitionism must endorse political activism. Douglass welcomed John Brown's abortive attempt to incite a slave insurrection at Harper's Ferry in Virginia in 1859 – although he had been unaware of Brown's intentions, despite their friendship, and applauded Abraham Lincoln's issuance of the Emancipation Proclamation in 1863. During the war, Douglass pressed for the acceptance of blacks into the Union armed forces, believing that a Northern victory would secure permanent abolition of slavery, and citizenship rights for the freedman. During Reconstruction, Douglass stood behind Republican attempts to enforce civil rights in the defeated South, and pushed for enactment of the 1875 Civil Rights Act, and the ratification of the Fourteenth and Fifteenth Amendments, with their guarantees of American citizenship for blacks and the right to vote. A loyal Republican, Douglass supported the corrupt administration of President Grant, and the Compromise of 1877, despite its abandonment of Southern blacks to local white rule.

As a reward for his faithful services to the Republican Party, Douglass was appointed a United States Marshal, Recorder of Deeds for the District of Columbia, and Ambassador to Haiti. With the worsening of race relations in the post-Reconstruction South, Douglass protested against disfranchisement, lynching and the spread of segregation, but also advised Southern blacks to make the best of their situation, and to adjust to the reality of white supremacy. Anticipating Booker T. Washington, who delivered his 'Atlanta Compromise' address in 1895, the year of Douglass's death, Douglass, as early as the 1850s, had advocated the founding of an Industrial College for Negroes. As he informed Harriet Beecher Stowe: 'We need mechanics as well as ministers. We need workers in iron, clay and leather. We have orators, authors and other professional men, but these reach only certain classes, and get respect for our race in certain select circles. We must not only be able to black boots but to make them.'

In 1873, Douglass moved to Washington, DC, where he settled on a fifteen-acre estate, a wealthy and respected 'elder statesman' of the Negro race. His marriage, following the death of his first wife, to Helen Pitts, a white woman from a prominent Rochester family, brought a storm of protest, to which Douglass is said to have responded: 'My first wife was the colour of my mother, and the second, the colour of my father.' A European tour from 1886 to 1887 added to his already prodigious international reputation. But, in his later years, Frederick Douglass was a shadow of his former self.

> His revolutionary fervour had abated. ... Accession to public office frequently has this effect, but it was a tragedy for the Southern blacks that their natural leader was now grown moderate and his counsels to them more designed to reassure his federal patrons than to awaken the resistance of his fellow blacks to the enormities being revived and practised against them. It was not that Douglass had ceased to speak out for his people, but his tone was now one of eunuchoid accommodation. ... He seemed no longer capable of flaming anger. ... It is not to detract from his indubitable greatness to say that he was never deficient in vanity. The misfortune from the standpoint of the black freedman was that this profoundly human weakness was too clearly evident to his enemies and theirs – the racist whites.[5]

FREDERICK DOUGLASS AND BOOKER T. WASHINGTON

Yet one black American, also born into slavery, welcomed Douglass's apparent accommodation to the fact (if not to the principle) of white supremacy. In *The Story of My Life and Work* (1910), intended primarily for a black readership, Booker T. Washington observed:

> Mr Douglass had the same idea concerning the importance and value of industrial education that I have tried to emphasize. He also held the same ideas that I do in regard to the emigration of the Negro to Africa, and was opposed to the diffusion and dissemination of the Negro throughout the North and North-West, believing as I do that the Southern section of the country where the Negro now resides is the best place for him. In fact the more I have studied the life of Mr Douglass the more I have been surprised to find his far-reaching and generous grasp of the whole condition and needs of the Negro race.[6]

In a later autobiographical piece, *My Larger Education* (1911), Washington paid Douglass a qualified tribute. His great achievement had been as a participant in the abolitionist crusade.

> But the long and difficult struggle in which he engaged against slavery had not prepared Mr Douglass to take up the equally difficult task of fitting the Negro for the opportunities and responsibilities of freedom. The same was true to a large extent of other Negro leaders.

At the time he expressed these sentiments, Washington had already emerged as the successor to, if not the ideological disciple of, Frederick Douglass. In the last year of his life, Douglass, when asked by a Negro student what advice he would give to the younger black generation, replied, 'Agitate! Agitate! Agitate!' When the same student posed the identical question to Booker T. Washington in 1899, he received the answer: 'Work! Work! Work! Be patient and win by superior service.'[7]

Writing in 1910, the Negro writer Kelly Miller, who had known both men, vividly contrasted their personalities and outlooks:

> Douglass was like a lion, bold and fearless; Washington is lamblike, meek and submissive. Douglass escaped from personal bondage which his soul abhorred; but for Lincoln's [Emancipation] Proclamation, Washington would have risen to esteem and favour in the eyes of his master as a good and faithful servant. Douglass insisted upon his rights; Washington insists upon duty. Douglass held up to public scorn the sins of the white man; Washington portrays the faults of his own race. Douglass spoke what he thought the world should hear; Washington speaks only what he feels it is disposed to listen to. Douglass' conduct was actuated by principle; Washington's by prudence.[8]

Yet Washington sincerely believed that the issues which Douglass had agitated were no longer of first importance. In his biography of Douglass, Washington noted:

> Frederick Douglass' career falls almost wholly within the period of revolution and liberation. That period is now closed. We are at present in the period of construction and readjustment. Many of the animosities engendered by the conflicts and controversies of half a century ago still survive. ... But changes are rapidly coming about that will remove, or at least greatly modify, these lingering animosities. This book will have failed of its purpose just so far as anything here said shall serve to revive or keep alive the bitterness of those controversies of which it gives the history.[9]

Despite his statements endorsing Douglass's ideas on industrial education, 'the career of Frederick Douglass had no contemporary significance to Booker T. Washington'.[10]

REFERENCES

1. Walker, D., *Appeal* (Boston, 1829).
2. Berlin, I., *Slaves without Masters: the free Negro in the antebellum South* (New York, 1974), p. 340.
3. Berlin, op. cit., p. 394.
4. Blassingame, J. W. (ed.), *The Frederick Douglass Papers, Series One: speeches, debates and interviews*, Vol. I, *1841–46* (Yale U.P., New Haven; London, 1979), p. xii.
5. Hercules, F., *American Society and Black Revolution* (New York, 1972), p. 159.

6. Harlan, L. *et al.* (eds), *The Booker T. Washington Papers;* Vol. I
    (University of Illinois Press, 1972), p. 56.
7. Foner, P. S. (ed), *The Life and Writings of Frederick Douglass;* Vol IV
    (New York, 1950), pp. 149–50.
8. Miller, K., *Race Adjustment* (New York, 1910), pp. 19–21.
9. Washington, Booker T., *Frederick Douglass* (London, 1906), pp. 3–4.
10. Foner, op. cit., p. 149.

Chapter three

BOOKER T. WASHINGTON (1865–1915): BLACK ENIGMA

I seed Booker Washington – after I was grown and got big enough. I'd heard a lot of talk about Booker Washington ... he was an important man, he was a principal there at that school. He was a noted man ... that had quite a bit of influence with the big people in the northern countries, and he was a businessman as a white man would be. I seed him and I heard him talk. And he'd travel yonder in them northern states and he'd go before them big moneyed men and the officials of the entire United States. They gived that man piles of money to run this school business here in the state of Alabama. But I wouldn't boost Booker Washington today up to everything that was industrious and right. Why? He didn't feel for and respect his race of people to go rock bottom with 'em. He leaned too much to the white people that controlled the money – lookin' out for what was his worth ... he had a political pull any way he turned and he was pullin' for Booker Washington.

(Theodore Rosengarten, *All God's Dangers: the life of Nate Shaw*)[1]

Booker T. Washington was not an easy person to know. ... He never expressed himself frankly or clearly until he knew exactly to whom he was talking and just what their wishes and desires were.

(W. E. B. Du Bois, *Dusk of Dawn*)[2]

SEPARATE BUT UNEQUAL: SOUTHERN RACE RELATIONS, 1865–1915

The withdrawal of the last remaining federal troops from the South in 1877 marked the formal end of Reconstruction – the attempt by the Republican Party to impose measures of civil and political equality for the freedmen in the former Confederate states. The Thirteenth, Fourteenth and Fifteenth Amendments to the Constitution, reforms

23

embodied in the new Southern state constitutions, the provision of education for blacks, and attempts to suppress such white supremacist organizations as the Ku-Klux-Klan, had been the notable achievements of Congressional Reconstruction – policies adopted in opposition to the lenient proposals favoured by Lincoln's successor, Andrew Johnson. By the terms of the Compromise of 1877, however, Rutherford B. Hayes, a Republican, gained the presidency over the rival claims of his Democratic opponent, Samuel J. Tilden, and, as part of the bargain, Northern Republicans abandoned the freedmen to the Democratic 'Redeemer' governments of the South. Unable to resurrect the slave system, Southern whites soon devised legal and extra-legal measures which effectively deprived blacks of the franchise, and the rights to hold public office or engage in political protest. Again, the 'Black Codes', adopted during Andrew Johnson's direction of the Reconstruction process, and designed to keep blacks as a landless and closely controlled labour force, although voided by Congressional Reconstruction, were to reappear in the form of various labour laws enacted by the Southern state legislatures in the 1870s and 1880s. Vagrancy laws, enticement acts, contract enforcement statutes and the criminal surety system, were all designed to replace slavery by forms of involuntary servitude for Southern blacks. Staple crop production was resumed on Southern farms and plantations with the share-cropping system, whereby planters and merchants kept black tenant farmers in a state of peonage, unable to clear themselves of debt, and required by law to work indefinitely for the owner. Socially, Southern race relations – both during and after Reconstruction – were marked by the increasing separation of the races, in public accommodations, hospitals, prisons, schools and places of entertainment. Historians have disagreed as to when segregation first appeared in the post-war South – whether it was before, during or at some period after Reconstruction – but point to its full-blown operation in both law and custom throughout the South by the 1890s, with segregation as the substitute for slavery. Yet, as a recent study suggests, segregation, whenever it occurred, marked a decisive change from the South's earlier and almost total exclusion of blacks from medical, welfare, educational and other facilities.[3] Thus one of the 'achievements' of Congressional Reconstruction in the South was to secure segregated facilities for blacks where, previously, they had faced exclusion. The Republican state governments in the South, while effecting the reforms mentioned, never pushed for racial integration as either a realizable or even desirable goal. With the ending of Reconstruction, the 'Redeemer' governments simply continued and extended segregationist practices. The best that blacks could hope for were separate accommodations equal to those provided for whites. Where idealistic Northern Republicans may have hoped that facilities for the two races might be made equal, the Democratic Redeemers had no such expectations or intentions.

One response to the restoration of white supremacy in the South was a renewed call for black emigration. Henry McNeal Turner, a black preacher in the African Methodist Episcopal Church, had been expelled from the Georgia state legislature following the return of the Democrats to power. Turner roundly denounced both Republicans and Democrats for their betrayal of the Negro and, from 1870, began to advocate the emigration to Africa of a select group of blacks with the skills and resources to build a new nation. In 1891, Turner visited West Africa for the first time, sent back enthusiastic reports, and returned to America determined to launch an intensive campaign to promote black emigration. A fierce black nationalist, Turner condemned the failings of American society, argued for racial separatism, and tried to get the federal government to pay reparations to blacks for their years in slavery – in a tone that anticipated the later nationalist separatism of the Garvey movement and the Nation of Islam. With the aid of white businessmen, who had organized the International Migration Society (IMS) in Alabama, Turner, from 1894, began to recruit emigrants, sell passages on the Afro-American Steamship Company, founded with his support, for transportation to Liberia. In March 1895, twenty-two blacks from Arkansas, Mississippi, Alabama, Florida and Tennessee, recruited by black representatives of the IMS, sailed for Africa. The following year, 325 blacks left for Liberia. On his third visit to West Africa, Turner reported that the settlers were making steady progress. In fact, the IMS officials had not provided them with promised food and help, and many of the emigrants died from malaria, while those who survived asked to return to America. Turner's emigrationist campaign appealed only to a small and desperate segment of the Southern black population. But Turner continued to advocate emigration for blacks for the remainder of his life (he died in the same year as Booker T. Washington), and can be considered as the immediate ideological forerunner of Marcus Garvey.

During and after Reconstruction, most Southern blacks rejected emigrationism, and placed their hopes in the securing of better schools and welfare facilities, rather than in gaining integrated institutions. Aware of their precarious position in a society pledged to restore white supremacy, those blacks who attended the first freedmen's conventions held in the South immediately after the Civil War, were careful not to offend white sensibilities by demanding political rights.

> To emphasize the mutuality of interest upon which a new South would arise, blacks attending the freedmen's conventions dwelled upon their own Southern roots and how their lives, experiences, and destinies were intertwined with those of white Southerners. ... Rather than affirming the need for government action and planning to protect the interests of black agricultural labourers, the black convention movement, like most

black newspapers, repeated the moral and economic injunctions and shibboleths that were standard fare in the nineteenth century.[4]

For a time it appeared that the Populist Movement or People's Party – the climax of the agrarian discontent of the 1880s and 1890s – with its rejection of both the Republicans and Democrats as the creatures of Northern business interests, might produce an alliance of Southern black and white farmers in a united protest. In the South, Populist leaders like Tom Watson of Georgia appealed for black support, arguing that economic distress cut across the colour line. In 1892, the Arkansas Populist platform included a resolution submitted by a black delegate, that 'it is the object of the People's Party to elevate the downtrodden, irrespective of race or colour'. Throughout the South, Populist platforms denounced lynchings and supported political rights for blacks. But these expressions of concern for the Negro were rooted in expediency rather than in idealism. When Southern planters used their influence to ensure that their black tenants voted for the Democrats, Southern Populists, alarmed at the prospect of white competition for the black vote, reversed their earlier pro-black statements, and joined with their political rivals in espousing black disfranchisement and racial segregation. By the 1890s, Southern whites of all political persuasions were beginning to unite under the banner of white supremacy. In the North, the radical impulse was on the wane, with the death or retirement from office of the old radical Republican leadership. The election of President Grant in 1868, and the subsequent rise of factionalism within the Republican Party, with liberal Republicans favouring an end to military rule in the South and sectional reconciliation, all pointed to the imminent abandonment of the freedman in the cause of sectional harmony. By the early 1870s, Northern business interests were demanding an end to Reconstruction because it was discouraging investment and commercial enterprise in the South. The Supreme Court, in a series of decisions, aided the segregation impulse in rulings which declared the provisions of the Fourteenth Amendment did not affect segregation by state law, if the facilities offered were 'separate but equal'. Mississippi in 1890, and South Carolina in 1895 were the first former Confederate states to amend their constitutions effectively to disfranchise nearly all blacks. Between 1896 and 1915, all Southern states enacted legislation that permitted the Democratic Party to declare only whites eligible for voting in primary elections. During the 1880s and 1890s, there were, on average, 150 lynchings of blacks a year – an appalling index of racial tensions in the South. Not surprisingly, Southern blacks, although they retained their loyalty to the Republican Party, became increasingly disillusioned with political activity. Yet black protest was not entirely extinguished in the South. From 1904 to 1908, Southern Negroes organized a series of unsuccessful boycotts following the introduction of segregated street cars in such cities as

Atlanta, New Orleans, Houston and Mobile. Given the helplessness of Southern blacks in the face of white hostility and violence, there is a certain irony in the observation that: 'It was an ex-slave who eventually framed the *modus vivendi* of race relations in the New South.'[5]

BOOKER T. WASHINGTON: EARLY LIFE

Booker Taliaferro Washington was born a slave in 1856, on James Burroughs's 207-acre farm in Franklin County, Virginia. The son of a house slave and an unknown white father, Washington later recalled:

> I was born in a typical log cabin, about fourteen by sixteen feet square. In this cabin I lived with my mother and a brother and sister till after the Civil War, when we were all declared free. Of my ancestry, I knew nothing.[6]

Washington spent nine years in slavery – the last four during the Civil War – and became very attached to his mother, Jane, the Burroughs's cook. As a slave, Washington was poorly clothed and inadequately fed, and denied any opportunities for education, apart from tantalizing glimpses into the schoolroom attended by his young white 'mistress'. His plantation duties consisted of taking water to slaves working in the fields, carrying corn for grinding to the local mill and operating a set of fans at the Burroughs's dinner table. Reflecting on this period of his life, Washington castigated slavery for having caused physical labour to 'be looked on as a badge of degradation, of inferiority' by both whites and blacks. In 1865, Washington went with his family to join his stepfather, Washington Ferguson, who had fled to Malden, West Virginia, during the war. In Malden, the reunited Washington family lived in a shanty town, and Washington worked for a time in the salt mines and later as a coal miner, experiences which may partly explain his adult addiction to the rituals of personal hygiene. An 'intense longing to read' was among Washington's earliest memories, and during his stay in Malden he began to acquire the rudiments of literacy when his mother obtained for him a copy of Noah Webster's spelling book, a traditional text in American primary schools. He also began to attend a local school started by Negro parents, after completing a 5.00 a.m. to 9.00 a.m. shift at the salt works, with a further two-hour shift after the end of afternoon classes. (In his later career, Washington became a strong advocate of the night school.) At some point during his Malden years, Washington heard about the existence of a school for freedmen – the Hampton Normal and Agricultural Institute, in Virginia – where blacks could receive academic training while working for their room and board. He recalled:

I resolved at once to go to that school, although I had no idea where it was, or how many miles away, or how I was going to reach it. .... I was on fire constantly with one ambition, and that was to go to Hampton.[7]

Hampton Institute had been founded in 1868 by Samuel Chapman Armstrong, the son of Hawaiian missionaries, and a former brigadier-general in the Union army. Armstrong was greatly interested in education for the freedman as the best means of smoothing the transition from slavery to freedom. The views of European educators stressing the value of industrial schools had been given a receptive hearing in America before the Civil War, and Frederick Douglass, as has been seen, was a notable black advocate of the idea. During Reconstruction, the Freedmen's Bureau had also supported the cause of industrial/agricultural education, in an attempt to improve the condition of Southern blacks. Armstrong had come to believe that such a programme, in addition to elevating 'dependent' and 'backward' races, might also provide a strategic ground of compromise between Southern whites, Northern whites and Negroes.

For Armstrong, the means of Negro advancement in a competitive, capitalist civilization lay essentially in combatting what seemed to him to be shiftlessness, extravagance, immorality, in working hard, buying land, saving money, creating stable Christian families, and learning trades.[8]

Armstrong also firmly believed that blacks should remain in the South, with their 'best friends' (Southern whites), engage primarily in agriculture, eschew politics and engage in programmes of individual and collective self-help. (Bishop Henry M. Turner, on a visit to Hampton in 1878, accused it of inculcating black inferiority.) Armstrong's ideas, grounded in the belief in education as a moral and conservative force, appealed to Southern whites and Northern capitalists, united in their wish to have a tractable and trained labour force in the post-war South.

Washington's desire to attend Hampton was increased during his eighteen-month service as a houseboy in the home of General Lewis Ruffner, owner of the Malden salt furnace and coal mine. His stay with the Ruffner family marked the beginning of Washington's lifelong association with upper-class whites, and it was from Mrs Viola Ruffner (a New Englander) that he began to imbibe 'the Puritan ethic of hard work, cleanliness and thrift on which his later social philosophy was based'.[9] Mrs Ruffner also encouraged Washington's efforts to acquire an education, allowing him to attend school for an hour a day during the winter.

In 1872, Washington, aged sixteen, set out from Malden to cover the 500 miles to Hampton, a journey that was to test his mental, physical and financial resources. At the first night's stagecoach stop, Washington, the only black passenger, was excluded from 'a common, unpainted house called a hotel', and refused a meal. When his meagre funds ran out in northern Virginia, Washington walked and begged rides until he reached Richmond, about eighty miles from Hampton, tired, hungry and completely out of money. Working at odd jobs in Richmond, Washington finally accumulated sufficient funds to undertake the last stage of his journey; he reached Hampton with fifty cents to spare. The head teacher at Hampton, Miss Mary F. Mackie (like Mrs Ruffner, a new Englander), was visibly unimpressed by the tramp-like figure who presented himself for admission to the school. After some deliberation, she ordered him to sweep the recitation room, a chore which Washington correctly surmised was his entrance examination. Thanks to Mrs Ruffner's training and his own unflagging enthusiasm, Washington passed the test. After a thorough inspection of the room Mrs Mackie informed the applicant: 'I guess you will do to enter this institution'.

Washington's three years at Hampton were to be the shaping experience of his life, and he later said that Hampton had given him a better education than he could have gained at Harvard or Yale. Working as a janitor for his room and board, and with his clothing and tuition provided by Northern benefactors, Washington gained the rudiments of a liberal education, acquired trade skills and was fully indoctrinated in the Hampton Christian work-and-cleanliness ethic. He also showed promise as a student debater and orator. In General Armstrong, Washington found a surrogate father, guide and mentor. 'Washington came to model his career, his school, his social outlook, and the very cut of his clothes after Armstrong's example.'[10] From 1875 to 1878, Washington disseminated the Hampton message as a schoolteacher in Malden; in 1878 he spent a year at Wayland Seminary, a small Baptist theological school in Washington, DC, but disliked both the atmosphere of the capital and the absence of moral and practical training in the Wayland curriculum. In particular, he disliked the frivolities and pretensions of the city's black population, and the insensitivity of Wayland's black graduates to the needs of the rural black peasantry. After a brief period spent studying law, Washington gratefully accepted Armstrong's invitation to return to Hampton as a teacher in 1879. In his second year at Hampton, Washington administered the first night-school class for preparatory students unable to afford part-time study during the day. Washington nicknamed them 'The Plucky Class' and under his driving force, the experiment was a success, confirming his belief that poverty was no excuse for ignorance.

TUSKEGEE

In May, 1881, General Armstrong received a letter from the state commissioners of a Negro normal school in Tuskegee, Alabama, asking him to recommend its first principal. Their assumption was that Armstrong would recommend a white teacher for the post. The 'school' in question consisted only of a dilapidated shack and an old church – both on loan – without teachers or pupils. Yet the founding of this school owed its origin to the persistence of the black vote in the Deep South in the period immediately after the end of Reconstruction. In the autumn elections of 1880, Colonel Wilbur F. Foster, a Confederate veteran, and former slaveholder, was a Democratic candidate for the Alabama state senate. Foster approached a black tinsmith, Lewis Adams, an ex-slave and the leading black citizen of Tuskegee, a town of 2,000, half-black and half-white, in Macon County, where the population was 75 per cent Negro. Foster promised that if Adams would deliver the black vote in the election, he could expect to be rewarded. Adams, formerly a Republican but now shrewdly decided on a course of political self-interest for the black community, secured Foster's promise to sponsor and aid the passage of a bill for a Negro normal school in Tuskegee. The Democrats won an overwhelming victory in 1880, and Foster fulfilled his part of the bargain: the Alabama legislature approved the project, named a Board of Commissioners, and appropriated $2,000 for teachers' salaries.

Armstrong recommended Washington for the Tuskegee position, and described him as 'a very competent capable mulatto, clear-headed, modest, sensible, polite and a thorough teacher and superior man'.[11] The Tuskegee commissioners accepted the nomination, and Washington went to Tuskegee determined to put into practice the lessons he had learned (and taught) at Hampton. From the outset, Washington demonstrated his talents as an interracial diplomat. Cultivating influential whites in the Tuskegee area, including one of the commissioners, George W. Campbell, a former slaveowner, merchant and banker, Washington persuaded and cajoled the white community into supporting the new school. He also travelled through Macon County, advertising the school to blacks, and soliciting whatever financial or other help they could offer. On the symbolically chosen 4 July 1881, Washington formally opened the school, with an intake of thirty students and one teacher – himself. Within a year, he moved the school to a new site, an abandoned slave plantation which he purchased for $500, half of which was borrowed from General James Marshall, treasurer of Hampton, with a promise to repay the other half within twelve months: he repaid both debts within five months. With the help of his first assistant, Olivia Davidson, who was to become his first wife, and the labours of the Tuskegee students, the school grew in size and scope. The student body erected buildings and built furniture – and in the process, learned skilled trades. After several failures, Tuskegee produced its own bricks; cabinet- and mattress-making shops were opened in 1887, and two years later, blacksmith operations, wagon-making and wheelwrights' work were added to the school 'catalogue'. In particular, Washington concentrated the school's efforts on teaching and devising modern agricultural techniques, training skilled artisans and preparing women students to be good housekeepers. New appointments to the Tuskegee staff included George Washington Carver, like Washington a former slave, who had become an agricultural chemist, and was to be a pioneer ecologist.

The regime at Tuskegee, modelled on that of Hampton, was even stricter and more Spartan. As principal, Washington ruled as a not-so-benevolent despot, alert to any infraction of school rules by either staff or students. Although Tuskegee was a non-sectarian school – and Washington always displayed a low regard for the moral and educational standards of black ministers – religious training, in the form of daily attendance at chapel and weekly Sunday evening talks by the principal himself, ensured that Tuskegee graduates would equate education with Christian precepts. Washington also steadily increased the influence of Tuskegee into the surrounding community, with extension courses and, after 1892, annual conferences for farmers which stressed not only innovative agricultural techniques but also the personal and moral qualities necessary for success. Even before he emerged as a national black spokesman, Washington, in speeches and letters to the Northern and Southern press, constantly stressed that good would come to the South – and to the nation – if the Tuskegee experiment was successful. He informed a meeting of the National Educational Association in Madison, Wisconsin, in 1884 that:

Any movement for the elevation of the Southern Negro in order to be successful, must have to a certain extent the cooperation of the Southern whites. They control the government and own property – whatever benefits the black man benefits the white man. ... In spite of all talk of exodus, the Negro's home is permanently in the South: for coming to the bread-and-meat side of the question, the white man needs the Negro, and the Negro needs the white man.[12]

Again, he could inform the editor of the Tuskegee *Macon Mail* in the same year: 'The race will grow in proportion as we learn to help ourselves in matters of education.'[13] In an address to the Alabama State Teachers' Association in 1882, Washington made an artful plea for the industrial education of blacks, one calculated to impress his white audience.

Two hundred years of forced labour taught the coloured man that there was no dignity in labour but rather a disgrace. The child of the ex-slave, naturally influenced by his parents' example, grows up believing that he sees what he thinks is the curse of work. To remove this idea is one of the great missions of the industrial school. The school teacher must be taught that it will not disgrace him to work with his hands when he cannot get a school.[14]

As Washington's fame grew, he was frequently absent from Tuskegee, often on fund-raising drives in the Northern states, where he impressed such millionaire industrial philanthropists as John D. Rockefeller, Andrew Carnegie, George Eastman and Henry C. Rogers with his own business-oriented and essentially conservative social philosophy. Washington (who also had unstinted admiration for the success symbolized by the possession of great wealth) directed their financial support not only to Tuskegee – which, by 1915, had an endowment of $1,945,000 – but to other black schools and colleges in the South. Washington was, then, the outstanding black educator of his day, and Tuskegee remains his great and lasting monument. In 1895, however, as the result of a single speech, Washington was to be catapulted into national prominence. Although his subsequent career was to take him on many occasions far from Tuskegee, it remained his great love and passion. It also became his power base and headquarters for the 'Tuskegee Machine'.

THE ATLANTA COMPROMISE ADDRESS

On 18 September 1895, at the opening of the Cotton States and International Exposition held in Atlanta, Georgia, Washington delivered a speech designed to 'cement the friendship of the races and bring about hearty cooperation between them'. Although there was nothing new in what Washington said at Atlanta, the timing and circumstances of his address ensured that it would reach and impress a national audience. Washington's purpose at Atlanta was to announce a pragmatic compromise that would resolve the antagonisms between Southern whites, Northern whites and the Negro. In a period of worsening race relations, Washington urged blacks (as he had before) to remain in the South, work at 'the common occupations of life', and accept the fact of white supremacy. He deprecated political action and black performances as voters and legislators during Reconstruction, reminded blacks that they were to live (and prosper) by manual labour, and, to whites, stressed the loyalty and fidelity of Southern Negroes – 'the most patient, faithful, law-abiding and unresentful people in the world'. Washington emphasized that blacks had no interest in securing social equality: 'In all things that are purely social we can be as separate as the five fingers, yet one as the hand in all things essential to human progress.' Reduced to their simplest terms, his proposals to the South were for economic cooperation and social separation (or segregation). But Washington went further than this, and assured whites that they had nothing to fear – and everything to gain – from trusting blacks.

As we have proved our loyalty to you in the past, in nursing your children, watching by the sick bed of your mothers and fathers, and often following them with tear-dimmed eyes to their graves, so in the future, in our humble way, we shall stand by you with a devotion that no foreigner can approach, ready to lay down our lives, if need be, in defence of yours.

Turning to blacks in the audience, Washington informed them:

Our greatest danger is that in the great leap from slavery to freedom we may overlook the fact that the masses of us are to live by the productions of our hands, and fail to keep in mind that we shall prosper in proportion as we learn to dignify and glorify common labour. No race can prosper till it learns that there is as much dignity in tilling a field as in writing a poem. No race that has anything to contribute to the markets of the world is long in any degree ostracized. It is important and right that all the privileges of the law be ours, but it is vastly more important that we be prepared for the exercise of these vast privileges. The opportunity to earn a dollar in a factory just now is worth infinitely more than the opportunity to spend a dollar in an opera house.

In conclusion, Washington assured white Southerners that in their efforts to resolve the race problem 'which God has laid at the doors of the South', they would 'have at all times the patient, sympathetic help of my race'. (The entire Atlanta Address is reprinted in *Up From Slavery*.)[15]

Washington's Atlanta Compromise Address caused a sensation at the time, and has been variously interpreted by commentators ever since. Not surprisingly, the Southern press heartily endorsed the sentiments it believed Washington had expressed. The *Atlanta Constitution* called the speech 'the most remarkable address delivered by a coloured man in America', and called Washington a 'sensible and progressive negro [*sic*] educator'. A South Carolina newspaper acclaimed him as 'one of the great men of the South', and added that 'his skin may be coloured, but his head is sound and his heart is in the right place'. Northern opinion (with only a few dissenting black voices) was almost as enthusiastic. Writing from Wilberforce University, the young black scholar W. E. B. Du Bois congratulated Washington on his 'phenomenal success at Atlanta – it was a word fitly spoken'. A Chicago newspaper, in an editorial widely reprinted in the South, declared that Washington's remarks at Atlanta and his personal example as an educator:

has done more for the improvement of the negro in the South than has been accomplished by all the political agitators. The possession of a vote does not always ensure respect, but the possession of a good character, a good home, and a little money reserve always ensure respect. If every Southern state had such an institution as that at Tuskegee, Alabama, presided over by such a man as Professor Washington, the race question would settle itself in ten years.[16]

Later estimates of Washington's most famous speech have viewed it either as an abject surrender of black civil and political rights to the forces of white racism, or as a masterly exercise in interracial diplomacy, and one which included ultimate goals which white Southerners could not support. 'Negroes must begin at the bottom, but surely Washington believed that eventually they would arrive at the top ... his Negro supporters emphasized the future implications of his remarks ... the dominant whites were impressed by his conciliatory phraseology, confused his means for his ends, and were satisfied with the immediate programme he enunciated.'[17] Whatever reading is given to the Atlanta Address, it made Washington the acknowledged and acclaimed leader, in the eyes of whites, of the Negro race. James Weldon Johnson, the Negro songwriter who became national organizer and executive secretary of the NAACP, reflecting on Washington's rise to fame, recalled:

> In 1895 Booker T. Washington made his epochal Atlanta speech. He had for ten years prior to that occasion been a rising figure, but after it his increase in power and prestige was so rapid that almost immediately he found himself the recognized leader of the Negro race. By his Atlanta speech he had at a stroke gained the sanction and support of both the South and the North – the South, in general, construing the speech to imply the Negro's abdication of his claim to full and equal citizenship rights, and his acceptance of the status of a contented and industrious peasantry; the North feeling that the opportunity had arisen to rid its conscience of a disturbing question and shift it over to the South. The great body of Negroes, discouraged, bewildered, and leaderless, hailed Mr Washington as a Moses. This was indeed a remarkable feat – his holding of the South in one hand, the North in the other, and at the same time carrying the major portion of his race along with him.[18]

UP FROM SLAVERY

From 1895 until his death in 1915, Washington's influence, power and determination made him a force to be reckoned with. He continued to act as the seemingly omnipotent and autocratic principal of Tuskegee, but also embarked on extensive fund-raising and lecturing tours. Washington's message, with few exceptions, was a restatement of the Atlanta Address: blacks should eschew politics, cultivate habits of thrift, economy and honesty, and concentrate on the acquisition of education, Christian character, property and industrial skills. Racial prejudice, he argued, could be endured by blacks, but inflicted permanent moral injury on its white practitioners. This was the message Washington also conveyed in his didactic autobiography, *Up From Slavery,* published in 1901, and a minor classic in American inspirational literature. Carefully designed to enhance Washington's image among the reading public, and to promote his school, career and philosophy, *Up From Slavery* presented him as a black Horatio Alger who had succeeded because of his application of the lessons of the Puritan ethic taught by his white mentors. An immediate publishing success, the book appealed to foreign readers as well, and was quickly translated into more foreign languages than any other American book of its time. Several of Tuskegee's most generous benefactors became converts to Washington's philosophy after reading his autobiography. *Up From Slavery* also appealed to blacks, who identified themselves with the protagonist's trials, tribulations and victories. One literary critic has aptly commented that *Up From Slavery*

> was written as a weapon for philanthropy and prestige by a Puritan materialist of astonishing proportions (and astonishing skill), and it served his purpose. The book is dominated by several inter-involved beliefs: an absolute faith in *laissez-faire* capitalism and the business ethic; an obsessive faith in hygiene and thrift and the dignity of manual labour; a limitless respect for Booker T. Washington – the book reads like a saint's life written by a saint. Like Dickens' virtuous co-narratress in *Bleak House,* Washington is forced to the artless ruse of quoting everyone's praises of him, so as not to be praising himself directly all the time. He does no wrong, has no enemies, suffers hardships willingly, is universally beloved, and is, for it all (as he confesses) quite humble.[19]

BLACK LEADER

In the last twenty years of his life, Washington had a dual career as educator and race leader. During the administrations of Theodore Roosevelt and William Howard Taft, Washington dispensed the limited federal patronage for blacks, established the intricate network of the 'Tuskegee Machine', and, with the help of his devoted secretary, Emmett J. Scott, monitored the activities of his Negro critics. In 1900, putting one of his favourite precepts into practice, Washington founded the National Negro Business League to promote black entrepreneurship and advertise the economic successes some blacks had achieved. The League not only reflected Washington's view that black advancement lay in economic progress, but also provided him with a cadre of loyal supporters in the major cities of the North. In the South, Washington, hypersensitively aware of the precarious position of blacks, ingratiated himself with successive governors of Alabama, promoted public health measures for Negroes, and supported such economic ventures as black owned-and-operated cotton mills and land purchase schemes.

By 1901, Washington was at the height of his fame, and received the presidential seal of approval when Theodore Roosevelt invited him to dinner at the White House. The episode angered Southern whites, but even Washington's black critics conceded that it had enhanced his reputation. Henry M. Turner informed Washington: 'You are about to be the great representative and hero of the Negro race, notwithstanding you have been very conservative.'[20] Yet although he had the ear of presidents and philanthropists, Washington was unable to halt, let alone improve, the deteriorating racial situation of the Progressive era. In 1896, the Supreme Court's decision in *Plessy* v. *Ferguson* appeared to give judicial sanction to the 'separate but equal' doctrine already endorsed by Washington. Again, while he helped to deliver the black vote to the Republicans in state and national elections, Washington appeared powerless when Theodore Roosevelt, in a blatantly racist act, summarily dismissed three companies of black troops in Brownsville, Texas, after they had resisted a white mob. The Brownsville affair 'highlighted Washington's lack of one essential attribute for the leader of an oppressed minority – the capacity for righteous public anger against injustice'.[21] Similarly, Taft's policy of removing Southern black office-holders indicated the very real limits to Washington's political influence.

Washington himself, on numerous occasions, was made painfully aware of the virulence of white racism. When a white chambermaid in an Indianapolis hotel was reported to have refused to make up Washington's bed and to have lost her job in consequence, a Texas newspaper solicited funds 'For a Self-Respecting Girl'. Washington also learned that segregation, imposed by whites on blacks, produced accommodations that were separate but decidedly unequal, and once confessed that 'the mere thought of a trip on a railroad brings to me feelings of intense dread'. Yet any summary of Washington's leadership must include the fact that he did protest and work against the more blatant forms of racial discrimination. He secretly sponsored legal suits against the exclusion of blacks from jury service, Jim Crow facilities on railroads, the various devices to deny blacks the exercise of the suffrage, and the persistence of involuntary servitude in the South. In his last years – possibly because of his failure to prevent presidents Roosevelt, Taft and Woodrow Wilson from giving executive approval to racial segregation – Washington became more outspoken against racial extremism. He criticized the conditions in the cars and waiting rooms of Southern railroads, lynching, a Congressional proposal to exclude African immigrants, and the blatant racism (with its romantic portrayal of the Ku-Klux-Klan) of D. W. Griffith's epic motion picture, *Birth of a Nation.* But Washington's strongest protest against discrimination did not appear until after his death, in a posthumously published article, 'My view of the segregation laws'.[22] Racial segregation Washington asserted, was 'ill-advised' because:

1. It is unjust. 2. It invites other unjust measures. 3. It will not be productive of good, because practically every thoughtful Negro resents its injustice and doubts its sincerity. 4. It is unnecessary. 5. It is inconsistent. The Negro is separated from his white neighbour, but white businessmen are not prevented from doing business in Negro neighbourhoods. 6. Wherever a form of segregation exists it will be found that it has been administered in such a way as to embitter the Negro and harms more or less the moral fibre of the white man. That the Negro does not express this constant sense of wrong is no proof that he does not feel it.

WASHINGTON AND THE WIDER WORLD

Washington travelled widely at home and abroad and had a world-wide following: Tuskegee was regularly visited by Africans, West Indians, Asians, European missionaries and white colonialists. On his three trips to Europe, Washington had tea with Queen Victoria, and met the Danish royal family. He stayed with – and impressed – H. G. Wells, who compared Washington favourably with W. E. B. Du Bois, a man who 'conceals his passionate resentment too thinly', whereas Washington 'looks before and after and keeps his counsel with the scope and range of a statesman'. On his 1910 visit to Denmark, Germany, Austria-Hungary, Italy and England, Washington concluded that despite handicaps, the American Negro was better off than 'the man farthest down' in Europe, in that he enjoyed a better standard of living, educational, economic and political opportunities. When Washington told a meeting of the London Anti-Slavery Society in 1910 that American race relations were improving, he drew an angry response from John E. Milholland of the NAACP, who was also in England. W. E. B. Du Bois, informed of the incident, published an 'Appeal to Europe' which appeared in the British and American press. Du Bois accused Washington of relating only selected items to European audiences because of his dependence on white support, and stressed instead the widespread discrimination, lynching and the failure of the courts to protect blacks as the less sanguine side of the American racial scene.

Despite his foreign travels, Washington did not alter his fundamental outlook which, throughout his life 'remained that of a provincial southern American'.[23] He never visited Africa, Asia or the West Indies, and before he sailed to Europe in 1910, resolved not to enter a single art gallery, museum or palace. Washington also had little interest in the African heritage of Afro-Americans. He was, however, quite prepared to advise the European colonial powers in Africa to the extent of supplying Tuskegee staff or graduates to promote programmes of

37

industrial education and self-reliance (within the existing political and racial order) among African peoples in Togo, Nigeria, the Belgian Congo and South Africa and Liberia. Washington also urged that Africans be taught English in order to give them a lingua franca, and promote their Western acculturation. Although he endorsed German colonialism in Africa, towards the end of his life Washington criticized white imperialist oppression in the Congo and South Africa – not because of any Pan-Africanist sentiments, but rather to highlight the impracticality of black emigration to Africa as a solution to the American race problem.

In 1915, on a speaking tour in New York, Washington collapsed from nervous exhaustion and arteriosclerosis. Informed that he had only a short time to live, he asked to be taken back to Tuskegee: 'I was born in the South, I have lived and laboured in the South, and I expect to be buried in the South.' He died at Tuskegee on 14 November 1915. Washington's statue on the Tuskegee campus expresses his life in the form of a parable. He is depicted lifting 'the veil of ignorance' from the kneeling figure of a young black man, holding on his knees an open book and agricultural and industrial tools. Washington's critics, in his lifetime, suggested another reading of the tableau: rather than lifting, Washington was lowering a 'veil of ignorance' over the eyes of his people.

WASHINGTON AND HIS BLACK CRITICS

Opposition to Washington's ideas and to his white-sanctioned position as race leader, came from a relatively small group of mainly Northern blacks – journalists, lawyers, clergymen and educators. Initially united only by their dislike of various elements of Washington's programme, his contemporary black critics accused him of a range of offences, miscalculations and misdemeanours. He was faulted for deprecating political action while at the same time functioning as a 'boss', condemned for attempting to impose a partisan and regional strategy for racial advancement on the country as a whole, and castigated for his control over the black press and friendships with white editors, with the resultant suppression of criticism. Washington's policies of industrial education were pronounced anachronistic, and his portrayals of race relations as travesties of the truth. An editorial in the *Christian Examiner* of November 1895 suggested that Washington should take every opportunity to 'bring home to the hearts and consciences of his hearers the ills his people suffer, and never allow any of his addresses to appear as if he were trying to temporize, palliate or lessen the facts as they exist'. In a letter published in an Atlanta journal, only three months after the

Atlanta Address, a black correspondent expressed alarm at the elevation of Washington to the position of race leader, and rejected as unseemly any comparisons between Washington and Frederick Douglass.

> Every race must make its own heroes. ... If another race selects our heroes, puts them upon pedestals, and tells us to bow down to them and serve them, woe be unto us. It is supreme folly to speak of Mr Washington as the Moses of the race. If we are where Mr Washington's Atlanta speech placed us, what need have we of a Moses? Who brought us from Egypt, through the wilderness to these happy conditions? Let us pray that the race will never have a leader, but leaders. Who is the leader of the white race in America? It has no leader, but leaders. So with us.[24]

John Hope, the black president of Atlanta University, made a thinly disguised reference to the 'Atlanta Compromise' when he declared in 1896: 'I regard it as cowardly and dishonest for any of our coloured men to tell white people and coloured people that we are not struggling for equality. Now catch your breath, for I am going to say that we demand social equality.' (Such criticisms were indicative of a more militant spirit among some southern blacks than Washington was prepared to admit.) As black migration to the North continued, and with the growth of a professional black élite, attacks on Washington became sharper and more concerted. Julius F. Taylor, Negro editor of the Chicago *Broad Axe,* was an ardent Democrat, and resented Washington's involvement in Republican patronage politics. Taylor typified Washington as 'the Great Beggar of Tuskegee' and 'the greatest white man's nigger in the world', and warned in 1899 that:

> The time is not far distant when Booker T. Washington will be repudiated as the leader of our race, for he believes that only mealy-mouthed Negroes like himself should be involved in politics.[25]

William Monroe Trotter, the fiery editor of the *Boston Guardian,* was also an early and bitter critic of Washington. When Andrew Carnegie donated $600,000 to Tuskegee, Trotter expressed the hope that Washington would no longer need to engage in fund-raising tours, and asserted:

> This man, whatever good he may do, has injured and is injuring the race more than he can aid it by his school. Let us hope that Booker Washington will remain mouth-closed at Tuskegee. If he will do this, all his former sins will be forgiven.

Taking issue with Washington's reported statement that the revised constitutions of the Southern states had placed 'a premium on intelligence, ownership of property, thrift and character', Trotter accused him of self-deception and asked:

What man is a worse enemy to the race than a leader who looks with equanimity on the disfranchisement of his race in a country where other races have universal suffrage, by constitutions that make one rule for his race and another for the dominant race?

Trotter deplored Washington's rise to fame, and charged him with being the 'Benedict Arnold' of the black race. He appealed for a 'black Patrick Henry' who would save his people from the dangers into which Washington had led them, one who would inspire his people with the words 'Give Me Liberty or Give Me Death'.[26]

The most searching and influential critique of Washington's policies was produced by W. E. B. Du Bois (see Ch. 4), in his essay 'Of Mr Booker T. Washington and others', in *The Souls of Black Folk* (1903). Although he began by conceding that 'Easily the most striking thing in the history of the American Negro since 1876 is the ascendancy of Mr Booker T. Washington', Du Bois charged that Washington's leadership had resulted in (or directly encouraged) black disfranchisement, the creation of an inferior civil status for Negroes, and the withdrawal of funds from institutions for the higher training of blacks. Washington, he suggested, faced a 'triple paradox' in that:

1. He is striving to make Negro artisans businessmen and property owners; but it is utterly impossible under modern competitive methods, for workingmen and property owners to defend their rights and exist without the right of suffrage.
2. He insists on thrift and self-respect, but at the same time counsels a silent submission to civic inferiority such as is bound to sap the manhood of any race in the long run.
3. He advocates common school and industrial training, and deprecates institutions of higher learning; but neither the Negro common schools, nor Tuskegee itself, could remain open a day were it not for teachers trained in Negro colleges, or trained by their graduates.[27]

Although he paid tribute to Washington's achievements in placating the white South, and in shrewdly appealing to the spirit of commercialism in the North, Du Bois pronounced Washington's vision narrow and essentially crass. 'Du Bois detested in Washington what he perceived as materialism, Philistinism, and, above all, spiritual pessimism.'[28] Du Bois' seminal essay concluded with a condemnation of Washington for representing 'in Negro thought the old attitude of adjustment and submission'. James Weldon Johnson recalled that Du Bois' critique provided a rallying point for blacks opposed to Washington 'and made them articulate, thereby creating a split of the race into two contending camps'.[29] The Niagara Movement of 1905, and its successor, the NAACP (see Ch. 4), were to institutionalize this opposition to Washington.

Washington's responses to his black critics consisted of a few abortive attempts at reconciliation and cooperation, together with unremitting efforts to influence, infiltrate or sabotage their organizations. In 1904, he persuaded the Du Bois-led faction to attend a meeting to iron out their differences. Held in secret in Carnegie Hall, this New York conference was marked by mutual suspicions, and failure to achieve a truce or agreement between the Washington and Du Bois camps. With the support of such white benefactors as Andrew Carnegie, Washington controlled the proceedings, outmanœuvred his opponents, and secured the election of loyal followers to a Committee of Twelve for the Advancement of the Negro Race, an advisory body which, for the brief period of its existence, reported directly back to Tuskegee.

Washington keenly resented any challenges to his leadership, and, as Du Bois later conceded, their conflict was essentially a power struggle, couched in terms of differences in educational and political ideology. With some justification, Washington argued that his Northern-based black critics had no real appreciation of conditions in the South. In a revealing letter of 1911, Washington summarized what he regarded as the outstanding differences between himself and Du Bois.

> I believe that the Negro race is making progress. I believe that it is better for the race to emphasize its opportunities than to lay over-much stress on its disadvantages. He believes that the Negro race is making little progress. I believe that we should cultivate an ever manly, straightforward manner and friendly relations between white people and black people. Du Bois pursues this policy of stirring up strife between white people and black people ... he fails to realize that it is a work of construction that is before us now and not a work of destruction.[30]

For his part, Du Bois, during his long life, continually revised his estimates of Washington, presenting him in a more sympathetic light, and stressing the significant differences in their respective backgrounds and education. But it was his essay 'Of Mr Booker T. Washington' that propelled Du Bois into the position of rival black leader. On Washington's death in 1915, Du Bois, as editor of the NAACP's journal *Crisis,* paid him a critical tribute:

> He was the greatest Negro leader since Frederick Douglass, and the most distinguished man, white or black, who has come out of the South since the Civil War. His fame was international and his influence far-reaching. Of the good that he accomplished there can be no doubt: he directed the attention of the Negro race in America to the pressing necessity of economic development; he emphasized technical education and did much to pave the way for an understanding between the white and darker races. [But] he never adequately grasped the growing bond of politics and industry; he did not understand the deeper foundations of human training, and his basis of better understanding between white and black was founded on caste. We may then generously lay on the grave of Booker T. Washington testimony of our thankfulness for his undoubted help in the accumulation of Negro property and land, his establishment of Tuskegee and spreading of industrial education and his compelling of

the white South to at least think of the Negro as a possible man. On the other hand, in stern justice, we must lay on the soul of this man a heavy responsibility for the consummation of Negro disfranchisement, the decline of the Negro college and public school, and the firmer establishment of colour caste in this land.[31]

REFERENCES

1. Rosengarten, T., *All God's Dangers: the life of Nate Shaw* (New York, 1974), pp. 568–9.
2. Du Bois, W. E. B., *Dusk of Dawn* (New York, 1940), pp. 78–9.
3. Rabinowitz, H. N., *Race Relations in the Urban South, 1865–1890* (Oxford U.P.; New York, 1978).
4. Litwack, L. F., *Been in the Storm So Long: the aftermath of slavery* (New York, 1980), p. 522.
5. Woodward, C. Vann, *Origins of the New South* (1951), p. 356.
6. Harlan, L. *et al.* (eds), *The Booker T. Washington Papers;* Vol. I (University of Illinois Press, 1972), p. 215.
7. Harlan *et al.* (eds), op. cit., p. 236.
8. Meier, A., *Negro Thought in America, 1880–1915* (Ann Arbor, Michigan, 1966), p. 88.
9. Harlan, L., *Booker T. Washington: the making of a black leader, 1865–1901* (Oxford U.P.; New York, 1972), pp. 42–3.
10. Harlan, op. cit., (1972), p. 58.
11. Harlan, op. cit., (1972), p. 110.
12. Harlan *et al.* (eds), op. cit., Vol. II, pp. 256, 258.
13. Harlan *et al.* (eds), op. cit., Vol. II, p. 249.
14. Harlan *et al.* (eds), op. cit., Vol. II, p. 194.
15. Harlan *et al.* (eds), op. cit., Vol. I.
16. Logan, R. W., *The Betrayal of the Negro* (1965), p. 285.
17. Meier, op. cit., p. 101.
18. Johnson, J. W., *Black Manhattan* (New York, 1930), pp. 131–2.
19. Littlejohn, D., *Black on White* (New York, 1966), p. 30.
20. Harlan, L., *Booker T. Washington: the wizard of Tuskegee.* (Oxford U.P.; New York, 1983), p. 5.
21. Harlan, op. cit., (1983), p. 323.
22. *New Republic,* 4 Dec. 1915.
23. Harlan, op. cit., (1983), p. 266.
24. Foner, P. S. (1970) 'Is Booker T. Washington's idea correct?', *JNH,* 55 (1970), 344.
25. Nielson, D. G., *Black Ethos: Northern urban Negro life and thought, 1890–1930* (London, 1977), pp. 199–200.
26. Meier, A. Rudwick, E. and Broderick, F. L., *Black Protest Thought in the Twentieth Century* (2nd edn, New York, 1971), pp. 32–5.
27. Du Bois, W. E. B., *Souls of Black Folk* (New York, 1968), pp. 48–9.
28. Rampersad, A., *Art and Imagination of W. E. B. Du Bois* (London, 1976), p. 85.

29. Johnson, op. cit., p. 134.
30. Harlan *et al.* (eds), op. cit., Vol. X, pp. 608–9.
31. *Crisis*, XI (1915–16), 82.

Chapter four

W. E. B. DU BOIS (1868–1963), TALENTED PROPAGANDIST

My first clear memory of Dr Du Bois was my pride in his recognized scholarship and his authority in his many fields of work and writing. We Negro students joined the NAACP which Dr Du Bois helped to organize and build; we read religiously *Crisis* of which he was editor for so many years, and in which he wrote clearly, constructively and militantly on the complex problems of the American scene, on the Negro question, on Africa, and on world affairs. We spoke of Dr Du Bois as Our Professor, The Doctor, The Dean, with great respect, paid close attention to his pronouncements. Dr Du Bois talked and wrote and marched for civil rights. He insisted upon first-class citizenship for all Americans ... he directed universal interest and attention to our Negro history and our rich African ancestry, to give us solid background for our struggle.

(Paul Robeson, 'The legacy of W. E. B. Du Bois')[1]

I first read Du Bois' *The Souls of Black Folk* in my home and his novel, *The Quest of the Silver Fleece.* He writes, my father would say, but he doesn't lead anybody.

(Harold R. Isaacs, *The New World of Negro Americans*)[2]

There is much bitterness among Southern Negro leaders because they are criticized for being 'Uncle Toms', especially by Northern Negro intellectuals. They will tell the observer that it takes little courage to stay in the safety of the North and to keep on protesting against Negro sufferings in the South.

(Myrdal, *An American Dilemma*)[3]

NORTHERN BLACKS ORGANIZE FOR PROTEST: 1890–1910

The late nineteenth century saw several attempts at the formation of Negro organizations to protest against discrimination and

Washingtonian accommodationism. In 1890, 141 delegates met in Chicago at the call of T. Thomas Fortune, editor of the New York *Age,* and the most able black journalist of his day. Three years earlier, Fortune had appealed to blacks to organize a National Afro-American League which would agitate for the removal of six principal grievances:

1. The suppression of voting rights in the South which had the effect of denying blacks political participation in the states where they were most numerous.
2. 'The universal and lamentable reign of lynch and mob rule.'
3. The inequitable distribution of funds between black and white schools.
4. 'The odious and demoralizing penitentiary system of the South.'
5. Discrimination and segregation on Southern railroads.
6. The denial of accommodations to blacks in public places.

Writing from Tuskegee, Booker T. Washington supported these proposals, and the Chicago convention adopted a constitution along lines recommended by Fortune, the desired goals to be secured by appeals to public opinion, litigation and non-violent demonstrations. By 1893, however, Fortune announced that the League was defunct because of lack of funds and mass support. In 1898, at a meeting in Rochester, New York, the League was revived as the National Afro-American Council, with a statement of objectives similar to those of the original League platform. Conceived as a comprehensive civil rights organization, the Council during its ten years of existence was largely ineffectual, and rent by faction. Although Washington did not hold any office in the Council, through his friendship with Fortune he became a dominant influence in its activities. Inevitably, black responses to the Council reflected, to a large extent, approval for, or opposition to, Washington's policies. When W. E. B. Du Bois, a young professor at Atlanta University, was made director of a Negro business league promoted by the Council, Washington sensed a challenge to his own leadership and formed the National Negro Business League (see Ch. 3) – with the help of a listing of black businessmen provided for him by Du Bois. While the Afro-American Council continued to be dominated by Washingtonians, a group of twenty-nine black radicals, responding to an appeal by Du Bois, met on the Canadian side of the Niagara Falls, in July 1905, to form an organization opposed to Washington and the influence of the Tuskegee Machine.

The Niagara Movement, which resulted from this meeting, placed responsibility for the racial problem squarely on whites. Its demands included:

1. Freedom of speech and criticism – an oblique reference to the Tuskegee Machine.
2. Manhood suffrage for all 'Negro Americans'.
3. The eradication of caste distinctions based on colour.

4. Universal common school education, federal aid to education, and the chance of higher education for all Negroes.
5. Equal employment opportunities.
6. Constant protest – 'persistent manly agitation' – as the strategy to secure Negro rights.

> The Niagara Movement reflected the personality of W. E. B. Du Bois. ... Where Washington proposed to improve the racial climate through conciliation, the Niagara Movement proposed to clear the air by frank protest of injustice. Where the Tuskegee Machine stood for the up-and-coming black businessman and farmer and such professional allies as these classes could attract, the Niagara Movement centred on the college-graduate professional class and spoke of its membership as the Talented Tenth. Where Washington emphasized economic means and self-help, the Niagara Movement depended on universal suffrage, civil rights, and an intellectual élite to bring about the promise of black opportunity in America.[4]

Predictably, Washington was opposed to the Niagara Movement from its inception, and his obstructionist tactics and influence undermined the movement, which was never able to gain white support. It was also unable to gain an appreciable following among the masses of blacks, and went down to short-term defeat as a protest organization. But the Niagara Movement was further evidence of the growing dissatisfaction of Northern blacks with Washington's Southern-style leadership and claim to be recognized as the spokesman for the race.

> The Niagara Movement represented the first organized attempt to raise the Negro protest against the great reaction after Reconstruction. Its main importance was that it brought to open conflict and wide public debate two types of Negro strategy – one stressing accommodation and the other raising the Negro protest. Booker T. Washington and W. E. B. Du Bois became national symbols for these two main streams of Negro thought.[5]

By 1903, the Niagara Movement had ceased to be an effective organization, but had laid the foundations for the emergence of the National Association for the Advancement of Coloured People (NAACP), a more serious challenge to Washington's leadership; a biracial coalition of black radicals and white Progressives, pledged to advance Negro civil and political rights.

THE RISE OF THE NAACP

In the summer of 1908, a race riot in Springfield, Illinois, home of Abraham Lincoln, resulted in the deaths of eight Negroes, fifty woundings, and a mass exodus of blacks from the city. William E. Walling, a white Kentuckian, socialist and social worker, reporting the incident in an article entitled 'The race war in the North', issued an appeal for a revival of the spirit of the abolitionist crusade, and urged the formation of a national organization of 'fair-minded whites and intelligent blacks' to work for social justice. Among those responding to Walling's appeal were Mary White Ovington, a white social worker from an abolitionist family, who had just completed a study of blacks in New York City, and Henry Moskowitz, another social worker. At their suggestion, Oswald Garrison Villard, grandson of William Lloyd Garrison, and editor of the New York *Post,* issued a 'call' on the centennial of Lincoln's birth, for a national conference for 'the renewal of the struggle for civil and political liberty'. Those who responded to the call included such leading white Progressives as Jane Addams, Rabbi Stephen S. Wise, and the 'muckraking' journalists Ray Stannard Baker and Lincoln Steffens. Negro respondents included Du Bois, Ida Wells Barnett, militant educationalist, and Bishop Alexander Walters, who had been active in the National Afro-American League and its successor, the Afro-American Council. The conference was held in the spring of 1909, as the National Negro Committee Conference. Booker T. Washington declined an invitation to attend on the grounds that he did not wish to jeopardize his work in the South, and was interested only in 'progressive, constructive' work for the race, not in 'agitation and criticism'. In his address to the conference, Du Bois emphasized the interrelatedness of politics and economics, but avoided attacking Washington directly. Among resolutions adopted by the conference were condemnations of the repression of blacks, appeals to the government to compel the Southern states to honour the Fourteenth and Fifteenth Amendments, and the demand that black children receive a proportional share of educational appropriations. The conference organizers were concerned to avoid alienating Washington, but Negro delegates rejected a proposal inviting him to join the steering committee, and forced through a resolution which indicated opposition to his policies.

> We fully agree with the prevailing opinion that the transformation of the unskilled coloured labourers in industry and agriculture into skilled workers is of vital importance to the race and to the nation, but we demand for the Negroes as for all others a free and complete education, whether by city, state, or nation, a grammar school and industrial training for all, and technical, professional and academic education for the most gifted.[6]

Although Villard attempted to maintain friendly relations with Washington, and tried to prevent the committee from taking an anti-Washingtonian stance, Washington stated that he would have no association with the National Negro Committee unless guarantees were given that neither Du Bois nor William Monroe Trotter would formulate its policies. At its 1910 conference, the National Negro Committee changed its name to the National Association for the Advancement of Coloured People, with the white lawyer and Progressive reformer Moorfield Storey as president. The aim of the new organization was 'to make 11,000,000 Americans physically free from peonage, mentally free from ignorance, politically free from disfranchisement, and socially free from insult'. From its inception, the NAACP put its emphasis on effecting change by lobbying for corrective legislation, educating public opinion and securing favourable court decisions. Its first judicial victory came in 1915, when it secured a Supreme Court ruling that Oklahoma's 'grandfather clause', designed to withhold the ballot from blacks, was unconstitutional. Its greatest victory was to be the Court's 1954 ruling that segregation in American schools was unconstitutional. By 1914, there were thirteen Negroes on the Association's board of directors, most of whom had earlier belonged to the Niagara Movement, and the NAACP had 6,000 members in 50 branches, and a circulation of its magazine, *Crisis,* of over 31,000.

Booker T. Washington declared his opposition to the NAACP, and expressed concern that white delegates to the 1910 meeting had gulled Negroes into believing that they could achieve progress 'by merely making demands, passing resolutions and cursing somebody'.[7] When W. E. B. Du Bois accepted an invitation to take up the post of Director of Publications and Research for the NAACP, any hope of a *rapprochement* between the organization and the Tuskegee Machine was lost.

> The NAACP was as diverse as the other reform coalitions of the Progressive Era, but the only one ... that dealt forthrightly with what W. E. B. Du Bois called 'the problem of the twentieth century – the problem of the colour line'. The NAACP came to represent the future, and Washington the past.[8]

The new Association's Director of Publications and Research had already emerged as Washington's most formidable black critic; as editor of *Crisis,* W. E. B. Du Bois consolidated his position as the supreme propagandist of the Negro protest movement.

W. E. B. DU BOIS: CURRICULUM VITAE

William Edward Burghardt Du Bois was born in Great Barrington, Massachusetts in 1868, the year of President Andrew Johnson's impeachment; he died in Ghana, in 1963, in self-imposed exile, at the time of the civil rights March on Washington. A poet, novelist, historian, sociologist and essayist, Du Bois occupies a commanding position in Afro-American letters. An outstanding scholar and teacher, Du Bois was also a political activist, founding member of the NAACP, editor of its journal *Crisis,* and, in all of these roles, the champion of racial justice. At various times in his long career, Du Bois was the declared opponent of Booker T. Washington and Marcus Garvey – yet had more in common with both these men than he cared to admit. Du Bois was also a socialist and Communist, an integrationist and advocate of a form of voluntary segregation, a black nationalist and a pioneering Pan-Africanist. A supporter of black American participation in the First World War, he became a Soviet and Chinese sympathizer and pacifist during the cold war of the 1950s. An élitist, who championed the cause of the 'Talented Tenth', Du Bois lacked the common touch, and was aloof, arrogant and visionary. During the 1930s he was to alienate the black bourgeoisie and intelligentsia who had earlier supported his integrationist radicalism. His intellectual biography is marked by ambivalence and inconsistency. An unashamed admirer of Western cultural values and achievements, he was also the impassioned spokesman for racial pride and solidarity as the prerequisites for black advancement. Du Bois expressed this ambivalence in the essay 'Of our spiritual strivings' in *The Souls of Black Folk:*

> One ever feels his two-ness – an American, a Negro; two souls, two thoughts, two unreconciled strivings; two warring ideals in one dark body, whose dogged strength alone keeps it from being torn asunder. The history of the American Negro is the history of this strife – this longing to attain self-conscious manhood, to merge his double self into a better and truer self. In this merging he wishes neither of the old selves to be lost. He would not Africanize America, for America has too much to teach the world and Africa. He would not bleach his soul in a flood of white Americanism, for he knows that Negro blood has a message to teach the world.[9]

To no black American is this statement more applicable than to Du Bois himself. Before considering his primary role as propagandist of the black protest movement, a summary of Du Bois' background, education and early academic career will serve to illustrate the remarkable strength of intellect which he was to bring to bear on his later role as agitator and ideologue.

THE EDUCATION OF W. E. B. DU BOIS

Du Bois, a free-born Negro, was of French Huguenot, Dutch and Negro ancestry, or as he chose to describe his racial background – 'with a flood of Negro blood, a strain of French, a bit of Dutch, but thank God! no

"Anglo-Saxon" '. Although his father deserted the family soon after Du Bois was born, his childhood in Great Barrington, a town of about 5,000 with only a few Negroes, was apparently a happy one. It was only when he and his classmates decided to exchange visiting cards, and one girl refused 'peremptorily, with a glance' to accept his card, that Du Bois, already conscious of his darker skin, felt that a 'vast veil' had shut him off from his white companions. An exceptional high school student, Du Bois, at the age of fifteen, contributed literary, political and social essays to the New York *Globe* and the New York *Freeman.* In these pieces, he urged blacks to join the local temperance movement, to form a literary society and to take a greater interest in politics. Already 'Du Bois had begun his self-appointed stewardship of the fortune of the race'.[10] In 1885 he won a scholarship to attend Fisk University, a black college in Tennessee, where he first encountered extreme racism and, simultaneously, began to cultivate his identity as an Afro-American. 'I was thrilled to be for the first time among so many people of my own colour or rather of such extraordinary colours, which I had only glimpsed before, but who it seemed were bound to me by new and exciting eternal ties. ... Into this world I leapt with enthusiasm: henceforward I was a Negro.'[11]

At Fisk Du Bois also encountered rural black poverty and ignorance at first hand, when for two summers he taught in black schools in Tennessee. This experience confirmed Du Bois' growing belief in the power of education and reason to resolve racial conflict and secure black advancement. At the same time, it also increased his awareness of the enormous intellectual gulf between himself and the generality of black people. Graduating from Fisk in 1888, Du Bois entered Harvard, where he was greatly influenced by the philosophers William James, Josiah Royce and George Santayana, and gained a BA degree in 1890, and an MA in the following year. As a graduate student in history at Harvard, Du Bois left for Europe in 1892, on a scholarship to study abroad. He enrolled at the University of Berlin for courses in history, economics and sociology, having already decided to take a Ph.D. in social science 'with a view to the ultimate application of its principles to the social and economic rise of the Negro people'. A declared admirer of Bismarck, who had created the German state through the force of his personality and will, Du Bois' later Pan-Africanism was undoubtedly influenced by his exposure to the rise of German national consciousness, just as his 'German years introduced him to meaningful socialist thought and practice'.[12]

On his return to America in 1894, Du Bois had arrived at his basic intellectual and ideological beliefs. 'To the end of his life he basically remained a nineteenth century liberal who believed in the power of ideas and declared "culture" as the highest human aim; who was convinced that only the educated and cultured man of "good manners" could deliver the world from evil.'[13] The Negro race, Du Bois believed, could only advance through its own self-help and the assistance of whites of goodwill. Black leadership must be provided by the race's intellectuals – the 'Talented Tenth' – who would inspire their own people while seeking aid and stimulation from whites. Du Bois' Ph.D. thesis, 'The suppression of the African slave trade to the USA, 1638–1870', asserted that it was moral cowardice in the face of economic opportunity that had seen the continuation of the trade after it was prohibited by law; its suppression had resulted from a mixture of humanitarian, political and economic pressures. A pioneering work, Du Bois' dissertation was published as the first volume in the Harvard Historical Studies series, and he seemed destined for an academic career.

From 1894 to 1896, Du Bois was Professor of Latin and Greek at Wilberforce University, a black college in Ohio, having rejected an offer from Booker T. Washington to teach mathematics at Tuskegee. (In his first autobiography, Du Bois noted wryly: 'It would be interesting to speculate just what would have happened if I had accepted the ... offer of Tuskegee instead of that of Wilberforce.')[14] Repelled by the religious fervour which frequently erupted at Wilberforce in the form of spiritual revivals, Du Bois was grateful to accept an invitation from the University of Pennsylvania to carry out a study of the black population of Philadelphia. *The Philadelphia Negro* (1899), a work of sociology, criticized the city's blacks for their immorality, criminality, lack of organization for social betterment, neglect of education, and the failure of the Negro middle class to assert its claims to leadership. White Philadelphians were judged guilty of racist attitudes and practices, and were urged to cooperate with 'better' Negroes by recognizing distinctions within the black community. Widely regarded as a model study of a black urban community, *The Philadelphia Negro* established Du Bois' academic reputation.

From 1897 to 1910, he was Professor of Sociology and History at Atlanta University, where he directed the preparation and publication of a series of studies which documented the existence of segregation in every area of black life – labour unions, prisons, business and industry. Yet, significantly, in view of Du Bois' controversial espousal of 'voluntary segregation' in the 1930s, the Atlanta Studies also acknowledged segregation as a unifying force in black life. In this period also, Du Bois refined and developed his conception of blackness and the meaning of the Afro-American experience. 'The conservation of races', an address delivered to the newly formed American Negro Academy in 1897, while disclaiming the existence of meaningful physical differences between the races, argued for 'spiritual and psychical differences'. Where the English had bestowed on the world the ideas of constitutional liberty and commercial freedom, and the Germans, science and philosophy, blacks had still to deliver their distinctive gifts and qualities. These gifts, as they were celebrated by Du Bois in *The Souls of Black Folk,* were said to be their 'pathos and humour', folk-tales and artistic and musical abilities. 'In both the address and the book, the black American was viewed as having a particular message to contribute to American life, just as the Negro race had a particular message to contribute to world civilization. His suffering had made him a seer.'[15] Although differing in emphases, Du Bois' notion of black distinctiveness was shared by Booker T. Washington, Marcus Garvey, Malcolm X and Martin Luther King.

During the early 1900s, Du Bois, although deeply engaged in scholarship, was increasingly convinced that the worsening racial situation required more direct action. The publication of *The Souls of Black Folk,* with its critical estimate of Booker T. Washington, his activities as an organizer of the Niagara Movement and author of its manifesto in 1905, and his response to the call which resulted in the founding of the NAACP, completed Du Bois' transition from academician to propagandist. Opposed to Washington's accommodationism, blind allegiance to the Republican Party, and the complete assimilation of Negroes into the white American way of life, Du Bois, as editor of *Crisis,* offered his alternative visions of the future of Afro-Americans.

DU BOIS: *CRISIS* EDITOR

The first issue of *Crisis* appeared in November 1910, with a circulation of 1,000 copies; within 12 months, it was selling 16,000 copies monthly. As editor of the magazine from 1910 to 1934, Du Bois later acknowledged that during this period 'the span of my life . . . is chiefly the story of *Crisis* under my editorship'.[16] One of his biographers asserts: 'As a writer Du Bois never surpassed the month-to-month prose of his editorials on social, political and economic topics in *Crisis.* His reputation as a writer will rest more on *Crisis* than on his forays into *belles lettres.*'[17] In the first issue, Du Bois declared that in *Crisis* he intended to 'set forth those facts and arguments which show the danger of race prejudice, particularly as manifested toward coloured people'. Determined from the start that the magazine would reflect his own ideas (even when they ran counter to those of the NAACP leadership), Du Bois aimed his editorial shafts at the literate and middle-class black public. Early issues featured editorials and articles on 'Coloured high schools', 'The coloured college athlete' and 'Women's clubs', and the repeated assertions that blacks possessed a superior spiritual sense and beauty that made them a chosen people. Du Bois called for resistance against attempts being made outside the South to institute segregated schools, attacked the black churches for their racial conservatism and defended the rights of women. The third issue carried Du Bois' avowal:

'I am resolved to be quiet and law-abiding, but refuse to cringe in body or soul, to resent deliberate insult, and to assert my just rights in the face of wanton aggression,' and *Crisis* recommended black self-defence against white vigilante mobs. Employing a variety of techniques and literary devices, Du Bois wrote in a clear, direct style, and used savage and sardonic humour to depict racial indignities and atrocities. In 1911, he dramatically described a lynching in Pennsylvania:

> Ah, the splendour of that Sunday night dance. The flames beat and curled against the moonlight sky. The church bells chimed. The scorched and crooked thing, self-wounded and chained to his cot, crawled to the edge of the ash with a stifled groan, but the brave and sturdy farmers pricked him back with the bloody pitchforks until the deed was done. Let the eagle scream! Civilization is again safe![18]

When two Kentucky Negroes who had been delayed by a train crash, were served in the same railroad car as whites, without encountering violence or abuse, and informed Du Bois of the episode, he responded in *Crisis:*

> The editor read this and read it yet again. At first he thought it was a banquet given to black men by white; then he thought it charity to the hungry poor; then – it dawned on his darkened soul: Two decently dressed, educated coloured men had been allowed to pay for their unobtrusive meal in a Pullman dining car 'WITHOUT ONE SINGLE WORD OF COMMENT OR PROTEST'! And in humble ecstasy at being treated for once like ordinary human beings they rushed from the car and sent a letter a thousand miles to say to the world: My God! Look! See! What more eloquent remark could be made on the white South? What more stinging indictment could be voiced? What must be the daily and hourly treatment of black men in Paducah, Ky., to bring this burst of applause at the sheerest and most negative decency? Yet every black man in America has known the same elation. ... We have all of us felt the sudden relief – the half-mad delight – when contrary to fixed expectation we were treated as men and not dogs; and then, in the next breath, we hated ourselves for elation over that which was but due any human being. This is the real tragedy of the Negro in America: the inner degradation, the hurt hound feeling; the sort of upturning of all values which leads some black men to 'rejoice' because 'only' sixty-four Negroes were lynched in the year of our Lord 1912. Conceive, O poet, a ghastlier tragedy than such a state of mind.[19]

In 1919, after an intensive investigation, the NAACP published *Thirty Years of Lynching in the United States, 1889–1918,* which estimated that 3,224 black men and women had been lynched during this period. During the First World War *Crisis* publicized the rising rate of lynch law, most dramatically in a 1916 account (published as an eight-page supplement) of the seizure and lynching of Jesse Washington, a mentally retarded adolescent, found guilty and sentenced to death for the murder of a white woman in Waco, Texas. 'The Waco horror', a report of the incident, complete with photographic evidence, was used as the opening move in an NAACP campaign for an Anti-Lynching Fund. Distributed to 42,000 *Crisis* subscribers, 50 Negro weeklies and 700 white newspapers, it was also sent to all members of Congress, and to a list of 500 'moneyed men' in New York, who were asked to subscribe to the appeal. 'The Waco horror' included the information that:

> Washington ... was dragged through the streets, stabbed, mutilated and finally burned to death in the presence of a crowd of 10,000. ... After the death what was left of his body was dragged through the streets and parts of it sold as souvenirs. His teeth brought $5 a piece and the chain that bound him 25 cents a link. ... He was lowered into the fire several times by means of the chain around his neck.

Du Bois' editorship was marked by almost constant friction between himself and the NAACP board. The issue was usually disagreement over the relationship between the journal and the Association – in its first number *Crisis* did not even mention the existence of the NAACP. Without consulting the board, Du Bois attacked large sections of the black press, asserting that they did not publish the true facts about the racial situation, and did not consistently support the cause of civil rights. Irritated black editors responded sharply to such attacks, and in 1914, at its annual convention, the NAACP passed a resolution praising the Negro press, and, indirectly, rebuking Du Bois. His response was to charge that some of his white critics within the NAACP were racists, and, as he stated in a 1915 editorial:

> I thank God that most of the money that supports the NAACP comes from black hands; a still larger proportion must so come ... we must not only support but control this and similar organizations, and hold them unwaveringly to our objects, our aims, and our ideals.

Du Bois repeatedly argued that the 'Negro problem' could not be separated from other humanitarian concerns and social problems of the day. In these, as in other views, his statements as editor often diverged from agreed NAACP policy.

In 1916, a year after Washington's death, Du Bois, with other leading blacks, attended a meeting called by Joel Spingarn, a white member of the NAACP, at his home in Amenia, New York. The Amenia conference, in a series of conciliatory resolutions, attempted to bridge the differences between the Washingtonians and their opponents. All forms of education were declared desirable for blacks; 'political freedom' was to be achieved through the cooperation of all black leaders, and 'antiquated subjects of controversy ... and factional alignments' were to be eliminated in the cause of racial progress. Yet Du Bois soon violated the Amenia principle of cooperative and concerted black protest. 'He minimized the social pressure which was placed upon Southern Negro leaders, and still blamed them for failing to propagandize on behalf of reforms he favoured.'[20] As *Crisis* editor, Du Bois continued to attack the principle of industrial education, and advised blacks to leave the South.

Although he viewed the First World War as the consequence of imperial rivalry between the European powers in Africa, Du Bois supported American intervention on the side of the Allies. 'Through my knowledge of Germany, I wished to see her militarism defeated and for that reason when America entered the war I believed we would in reality fight for democracy including coloured folk and not merely for war investments.'[21] Du Bois also realized that the American war effort encouraged migration from the South, expanded job opportunities and gave blacks a chance to prove their American loyalties. The most controversial editorial ever published in *Crisis* was Du Bois' 'Close ranks' plea of July 1918, which called upon blacks to 'forget our special grievances and close ranks shoulder to shoulder with our fellow citizens and the allied nations that are fighting for democracy'. (Du Bois had earlier supported the Democrat, Woodrow Wilson for the presidency, under the mistaken impression that he would support Negro rights.) Black radicals denounced the sentiments expressed in 'Close ranks'. A. Philip Randolph, the leading black socialist, said it would 'rank in shame and reeking disgrace with the Atlanta Compromise', and typified its author as a 'hand-picked, me-too-boss, hat-in-hand sycophant, lick spittling Negro'. When, after the publication of 'Close ranks', Du Bois was offered a commission in the Intelligence branch of the United States Army, his critics accused him of having been bribed to support the policies of the Wilson administration. In the event, the army withdrew the offer, but Du Bois' behaviour in the affair, which included the demand that he should receive $1,000 a year from the NAACP to supplement his army pay, called into question his commitment to black protest. If, as his critics maintained, Du Bois had been an accommodationist in wartime, he more than made amends by his editorial 'Returning soldiers' of May 1919, which advised blacks to 'return fighting' in the struggle at home against racism. America, victorious over German imperialism, was yet a 'shameful land':

It *lynches*. And lynching is barbarism of a degree of contemptible nastiness unparalleled in human history. Yet for fifty years we have lynched two Negroes a week, and we have kept this up right through the war. It *disfranchises* its own citizens. ... It encourages *ignorance*. ... It *steals* from us. ... It *insults* us ... we are cowards and jackasses if now that the war is over we do not marshal every ounce of our brain and brawn to fight a sterner, longer, more unbending battle against the forces of hell in our own land. We *return*. We *return from fighting*. We *return fighting*. Make way for Democracy![22]

'Returning soldiers' prompted the United States Department of Justice to investigate *Crisis* and other black journals. It published a condemnatory report, *Radicalism and Sedition Among Negroes as Reflected in Their Publications,* but did not prosecute.

Between 1918 and 1928, Du Bois (who had earlier made three trips to Europe), visited France, England, Belgium, Switzerland, Portugal, Germany, Russia and Africa. As he later wrote, these journeys 'gave me a depth of knowledge and a breadth of view which was of incalculable value for realizing and judging modern conditions and, above all, the problem of race in America and the world'.[23] While America's racial conflicts continued to engage most of his attention, Du Bois increasingly came to believe that these conflicts must be set in the context of the universal problem of the 'colour line'. During the 1920s, he directed a *Crisis* campaign against black colleges and universities which did not have representative numbers of Negroes on their faculties or in administrative positions. In 1924, Du Bois suggested that the NAACP, the American Federation of Labour and the Railroad Brotherhoods should organize an interracial commission, with the aim of creating integrated labour unions. But the NAACP leadership, primarily concerned with issues of political and civil rights, did not regard the promotion of unionism among blacks as an objective it could officially support. Du Bois himself was soon to abandon his earlier tolerant attitude towards organized labour, in the face of continuing discrimination within the labour movement, and his growing conviction that blacks could not expect white goodwill and support. The onset of the Great Depression confirmed Du Bois in his belief that the NAACP was untouched by or indifferent to the economic plight of the black masses.

> What distinguished Du Bois ... from other black and white spokesmen in the 1930s and 1940s was his belief that race was seriously underestimated in the theories and strategies proposed to bring racial change. To emphasize the larger social, economic, and political questions at the expense of racial considerations was, to him, naive and dangerous. ... Even though Du Bois agreed with the militants that economic considerations were of major importance to the black masses, he no longer held, as he had earlier, that black and white class solidarity was a practical or meaningful strategy for Negroes to pursue. ... Du Bois proposed the formation of a black economic cooperative enterprise based on socialist principles, racial self-help, and cultural racial nationalism. ... Central to his theory was the assumption that black people as consumers held in their own hands a powerful tool which, if properly utilized, could provide a foundation for developing within the black community an independent base of power.[24]

Du Bois accordingly proposed in the financially ailing *Crisis,* that blacks should develop a separate economy, and, to the consternation of the NAACP and many black radicals, advocated racial 'self-segregation' as the path to ultimate black political and economic power. While he welcomed the expansion of government activities under Franklin D.

Roosevelt's New Deal (see Ch. 7), Du Bois did not expect the administration's policies to effect any sea change in black–white relations. Although blacks had undoubtedly gained from New Deal welfare and public works programmes, Du Bois did not want blacks to remain dependent on a supposedly benevolent president. Rather, blacks should accept the persistence of racial prejudice, including the reality of segregation, and develop their own institutions and self-respect.

'A NEGRO NATION WITHIN A NATION'

In presenting the case for black economic separatism, Du Bois attempted to reassure *Crisis* readers that his ideas – valid in themselves – also did not contradict NAACP policies. The Association's traditional opposition to segregation, he asserted, had been in fact opposition to discrimination, and the two were not necessarily synonymous. Moreover, the NAACP had long supported such segregated institutions as churches, schools and newspapers; a self-segregated black economy was, therefore, simply another step in the formation of institutions which would bolster black morale and solidarity. Du Bois urged blacks (and the NAACP) to face the fact of enforced segregation and turn it to advantage. Members of the Talented Tenth should become planners of producer and consumer cooperatives which would form 'a Negro nation within a nation'. Blacks should patronize Negro-owned stores and use the services of the black professional classes.

> With the use of their political power, their power as consumers, and their brain power, added to that chance of personal appeal which proximity and neighbourhood always give to human beings, Negroes can develop in the United States an economic nation within a nation, able to work through inner cooperation, to found its own institutions, to educate its genius, and at the same time ... to keep in helpful touch with and cooperate with the mass of the nation. This has happened more often than most people realize, in the case of groups not so obviously separated from the mass of people as are American Negroes. It must happen in our case, or there is no hope for the Negro in America.[25]

When the NAACP passed a resolution condemning 'enforced segregation', Du Bois launched a campaign to reorganize the Association along more progressive lines. Yet in advocating black economic self-sufficiency, and in appearing to condone – if not actively encourage – racial segregation, Du Bois was running against the tide of dominant black ideology. To his critics, 'a Negro nation within a nation' smacked of Booker T. Washington's accommodationism and petty capitalism. 'Negroes had followed too long the old Du Bois, uncompromising fighter for social equality, to turn to a new Du Bois who sounded like Booker T. Washington.'[26] Francis Grimke, a black minister who had participated in the founding of the NAACP, asserted that Du Bois' acceptance of Jim Crow signalled the end of his role as black leader. A Chicago black newspaper mourned the passing of a 'race champion' and over a picture of Booker T. Washington, placed the caption 'Was He Right After All?'; above Du Bois' picture it asked 'Is He a Quitter?' Du Bois denied that his proposals bore any resemblance to Washington's National Negro Business League, which sought to develop a black economy on the basis of free competition and private profit, since his own recommendations called for the organization of an economy based on producers' and consumers' cooperatives. Distorting the truth, Du Bois also argued that his opposition to Washington had not been because of 'his programme of separation for Coloured people' but had been 'based upon the fact that he taught Coloured children to use certain tools which were almost always obsolete by the time they had finished their courses'. Such a statement misrepresented the whole rationale of the Niagara Movement and the NAACP, both of which had been integrationist.

When the NAACP resolved that no official could criticize the Association in *Crisis* without prior approval, Du Bois ignored the ruling. He continued to regard the magazine as his own personal medium to counter pejorative stereotypes of the Negro. 'He resisted all efforts by the board to make it a "house organ" that simply reported the policies of an institution, as he alleged the New York *Age* and other black newspapers did for Booker T. Washington.'[27] Black newspaper editors now expressed concern over the open rift in the Association, and sided with the NAACP against Du Bois. Walter White, who had succeeded James Weldon Johnson as executive secretary of the NAACP, charged Du Bois with having compromised with white supremacy, and undermined the Association's integrationist ideal. Du Bois retorted that White had 'more white companions and friends than coloured', and of being too light skinned to understand what segregation and discrimination really meant to blacks – 'the very same charges that Garvey had levelled at Du Bois a decade earlier' (see Ch. 5).'[28] On 26 June 1934, Du Bois resigned from the NAACP and returned to Atlanta University. In accepting his resignation, the board of the NAACP, while noting that it had not always 'seen eye to eye' with Du Bois, and could 'not subscribe to some of his criticism of the Association and its officials', paid him a generous (and deserved) tribute. Through *Crisis,* he had:

> ... created what never existed before, a Negro intelligentsia, and many
> who have never read a word of his writings are his spiritual disciples and
> descendants. ... We shall be the poorer for his loss, in intellectual
> stimulus, and in searching analysis of the vital problems of the American

Negro; no one in the Association can fill his place with the same intellectual grasp.[29]

If Du Bois' obsession with a separate black economy failed to win support among the majority of blacks or black leaders – who were concerned more with local problems than with ideological projections – his Pan-African enthusiasms (unlike those of Marcus Garvey) also failed to communicate themselves to *Crisis* readers or to the executive board of the NAACP.

DU BOIS AND PAN-AFRICANISM

As a young child, Du Bois heard his great-grandmother singing a 'heathen melody' to her children:

Do ba-na co-ba, ge-ne me, ge-ne me!
Ben d'nu-li, nu-li, nu-li, nu-li, bend' le.

These lines were handed down in the Du Bois family – 'we sing it to our children, knowing as little as our fathers what its words may mean, but knowing well the meaning of its music'.[30] After his rejection by white children in Great Barrington, and his experiences at Fisk, Du Bois discovered his 'African racial feeling' and felt himself to be both African by 'race' and 'an integral member of the group of dark Americans who are called Negroes'.[31] Concern with Africa, the ancestry and culture of Afro-Americans, and the deliverance of the African continent from the European colonizing powers, became central themes of Du Bois' thought and writings. Yet whether as a scholar, propagandist or the organizer of four Pan-African Congresses between 1919 and 1927 (a fifth was held in Manchester, England, in 1945), Du Bois' conception of Africa was that of a romantic racialist. Reporting on his first experiences of Africa in 1923, as 'Envoy Extraordinary and Minister Plenipotentiary of the President of the United States to the Inauguration of the President of Liberia', Du Bois apprised *Crisis* readers:

The spell of Africa is upon me. The ancient witchery of her medicine is burning my drowsy, dreary blood. This is not a country, it is a world, a universe of itself and for itself, a thing Different, Menacing, Alluring. It is a great black bosom where the spirit longs to die. Things move – black shiny bodies, perfect bodies, bodies of sleek and unearthly poise and beauty.[32]

Idyllic pictures of African village and tribal life, with 'well-bred and courteous children, playing happily and never sniffling or whining', were intended to awake in black Americans pride in Africa, and, by implication, pride in themselves. Although he was to ridicule Marcus

Garvey's glorification of blackness, Du Bois was himself a 'racial chauvinist', holding for all of his life a near-obsession with colour. 'At times he became involved in a black "Aryanism", tracing every civilized worldly thing to an African origin.'[33]

Du Bois' active interest in Africa began in 1900, when he attended the First Pan-African Congress held in London, attended by delegates from Ethiopia, the Gold Coast, Sierra Leone, Liberia, the United States and the Caribbean. As Chairman of the Committee on the Address to the Nations of the World, Du Bois issued a call to action:

> Let the Nations of the World respect the integrity and independence of the free Negro states of Abyssinia (properly Ethiopia), Liberia, Haiti, etc. and let the inhabitants of these states, the independent tribes of Africa, the Negroes (people of African descent) of the West Indies and America, and the black subjects of all Nations take courage, strive ceaselessly, and fight bravely, that they may prove to the world their incontestable right to be counted among the great brotherhood of mankind.[34]

The Second Pan-African Congress, organized by Du Bois, and held in Paris in 1919, was attended by fifty-seven delegates from fifteen countries. They resolved that Germany's African colonies should be turned over to an international organization, and that a code of laws be drawn up for the protection of Africans. At the Third Pan-African Congress, held in London, Brussels and Paris in 1921, a committee, headed by Du Bois, was sent to petition the League of Nations on behalf of the African colonies. The Fourth Pan-African Congress, which met in Paris and Lisbon in 1923, issued a set of eight demands seeking equality for black people throughout the world. At the Fifth Pan-African Congress, held in New York in 1927, the major resolution adopted by the delegates sought 'the development of Africa for the Africans and not merely for the profit of Europeans', and, in addition, demanded independence for India, China and Egypt. Du Bois either organized or played a leading role in each of these Congresses, yet, as he was to admit, black Americans (not to mention the European powers) were not inspired by his Pan-Africanist visions.

> The Pan-African movement ... was a curious international revival of the Niagara Movement: a handful of self-appointed spokesmen challenged a staggering problem by passing resolutions. Even the principal techniques were similar: the periodic conferences to recodify the platform, refresh personal contacts, and exchange enthusiasm and information, and the manifestoes designed to rally coloured support and to convert white opinion. In the end the congresses accomplished, if anything, less than Niagara.[35]

Such a judgement is not entirely fair. Just as the Niagara Movement was the forerunner of organized black protest in twentieth-century America, the Pan-African Congresses pointed to the later course of political independence in Africa. African nationalists like Kwame Nkrumah and

Jomo Kenyatta were to acknowledge Du Bois as a founding father of Pan-Africanism. In the United States, such ideologically divergent leaders as Malcolm X and Martin Luther King were also to pay tribute to Du Bois' African dream.

Unlike his great rival in the 1920s, Marcus Garvey (see Ch. 5), Du Bois, for all his romanticization of Africa never advocated the 'return' of Afro-Americans to their ancestral homeland, and his African nationalism was more democratic than Garvey's. Du Bois informed *Crisis* readers:

> The African movement means to us what the Zionist movement must mean to the Jews, the centralization of race effort and the recognition of a racial fount.

At the height of the Garvey movement in America, Du Bois warned:

> Africa belongs to the Africans. They have not the slightest intention of giving it up to foreigners, white or black. .... They resent the attitude that other folk of any colour are coming in to take and rule their land.
> Liberia is not going to allow American Negroes to assume control and direct her government. Liberia, in her mind, is for Liberians.[36]

Du Bois himself blamed the failure of Pan-Africanism in the short term on the opposition of the colonial powers, the patronizing and selfish attitudes of whites to Africa, and the indifference of American blacks to the plight of their African contemporaries. To these reasons should be added the sheer enormity of the task, and Du Bois' own limitations as a leader. Yet, as one authority suggests:

> Du Bois had the imagination and the intelligence to see, long before anyone else, that the meaningful slogan for beleaguered American Negroes as far as Africa was concerned was not *Back to Africa* but *Africa for the Africans,* and this is what he tried to promote with his Pan-African movement. He tried to win both the rulers of the white world and the Negroes of his own world to the self-serving good sense of his idea, and he failed with both.[37]

Ironically, Marcus Garvey's flamboyant and fantastic notion of uniting all the Negroes of the world into one great organization was to eclipse Du Bois' Pan-Africanism, as it also underlined his inability to reach a mass audience.

'A LEADER WITHOUT FOLLOWERS': W. E. B. DU BOIS, 1934–1963

The most prolific and gifted of all Afro-American writers and intellectuals, Du Bois was never a successful leader or organizer. After his resignation from the NAACP in 1934, at the age of sixty-six, he became, more than ever, isolated and embittered, in F. L. Broderick's phrase, 'a leader without followers'.

> Du Bois had come North to win the Negro from Washington's patient gradualism, and by 1920, he had stood as a prophet preaching a successful gospel. [But] new proposals had to win in a market crowded with leaders who, though ready to canonize Du Bois, were unwilling to surrender to him their independent power in specific areas of Negro life. Du Bois never really grasped this new situation. Coming to full maturity in the era of Booker T. Washington, Du Bois inherited an image of an all-embracing leader, the universal pundit creating total solutions for the Negro problem. He thought that his victory over Washington made him lead dog in a pack, when actually it made him one caravan leader on a very broad frontier. Such an attitude led him into two errors fatal to his continuing leadership. First, it teased him into explorations of universal movements like Pan-Africanism and world socialism so remote from the Negro's humdrum day-to-day struggle for existence that they commanded neither attention nor support. Second, it forbade deviation from Du Bois' views under pain of anathema.[38]

From the time of his return to Atlanta in 1934, to his death in Ghana in 1963, Du Bois remained estranged from the Talented Tenth, because of their opposition to socialism and voluntary self-segregation, and their support for integration and increased opportunity within the capitalist system. During the Depression and New Deal, Du Bois, as mentioned, was very much a prophet without honour in his own country.

> Du Bois' denial of interracial cooperation ... his affirmation of distinctive social and cultural characteristics and the necessity of black self-help and racial unity, and his assertion that race prejudice was not on the decline as a result of the Depression crisis or liberal reformism, but remained permanent features of American life, challenged the basic assumptions of most black and white thinkers during the period.[39]

Shortly after his return to Atlanta, Du Bois published two major works. *Black Reconstruction in America: an essay toward a history of the part which black folk played in the attempt to reconstruct democracy in America, 1860–1880* (1935), offered a Marxist-derived interpretation of the role played by blacks in securing Confederate defeat. Southern slaves, Du Bois argued, had engaged in a 'general strike' when they fled from the plantations to join the invading Union armies. More realistically, *Black Reconstruction* stressed the roles played by blacks during the Civil War and in the post-war governments in the South. As one contemporary reviewer noted, the book, although too bulky and marked by radical terminology, presented 'a mass of material, formerly ignored, that every future historian must deal with'. *Dusk of Dawn,* which appeared in 1940, was subtitled 'An Autobiography of a Race Concept', and presented Du Bois' account – and defence – of his dual careers as an Afro-American and Pan-African propagandist. It reiterated his belief in voluntary self-segregation as the best means of securing racial progress, expressed a favourable view of the Marxist interpretation of history, and recounted the author's search for fulfilment in a materialistic and racially divided world. 'He viewed his own career as an ideological case study illuminating the varied facets of the Negro–white conflict.'[40] The principal fault (and characteristic) of *Dusk of Dawn,* as Oswald Garrison Villard observed, was 'the very real egotism which shines through these pages in which few others are praised – chiefly those who contributed to his success'.

In *Dusk of Dawn,* Du Bois also reviewed his controversy with Booker T. Washington, and carefully presented himself as the injured party.

> I was in my imagination a scientist, and neither a leader nor an agitator;
> I had nothing but the greatest admiration for Mr Washington and
> Tuskegee, and I had applied at both Tuskegee and Hampton for work.

There had been, Du Bois conceded, significant differences between himself and Washington. Where Washington had placed his faith in industrial education and 'common labour': 'I believed in the higher education of a Talented Tenth who through their knowledge of modern culture could guide the American Negro into a higher civilization.' These theories, Du Bois maintained, were not necessarily opposed, and indeed could have been complementary. But the striking feature of Washington's leadership was 'that whatever he or anybody believed in or wanted must be subordinated to dominant public opinion and that opinion deferred to and cajoled until it allowed a deviation toward better ways'. The root cause of the controversy, however, lay in the 'discrepancies and paradoxes' of Washington's influence and leadership.

> It did not seem fair ... that on the one hand Mr Washington should
> decry political activities among Negroes, and on the other dictate Negro
> political objectives from Tuskegee. At a time when Negro civil rights
> called for organized and aggressive defence, he broke down that defence
> by advising acquiescence or at least no open agitation.

Above all, Du Bois remembered, the power of the Tuskegee Machine – which reached out to governors, congressmen, presidents and philanthropists – had had to be resisted.

> Contrary to most opinion, the controversy as it developed was not
> entirely against Mr Washington's ideas, but became the insistence upon
> the right of other Negroes to have and express their ideas. ... I was
> greatly disturbed at this time, not because I was in absolute opposition
> to the things that Mr Washington was advocating, but because I was
> strongly in favour of more open agitation against wrongs and above all I
> resented the practical buying up of the Negro press and choking off even

mild and reasonable opposition to Mr Washington in both the Negro press and the white.

Yet in his essay 'Of Mr Booker T. Washington and others', Du Bois reminded readers of *Dusk of Dawn,* he had left out 'the more controversial matter: the bitter resentment which young Negroes felt at the continued and increasing activity of the Tuskegee Machine'. Instead, he had concentrated on Washington's 'general philosophy', and now 'a generation later' was still satisfied with that critique – 'I can see no word that I would change.'[41] (Surprisingly, in view of their deep enmity, Du Bois devoted only a few lines in his autobiography to his disagreements with Marcus Garvey.)

Du Bois' other scholarly publications (after a brief return to the NAACP in 1945) included *Colour and Democracy* (1945), in which he attempted to link the future of Africa with that of the rest of the world, and to align African nationalism with socialist thought. By this time, Du Bois was identified with international peace movements, socialism, and in lobbying the United Nations to permit the representation of African colonial peoples. In 1947, as editor of the NAACP 'Appeal to the World', he again petitioned the United Nations to mobilize world public opinion on the United States to redress the wrongs suffered by black Americans. (In 1945, he had served as an associate consultant to the American delegation at the founding session of the UN in San Francisco.) Du Bois' expressed sympathies for the Soviet Union, his condemnation of the Korean conflict as a capitalist war, an abortive attempt to become the American Labour Party's representative for New York in the United States Senate in 1950 (when he received less than 4 per cent of the vote), and his chairmanship of the Peace Information Centre which circulated the 1951 'Stockholm Peace Appeal', a Russian-inspired nuclear disarmament proposal, were all indications of his continuing radicalism. When he refused to comply with a US Department of Justice order to register as an agent of a 'foreign principal', Du Bois was indicted by a federal grand jury, but was acquitted. Excoriated in the United States, at the height of the McCarthy witch-hunting era, Du Bois was fêted in the Communist world, on visits to China and the Soviet Union. In 1953, he was awarded the Communist-sponsored World Peace Prize, and ten years later, the Lenin Prize. On his ninety-first birthday in Peking, Du Bois informed a large and responsive audience that 'in my own country for nearly a century I have been nothing but a "nigger" '.[42]

Although he welcomed the Supreme Court's 1954 school desegregation decision, and applauded the action of 'black workers' in the Montgomery, Alabama, bus boycott (see Ch. 7), and student involvement in the lunch-counter 'sit-ins' of the 1960s, Du Bois, during his last years in America, remained aloof from the black–white civil rights coalition. He was not, however, indifferent to scholarly assessments of Booker T. Washington which suggested that he had made a realistic pragmatic adjustment to the conditions of his time. Reviewing Samuel R. Spencer's biography, *Booker T. Washington and the Negro's Place in American Life* (1955), Du Bois dissented from Spencer's view that Washington anticipated the civil rights movement of the 1950s, but in his own day 'did what was possible, given the time and place in which he lived, and did it to the utmost'. After noting that Spencer, 'a Southern white man', was bound to reach a favourable verdict on Washington, Du Bois reiterated his contention that if the Negro, contrary to Washington's advice and example, 'had not fought desperately to retain the right to vote, to gain civil rights and social recognition ... for the education of his gifted children, for a place among modern men, their situation today would have been disastrous'. Southern whites, by their subsequent behaviour, had dishonoured the terms of the compromise offered by Washington at Atlanta. Yet, Du Bois maintained, Washington had been 'treated with extraordinary respect by his fellow Negroes, even when they believed he was bartering their rights for a mess of pottage'. Du Bois was not simply restating his differences with Washington, but was also, by implication, linking the militant protest of the NAACP in its early years, and his own editorship of *Crisis* in particular, with the emerging civil rights coalition that was to thrust Martin Luther King into the role of race leader.[43] On an even more personal note, Du Bois could hardly approve of a book in which he was characterized as having had 'delusions of grandeur' when he dared to challenge the Tuskegee Machine, or the typification that he 'was imperious, egocentric, aloof'.

In 1961, Du Bois applied for membership of the American Communist Party, having reached the 'firm conclusion' that 'capitalism cannot reform itself; it is doomed to self-destruction. No universal selfishness can bring social good to all.' Before the announcement of his application was made public, Du Bois, at the urging of President Nkrumah, went to Ghana – where in 1960 he had begun work on the preparation of an *Encyclopedia Africana,* a project he had already attempted in 1909 and in 1934 – and became a Ghanaian citizen in the last months of his life. Yet:

> ... in spite of his Ghanaian citizenship ... Du Bois died an American in exile. ... To the end, the attempted reconciliation of his divided souls, African and American, tested his greatest strength. His place in Ghana was in fact far more tenuous than he might have imagined. Had he lived three more years, he would have witnessed the military coup that routed Nkrumah and his government, suppressed socialism and the doctrine of Pan-Africanism, and aborted the scheme for the *Encyclopedia Africana.*[44]

But, as one of his last letters revealed, Du Bois retained an optimistic belief in his contribution to black advancement:

... always I have been uplifted by the thought that what I have done well will live long and justify my life; that what I have done ill or never finished can now be handed on to others for endless days to be finished, perhaps better than I could have done.[45]

REFERENCES

1. Robeson, P., 'The legacy of W. E. B. Du Bois', in P. S. Foner (ed.) *Paul Robeson Speaks: writings, speeches and interviews, 1918–1974* (New York, 1978), pp. 474–5.
2. Isaacs, H. R., *The New World of Negro Americans* (London, 1963), p. 195.
3. Myrdal, G., *An American Dilemma* (New York, 1944, 1962), p. 770.
4. Harlan, L., *Booker T. Washington: the wizard of Tuskegee* (Oxford U.P.; New York, 1983), pp. 84–5.
5. Myrdal, op. cit., p. 743.
6. Rudwick, E. M., *W. E. B. Du Bois: propagandist of the Negro protest* (New York, 1969), p. 126.
7. Rudwick, op. cit., p. 131.
8. Harlan, op. cit., p. 360.
9. Du Bois, W. E. B., *Souls of Black Folk* (New York, 1961), p. 17.
10. Rampersad, A., *The Art and Imagination of W. E. B. Du Bois* (London, 1976), p. 11.
11. Du Bois, W. E. B., *The Autobiography of W. E. B. Du Bois: a soliloquy on viewing my life from the last decade of its first century* (1968), pp. 107–8.
12. Rampersad, op. cit., p. 45.
13. Berghahn, M., *Images of Africa in Black American Literature* (1977), p. 76.
14. Du Bois, W. E. B., *Dusk of Dawn* (1940), p. 49.
15. Moses, W. J., *The Golden Age of Black Nationalism* (Connecticut, 1978), p. 136.
16. Du Bois, op. cit., (1968), p. 258.
17. Broderick, F. L., *W. E. B. Du Bois: Negro leader in a time of crisis* (Stanford, California, 1959), p. 229.
18. *Crisis,* II (1911), 195.
19. *Crisis,* V (1912–13), 290–1.
20. Rudwick, op. cit., p. 187.
21. Du Bois, op. cit., (1940), p. 253.
22. *Crisis,* XVIII (1919), 13–14.
23. Du Bois, op. cit., (1940), p. 267.
24. Kirby, J. B., *Black Americans in the Roosevelt Era* (Knoxville, Tennessee, 1980), pp. 191–3.
25. Lester, J. (ed.), *The Seventh Son: the thought and writings of W. E. B. Du Bois,* Vol. II (New York, 1971), p. 405.
26. Broderick, op. cit., p. 177.
27. Toll, W., *The Resurgence of Race: black social theory from Reconstruction to the Pan-African Conferences* (University of Pennsylvania Press, 1979), p. 158.

28. Sitkoff, H., *A New Deal for Blacks: the emergence of civil rights as a national issue.* Vol. I, *The Depression Decade* (Oxford U.P., New York, 1978), p. 251.
29. Du Bois, op. cit., (1940), pp. 314–15.
30. Du Bois, op. cit., (1961), p. 184.
31. Du Bois, op. cit., (1940), pp. 114–15.
32. *Crisis,* XXVII (1924), 273–4.
33. Moses, op. cit., p. 144.
34. Clarke, J.H. *et al. Black Titan: W. E. B. Du Bois, an anthology by the editors of Freedomways* (Boston, 1970), pp. 191–2.
35. Broderick, op. cit., p. 130.
36. *Crisis,* July 1924, p. 106.
37. Isaacs, op. cit., p. 221.
38. Broderick, op. cit., pp. 175–6.
39. Kirby, op. cit., p. 196.
40. Rudwick, op. cit., p. 287.
41. Du Bois, op. cit., (1940), pp. 69–80.
42. Rudwick, op. cit., p. 293.
43. *Science and Society,* 20 (1956), 183–5.
44. Rampersad, op. cit., p. 291.
45. Brewer, W. H., 'Some memories of Dr W. E. B. Du Bois', *JNH,* 53 (1969), 348.

Chapter five

MARCUS GARVEY (1880–1940): GHETTO MESSIAH

Since the death of Booker T. Washington there was no one with a positive and practical uplift programme for the masses – North or South. Said a coloured woman after she had joined the organization, 'Garvey is giving my people backbones where they had wish-bones.'

(Amy Jaques-Garvey, *Garvey and Garveyism*)[1]

As a kid I heard about Marcus Garvey. We used to sing a song ridiculing him. 'Marcus Garvey is a big monkey man. Marcus Garvey will catch you if he can. All you black folks get in line. Buy your tickets on the Black Star Line.'

(Harold R. Isaacs, *The New World of Negro Americans*)[2]

WAITING FOR GARVEY? THE NORTHERN GHETTO, 1900–1920

From the end of the Civil War, Southern blacks began to move from rural areas to the cities of the South, and increasingly, to those of the North. A series of economic crises and natural disasters (the ravages of the boll weevil and catastrophic floods in Mississippi and Alabama), the increasing mechanization of Southern agriculture, the perfection of disfranchisement techniques and the spread of Jim Crow legislation and practices, combined to drive blacks from the land to the large urban centres. In 1879, thousands of black tenant farmers, the victims of a vicious credit system that kept them in unending poverty, and of returning Democratic 'Redeemer' governments which stripped them of the civil and political rights gained during Reconstruction, left the states of Tennessee, Texas, Mississippi and Louisiana, and headed for Kansas. These black 'Exodusters' were the advance wave of the 'Great Migration' of Southern blacks, attracted by the promise of greater opportunities in the cities of the North-east and Middle West. Between

1890 and 1910, the black population of Chicago increased from 1.3 to 2.00 per cent; that of Philadelphia, from 3.8 to 5.5 per cent and that of Pittsburgh from 3.3 to 4.8 per cent. By the early 1900s, well-developed black ghettos had begun to emerge in these and other cities, marked by patterns of residential segregation and the growth of separate institutions. In New York City, between 1890 and 1920, the black population increased from less than 70,000 to over 152,000, the majority Southern-born, but with a significant influx from the West Indies. In this same period, one area of New York City – Harlem – was transformed from an all-white upper-class and fashionable section into a ghetto slum.

HARLEM

Although there were significant differences in the urban experiences of Negroes, which reflected the nature of race relations, the origins and composition of the black population, economic opportunities and the structure of the black leadership class, there was also a marked similarity in the forces which combined to produce all-black residential areas in the major cities. In all cases, the Negro ghetto was both the product of white racism, which confined blacks to less desirable areas of settlement, and of black entrepreneurship, adaptability and community spirit. In Harlem, the Afro-American Realty Company, formed in 1904, originated in a partnership of ten Negroes, organized by Philip A. Payton, a friend and admirer of Booker T. Washington, who saw the possibilities of exploiting Harlem's depressed property market. The Afro-American Realty Company specialized in acquiring five-year leases on property owned by whites, and then renting it to blacks. Charles W. Anderson, the leading New York Negro Republican, and T. Thomas Fortune, editor of the New York *Age,* supported Payton's enterprises. All were protégés of Washington, and members of his National Negro Business League; ironically, Washington, despite his anti-urban bias, can be considered a founding father of Harlem, which by the 1920s had become, in the words of James Weldon Johnson, 'the intellectual and artistic capital of the Negro world'. By the 1920s, Negro churches had become the largest black property holders in Harlem, investing heavily in local real estate and building new places of worship. In addition, by the early 1920s:

> Practically every major Negro institution moved from its downtown headquarters to Harlem ... the United Order of True Reformers; Odd Fellows, Masons, Elks, Pythians and other fraternal orders; the Music School Settlement; the Coachman's Union League; the African Society of

Mutual Relief; The New York *Age;* West Fifty-third Street YMCA and YWCA; almost all the Negro social service agencies, including local offices of the Urban League (see below) and the NAACP; the African Methodist Episcopal Home and Foreign Missionary Society; all the major churches. The virtual monopoly The New York *Age* had for generations as the city's only leading Negro journal was broken, and two other weeklies were established: the *New York News* and the *Amsterdam News.*[3]

In 1914, blacks lived in 1,100 different houses within a 23-block area of Harlem; in the same year, an Urban League survey estimated Harlem's black population at 49,555. By 1930, its Negro population was approximately 200,000, of whom 55,000 had been born in the West Indies. By this date, Harlem had become a gigantic slum as housing and welfare facilities deteriorated under the sheer weight of numbers.

THE NATIONAL URBAN LEAGUE

Booker T. Washington was also to see his policies of moral and economic progress, vocational training and the de-emphasis of civil and political rights reflected in the programme of the National Urban League. Founded in 1911, the League grew out of two earlier organizations, the National League for the Protection of Coloured Women, and the Committee for Improving the Industrial Conditions of Negroes in New York. Concerned to offer for recently arrived rural blacks the kinds of welfare and employment services already available to native and foreign-born whites through settlement houses, charities and immigrant-aid societies, the Urban League, a biracial coalition of Progressive whites and professional blacks, was considerably to the right of the NAACP. Where the NAACP worked for the recognition and exercise of legal and civil rights by Negroes, the Urban League's declared aim was 'to promote, encourage, assist and engage in any and all kinds of work for improving the industrial, economic, social and spiritual condition among Negroes'.

It sought jobs and decent homes for migrants, and counselled them on behaviour, dress, sanitation, health and homemaking. It trained Negro social workers and placed them in community service positions as family caseworkers, settlement house workers, supervisors of day nurseries. The League unsuccessfully petitioned the American Federation of Labour to end lily-white union policies. And it conducted scientific investigations among urban Negroes as a basis for practical reform. While the NAACP dealt in protest and agitation, the Urban League's tools were primarily those of negotiation, persuasion, education and investigation.[4]

Echoing Washingtonian precepts, the League urged blacks to make free use of the toothbrush, the comb, and soap and water. In 1911, the League and the NAACP agreed to adhere to their respective goals and strategies of racial advancement, but neither organization was able to avoid the charges of black militants like the socialist A. Philip Randolph, that they were basically middle-class and white-dominated agencies, pledged to the perpetuation of the capitalist system.

American involvement in the First World War encouraged further black migration from the South, as Northern industries supplied the needs of the Allies and, with European immigration closed off, called for skilled and unskilled labour. Black migrants, however, met with the hostility of white workers in the competition for jobs and housing. After the United States Supreme Court, in a decision of 1917, declared municipal segregation ordinances unconstitutional, 'white improvement associations' utilized restrictive covenants – agreements among property holders not to sell housing in specified areas to Negroes. As urban conditions worsened, 'earlier Negro settlers blamed the mass of Southern newcomers, with their awkward and unrefined ways, for the more intense prejudice which all blacks in the North now faced'.[5] In Harlem, tensions between American blacks and West Indian immigrants resulted from fears of economic competition, and jealousy of the business and social mores of the growing West Indian community. Afro-Americans asserted that West Indians were too clannish, overly ambitious – often willing to work for lower wages than native-born blacks – and arrogant. West Indians were charged with disregarding the norms of American racial etiquette, as seen in their seeking jobs which American custom designated as 'white', while holding aloof from black protest organizations.

> The propensity of West Indians to isolate themselves from the struggles of the Afro-American while criticizing him and his nation especially irritated natives. ... Worse, some retreated to the protection of foreign citizenship when they experienced discrimination or insults from race-conscious whites. ... Black Americans resented West Indians for enjoying the best of two worlds – the British and the American – while making it more difficult for Afro-Americans to secure the economic advantages of American citizenship. ... American blacks were deeply disturbed by the reluctance of the West Indians to abandon old allegiances and become citizens. They viewed the slow rate of naturalization as evidence of West Indian refusal to assimilate and form a united front with them.[6]

These tensions, together with race riots in Northern cities, culminating in the 'Red Summer' of 1919, which witnessed over twenty major racial disturbances and the revival of the Ku-Klux-Klan, segregation and discrimination in the American armed forces and the continuing deterioration of conditions in the urban ghettos, produced an intensified racial awareness and militancy among black Americans. W. E. B. Du

Bois and A. Philip Randolph advocated black resistance to white mobs, and the united action of white and black workers against the capitalists. In literature, the arts and music, the 'Harlem Renaissance' signified the advent of a 'New Negro' – racially proud, and searching for an Afro-American identity. Into this climate, soon to be overladen by the effects of the Great Depression, a West Indian prophet and visionary injected a compelling appeal to urban blacks who were, for all practical purposes, already living in a social environment that resembled an all-black and separatist nation. Moreover, as his fellow West Indian, the poet and novelist Claude McKay, observed, Marcus Garvey came to America 'as a humble disciple of the late Booker T. Washington, Founder of Tuskegee Institute'.[7]

MARCUS GARVEY: BLACK JAMAICAN

Marcus Moziah Garvey was born in St Ann's Bay, Jamaica, the youngest of eleven children. His parents were of unmixed Negro ancestry, descended from Maroons – African slaves who had successfully defied the Jamaican slave regime and formed virtually independent black communities in the mountains from 1664 to 1795. Because of his Maroon heritage, Garvey was fiercely proud of his blackness, and came to display a distrust for light-skinned Negroes. In a 'chapter of autobiography' published in 1925, Garvey recalled:

> My parents were black Negroes. My father was a man of brilliant intellect and dashing courage. He once had a fortune; he died poor. My mother was a sober and conscientious Christian; too soft and good for the time in which she lived.[8]

Garvey's father, a skilled stonemason, was also literate, possessed a private library and acted as a local lawyer. After a few years of elementary education, Garvey, already apprenticed to a printer, left school at the age of fourteen. As a child, Garvey maintained friendly relations with the white children in his neighbourhood, played with the children of a Wesleyan minister whose church his family attended, and was especially attached to one of the minister's daughters. But at the age of fourteen, her parents separated her from Garvey, and the effect was traumatic.

> They sent her and another sister to Edinburgh, Scotland, and told her that she was never to write or try to get in touch with me, for I was a 'nigger'. It was then that I found for the first time that there was some difference in humanity, and that there were different races, each having its own separate and distinct social life. ... After my first lesson in race distinction, I never thought of playing with white girls any more.[9]

Moving to Kingston, where he hoped to continue his education, Garvey was forced to work in a printing shop owned by his godfather. By the age of twenty, he had become the youngest foreman printer in Kingston, at a time when British and Canadian immigrants were generally taking such jobs. When the printer's union went on strike for higher wages, Garvey was elected leader. The strike failed when the printer imported new machinery and immigrant labour, and the treasurer absconded with the union's funds. Garvey was fired and blacklisted. He became sceptical of the value of the labour movement and of socialism, and went to work for the government printing office. Increasingly conscious of the related issues of race and politics, Garvey also began to oppose British colonial rule in Jamaica. In 1910, he published his first newspaper, *Garvey's Watchman,* a weekly with a circulation of about 3,000 copies. The venture was short-lived, and Garvey went to Costa Rica, where he worked as a timekeeper on a United Fruit Company banana plantation. He observed the exploitation of West Indian immigrant workers, and founded his second paper, *La Nacion,* in which he attacked the British consul for his indifference to the situation. Garvey then moved on to Panama, witnessed the depressed condition of Jamaican workers on the Panama Canal, and produced another newspaper, *La Prensa.* Moving on through Ecuador, Nicaragua, Honduras, Columbia and Venezuela, he discovered essentially similar situations, and in each case attempted to organize the black labour forces. Then, according to his wife, Garvey:

> Sickened with fever, and sick at heart over appeals from his people for help on their behalf ... decided to return to Jamaica in 1911, and try with Government there, as well as to awaken Jamaicans at home, to the true conditions on the Spanish mainland.[10]

Unable to interest the government in the appalling conditions faced by Jamaican workers abroad, Garvey travelled through Europe, and settled for a time in London, where he met and worked with the Egyptian nationalist Duse Mohammad Ali, an admirer of Booker T. Washington, and publisher of the *African Times and Orient Review.* From Ali, Garvey learned of the subjugation of blacks throughout Africa, and increased his knowledge of African history. In London Garvey also first read Washington's *Up From Slavery,* and later remembered: 'I read of conditions in America ... and then my doom – if I may so call it – of being a race leader dawned upon me.'[11] In 1914, Garvey returned to Jamaica with the plan of 'uniting all the Negro peoples in the world into one great body to establish a country and Government absolutely their own'. On 1 August 1914, he established the Universal Negro Improvement and Conservation Association and African Communities League – the UNIA. As defined by Garvey, the UNIA's grandiose objectives were:

> To establish a Universal Confraternity among the race; to promote the spirit of pride and love; to reclaim the fallen; to administer to and assist

the needy; to assist in civilizing the backward tribes of Africa; to assist in the development of independent Negro Nations and communities; to establish a central nation for the race, where they will be given the opportunity to develop themselves; to establish Commissaries and Agencies in the principal countries and cities of the world for the representation of all Negroes; to promote a conscientious spiritual worship among the native tribes of Africa; to establish Universities, Colleges, and Academies and Schools for racial education and culture of the people; to improve the general conditions of Negroes everywhere.

The motto of the new organization was 'One God! One Aim! One Destiny!' More immediately, the UNIA planned to establish educational and industrial colleges for Jamaican blacks – a reflection of Booker T. Washington's guiding influence on Garvey's thought and career. Planning to visit the United States in 1915 on a fund-raising tour, Garvey (who had earlier been invited by Washington to visit Tuskegee) informed him in a letter: 'I need not reacquaint you of the horrible condition prevailing among our people in the West Indies as you are so well informed of happenings over Negrodom.'[12] Garvey also enclosed a copy of the UNIA manifesto, which included among its objects the establishment of industrial schools. Washington, in reply, wished Garvey every success, yet failed to appreciate the heroic aims of the UNIA, treating it 'as though it were a variant of the National Negro Business League'. He informed his Jamaican admirer:

This is the age of 'getting together', and everywhere we look we see evidence of that constructive accomplishment which are [*sic*] the result of friendly cooperation and mutual helpfulness. Such, I am sure, is the object of your Association, and I am only too sorry that I cannot afford the time just now to give more careful study to your plans so outlined.[13]

At this stage, Garvey saw himself as a Washingtonian, but never met his mentor, who died before Garvey reached America in 1916. Throughout his life, Garvey expressed admiration – although often qualified – for Washington. Following his second visit to Tuskegee in 1923, Garvey wrote: 'Language fails me to express my high appreciation for the service Dr Washington has rendered to us as a people.' He was 'an originator and builder who, out of nothing, constructed the greatest educational and industrial institution of the race in modern times'.[14] Garvey also, on this occasion, expressed enthusiasm for Washington's emphasis on self-help, race pride, and his hostility to social equality. But in a later appraisal of Washington's leadership, Garvey qualified his admiration:

The world held up the great Sage of Tuskegee ... as the only leader for the race. They looked forward to him and his teachings as the leadership for all times, not calculating that the industrially educated Negro would himself evolve a new ideal.

Echoing one of Du Bois' criticisms of Washington, Garvey asserted that:

> If Washington had lived he would have had to change his programme. No leader can successfully lead this race of ours without giving an interpretation of the awakened spirit of the New Negro, who does not seek industrial opportunity alone, but a political voice.[15]

At the height of his power in the United States, Garvey could argue that whereas Washington had looked for concessions from whites, the true race leader must be more aggressive and demanding. Reversing his earlier estimate, Garvey concluded that 'Booker T. Washington was not a leader of the Negro race. We do not look to Tuskegee. The world has recognized him as a leader, but we do not. We are going to make demands.'[16] When Washington's successor at Tuskegee, R. R. Moton, failed to provide the kind of leadership which Garvey believed the changed situation demanded, he was denounced as the captive of 'white philanthropists' and therefore unfit to speak for the Negro race.

In Jamaica, the UNIA failed to attract the mulatto group, while the use of the term 'Negro' in its title was resented by many native Jamaicans who preferred the word 'coloured'. After a year, the movement had only about 100 members. Reflecting bitterly on this period, Garvey declared:

> I really never knew there was so much colour prejudice in Jamaica ... until I started the work of the UNIA. ... I had just returned from a successful trip to Europe, which was an exceptional achievement for a black man. The daily press wrote me up with big headlines and told of my movement. But nobody wanted to be a Negro. ... Men and women as black as I, and even more so, had believed themselves white under the West Indian order of society ... yet everyone beneath his breath was calling the black man a nigger. I had to decide whether to please my friends and be one of the 'black–whites' of Jamaica, and be reasonably prosperous, or come out openly, and defend and help and improve and protect the integrity of black millions and suffer. I decided to do the latter, hence my offence against 'coloured–black–white' society in the colonies and America ... in the opinion of the 'coloured' element, leadership should have been in the hands of a yellow or a very light man. There is more bitterness among us Negroes because of the caste of colour than there is between any other peoples, not excluding the peoples of India.[17]

Garvey arrived in New York on 23 March 1916, on a fund-raising lecture tour for an industrial institute to be established in Jamaica, intending to stay for five months. He visited Tuskegee 'and paid my respects to the dead hero, Booker Washington', toured thirty-eight states and, at the end of the year, returned to New York City and set up a base in Harlem. Scornful of existing Afro-American leadership, with its dependence on white support and neglect of the black masses, Garvey decided to set up a division of the UNIA in America, and turned to the West Indian element in Harlem for support. Initially, Garvey planned to return to Jamaica 'after instructing people in the aims and objectives' of the UNIA. But, faced with the opposition of Harlem's established black leadership, who attempted to 'turn the movement into a political club', he resigned as president of the Jamaican chapter, decided to remain in Harlem, and began a campaign to recruit members. Within three weeks, Garvey claimed to have recruited 2,000 members in Harlem; by 1921, he estimated that the UNIA had 6 million members throughout the world. Neither contemporary observers nor later historians of the Garvey movement have agreed on its due-paying membership. In 1923, Du Bois claimed that the UNIA had fewer than 20,000 members. By 1923, Garvey could reasonably claim that within the United States the UNIA had twenty times the membership and support of all the other Negro organizations combined. 'Arguments about the number of his followers dispute the millions.'[18]

In 1919, Garvey began publication of a weekly newspaper, *The Negro World,* the official organ of the UNIA. It was, as its masthead proclaimed, 'A Newspaper Devoted Solely to the Interests of the Negro Race'. Other slogans declared that it was: 'The indispensable weekly, the voice of the awakened Negro, reaching the masses everywhere'. With a weekly circulation of about 200,000, *The Negro World* was Garvey's greatest propaganda device and his most successful publishing venture. It appeared in English, Spanish and French editions, and lasted until 1933. Every issue carried a front-page polemic by Garvey, and articles on black history and culture, racial news and UNIA activities. Garvey's ideological statements in *The Negro World* spread the UNIA message not only throughout the United States, but also in Latin America, the Caribbean and Africa – much to the consternation of the colonial powers. C. L. R. James relates a conversation with the Kenyan nationalist Jomo Kenyatta in 1921, in which he was informed that illiterate Kenyans 'would gather round a reader of Garvey's newspaper ... and listen to an article two or three times'. They would then run into surrounding areas 'carefully to repeat the whole, which they had memorized, to Africans, hungry for some doctrine which lifted them from the servile consciousness in which Africans lived'.[19]

The programme of the UNIA was succinctly stated in an eight-point platform in one issue of *The Negro World.*[20]

1. To champion Negro nationhood by redemption of Africa.
2. To make the Negro Race conscious.
3. To breathe ideals of manhood and womanhood into every Negro.
4. To advocate self-determination.
5. To make the Negro world-conscious.
6. To print all the news that will be interesting and instructive to the Negro.
7. To instill Racial self-help.
8. To inspire Racial love and self-respect.

To underline this last point, *The Negro World* refused to print advertising copy for skin-whitening and hair-straightening compounds – staple revenue sources for much of the black press in America.

In July 1919, Garvey purchased a large auditorium in Harlem, Liberty Hall, for UNIA meetings, and Liberty Halls were also opened by other UNIA branches. (By 1926, there were sixteen divisions and chapters of the UNIA in California.) Amy Jacques-Garvey described the multiple functions of these halls, designed to serve 'the needs of the people'.

> Sunday morning worship, afternoon Sunday schools, Public Meetings at nights, concerts and dances were held. Notice boards were put up where one could look for a room, a job, or a lost article. In localities where there were many members out of work during the winter, Black Cross Nurses would organize soup kitchens, and give them a warm meal daily. The Legions would make portable screens for a corner of the Hall, where men who could not be temporarily housed with fellow members would sleep on benches at nights. In the freezing winter days stoves had to be kept going to accommodate the cold and homeless until they 'got on their feet again'.[21]

The following month, the Negro Factories Corporation was founded 'to build and operate factories in the big industrial centres of the United States, Central America, the West Indies, and Africa to manufacture every marketable commodity'. The Corporation developed a chain of grocery stores, a restaurant, steam laundry, tailoring establishment, hotel, doll factory and printing press in Harlem. By 1920, the UNIA and its allied enterprises employed 300 people – putting into practice the Washington-derived precept of economic self-help.

Garvey's most spectacular undertaking was the organization of an all-Negro steamship company that would link the coloured peoples of the world in commercial and industrial intercourse. The Black Star Steamship Line, incorporated in Delaware on 26 June 1919, was capitalized at $500,000, with 100,000 shares of stock at $5.00 a share. The Black Star Line (BSL) also derived from Washington's axiom that blacks must become independent of white capital, and stock circulars for the projected line appealed directly to racial pride. 'The Black Star Corporation presents to every Black Man, Woman, and Child, the opportunity to climb the great ladder of industrial and commercial progress.' Sale of BSL stock was limited to Negroes, with a maximum of 200 shares per person. 'Holding a share in the BSL gave the black American, at least vicariously, some connection with the world of international finance.'[22] In February 1920, the BSL was recapitalized at $10,000,000.

Garvey never intended that the line would be the agency for the mass transportation of Negroes back to Africa; rather was it conceived as a commercial operation, a source of justifiable racial pride and a demonstration of black entrepreneurial skills.

> The main purpose of the formation and promotion of the Black Star
> Line was to acquire ships to trade between the units of the Race – in
> Africa, the USA, the West Indies, and Central America, thereby building
> up an independent economy of business, industry, and commerce, and to
> transport our people ... on business and pleasure, without being given
> inferior accommodation ... or refusal of any sort of accommodation.[23]

Unfortunately, the BSL's operations were marked by financial (and
navigational) failure, as well as by elements of farce and ineptitude.

In August 1920, Garvey and the Harlem branch of the UNIA staged
the First International Convention of Negro Peoples of the World.
Delegates from twenty-five countries attended the proceedings in New
York. Roi Ottley, the black journalist and social worker, remembered
that as a child he had seen the UNIA carnival.

> It was a monster affair almost approaching medieval splendour in regalia
> of lush colours. During the whole month of August, 1920, delegates from
> all the states, the West Indies, South America and Africa assembled in
> Liberty Hall, in a demonstration that proved to be a series of rousing
> 'bravos' and 'hallelujahs' to the black leader. People were fascinated by
> all the bustle, colour, and animation in the streets. There were loud
> speeches, stock-selling from the curbstones, and indeed fisticuffs as men
> clashed. 'Is Garvey greater than Jesus Christ?' people asked. 'Give he a
> chance,' shot back his devout West Indian followers in their quaint
> English dialect. 'He's a young mon yet!'[24]

The 1920 convention was certainly a splendid and glamorous affair.
Parades through Harlem of the various elements of the UNIA – the
African Legion in blue and red uniforms, the Black Cross Nurses,
dressed in dazzling white, the Black Flying Eagles and the Universal
African Motor Corps – attracted and delighted the Negro community.
The UNIA flag, red for Negro blood, green for Negro hopes and black
for Negro skin, was prominently displayed, while the UNIA anthem,
'Ethiopia, Thou Land of Our Fathers' was sung rousingly. Convention
speeches stressed the theme of African nationalism, and Garvey was
elected Provisional President of the African Republic. (Charles S.
Johnson, writing in *Opportunity,* the magazine of the National Urban
League, detected the possible source of Garvey's exalted title. 'Just prior
to the first International Convention of the UNIA, De Valera was
elected Provisional President of Ireland. Garvey then became
Provisional President of Africa.')[25] The UNIA convention also created a
nobility, Knights of the Nile, and honours, the Distinguished Service
Order of Ethiopia. Delegates drafted a 'Declaration of the Rights of the
Negro Peoples of the World', which included the demand that 'Negro'
be spelt with a capital N, and condemnations of European imperialism
in Africa, and lynchings in the United States.

But the UNIA rested on Garvey's charisma, rather than on his
administrative or organizational abilities. After 1920, a series of

misfortunes, miscalculations and tactical blunders hastened his eventual downfall. In 1921, President Warren G. Harding, speaking in Alabama, asserted his belief in the Washingtonian ideal of separation of the races. Garvey endorsed the speech, and was roundly condemned by other black spokesmen. The following year, Garvey went to Georgia for a meeting with Edward Young Clark, Imperial Giant of the racist and terroristic Ku-Klux-Klan, in an attempt to elicit Klan support for the UNIA's African programme. From their opposing perspectives, Clark and Garvey shared a common belief in racial purity and racial separation. Garvey later declared: 'I was speaking to a man who was brutally a white man, and I was speaking to him as a man who was brutally a Negro.'[26] Garvey's black critics were outraged by the episode and redoubled their attacks on the 'Klan's Negro Leader'. William Pickens of the NAACP, who had earlier shown an interest in the UNIA, broke with Garvey over the Klan meeting, and informed him bitterly:

> I gather from your recent utterances that you are now endorsing the Ku-Klux-Klan, or at least conceding the justice of its aim to crush and repress Coloured Americans and incidentally other racial and religious groups in the United States.[27]

Garvey's continuing support for white segregationists, and his contacts with Theodore G. Bilbo, the Mississippi senator actively opposed to racial intermixing, who also espoused the repatriation of black Americans to West Africa, indicated that in his quest and zeal for black separatism, Garvey disregarded the sensibilities of his black (and white) critics.

After 1920 also, Garvey was repeatedly in financial and legal difficulties. The BSL was economically unsound, and its operations were less than seaworthy. For example, the BSL's first ship, a small freighter, the SS *Yarmouth,* cost $165,000, and was in constant operational and financial trouble. Other ships purchased by the line, the aptly named *Shadyside,* an old Hudson River excursion boat, and the steam yacht *Kanawha,* never realized a fraction of their purchase prices. The *Yarmouth* (later renamed the SS *Frederick Douglass*), sailed for Cuba with a cargo of whiskey, narrowly escaped sinking, and arrived at its destination with a good part of the cargo having been disposed of by the crew. The Pan Union Company, the importers of the whiskey, were awarded $6,000 by a court for its losses. In less than five months' active service, the *Shadyside* cost the BSL $11,000 in operating losses.

In 1922, Garvey and three of his associates were arrested and charged with using the United States mails to defraud. At his trial, the prosecution declared that Garvey had used the mails to promote the sale of BSL stock, although knowing that the line was in serious financial trouble. Garvey conducted his own defence in a melodramatic fashion, and blamed his colleagues, white competitors, the NAACP and other enemies for the line's collapse. He was fined $1,000, and sentenced to five years in prison. Released on bond, he returned to UNIA activity, and in particular to attempts to obtain permission from the Liberian government to establish a UNIA base in that country. The Liberians, already engaged in financial transactions with the Firestone Rubber Company, informed the American government that they were 'irrevocably opposed, both in principle and fact to the incendiary policy of the UNIA headed by Marcus Garvey'. In addition, Garvey faced the opposition of the European imperialist powers (and of W. E. B. Du Bois) to his Liberian scheme. In 1925, Garvey's appeal of his mails fraud conviction was rejected by the United States Circuit Court of Appeals, and he was sent to Atlanta penitentiary. After two years, President Calvin Coolidge (who had gained Garvey's declaration of support in the 1924 elections) commuted the sentence, and as an alien convicted of a felony, he was deported to Jamaica.

From 1927 to 1940, Garvey worked to rebuild the UNIA, and branches were opened in Paris and London – where he established an office in West Kensington. In 1929, the Sixth International Convention of Negro Peoples of the World met in Jamaica, but Garvey disputed with the American delegates, whom he accused of financial malpractices. He also refused to accept their demand that the headquarters of the organization remain in New York, and with the defection of his remaining American followers, Garvey's influence in the United States declined even further, although offshoots of the UNIA were to reappear from time to time in the 1930s and the 1940s. Garvey himself remained active throughout the 1930s – he denounced Italy's attack on Ethiopia in 1935 – but none of his enthusiasms aroused the mass support which they had provoked in America. Garvey died in London in 1940 (after reading false reports of his death), impoverished and without ever having set foot in Africa.

GARVEYISM

The racial ideology of Marcus Garvey and the UNIA combined various elements of black nationalism – religious, cultural, economic and territorial – into a distinctive philosophy. Basic to this world view was the power of blackness. Garvey was essentially a racial Zionist, offering a doctrine of blackness in which black was good, and white was evil. No race leader before the advent of Malcolm X made such a powerful appeal to the ethnic consciousness of black Americans.

> Psychological and religious independence from the white man were
> essential to Garveyism. Even more crucial was economic self-
> determination by blacks. ... Much of Garvey's sulfurous rhetoric was
> directed at the need for African redemption. ... Garvey unremittingly

advocated the cause of Africa for Africans, both those at home and abroad. ... He was exceedingly pessimistic about the future of the heavily outnumbered black man in the western hemisphere.[28]

The religious component of Garveyism was the African Orthodox Church, established in 1921, with the West Indian George Alexander McGuire as chaplain-general. Garvey believed that as God was made in the image of man, black people ought to visualize a Black God and a Black Christ.

Since the white people have seen their own God through white spectacles, we have now started out to see our God through our own spectacles. We Negroes believe in the God of Ethiopia, the everlasting God – God the Father, God the Son and God the Holy Ghost – but we shall worship Him through the spectacles of Ethiopia.[29]

For many of its followers, the UNIA was itself a surrogate religion, Garvey the 'Black Moses', and blacks the Chosen People. Benjamin E. Mays, the Negro theologian and teacher (and the intellectual mentor of Martin Luther King, Jr), observed that Garvey used the idea of a black God 'to arouse the Negro to a sense of deep appreciation for his race ... to stimulate the Negro to work to improve his social and economic conditions'.[30] The black sociologist E. Franklin Frazier believed that one of the 'most picturesque phases' of Garveyism had been 'the glorification of blackness, which has been made an attribute of the celestial hierarchy'.

Culturally, Garveyism extolled and instilled racial pride among blacks throughout the world. In America, the 1920s saw the rise of a creative impulse among black intellectuals, writers and artists, which attained its fullest expression in the Harlem Renaissance.

Garveyism was at bottom an expression of nationalism on the part of lower-class black urban America. The Renaissance was at bottom an expression of cultural nationalism on the part of the middle class. The former found its support within the black community alone; the latter in the white community as well as in black intellectual circles. Both, obviously, registered the heightened racial consciousness of the time.[31]

In 1915, the Association for the Study of Negro Life and History and its pioneering publication, the *Journal of Negro History* had been founded by Carter G. Woodson. 'When Garvey exalted the historical background of the Negro people, he stole weapons from his enemies, the Negro intellectuals.'[32]

As an exponent of economic nationalism, Garvey (deriving many of his ideas from Booker T. Washington) espoused black economic independence and self-sufficiency, but avoided endorsing either capitalism or socialism.

> ... if any economic label fits Garvey, it would be 'welfare state liberal';
> his People's Political Party platform for Jamaica, drawn up in 1929,
> states that the government of a black nation should guarantee the
> workers social security, steady employment, and compensation in case of
> injury, and that it should have the right to appropriate private lands for
> public use. The UNIA Negro Factories Corporation and the Black Star
> Line were more cooperatives than corporations, and the proposed colony
> in Liberia was to consist of family-unit farms along with five thousand-
> acre cooperative farms run by the Association.[33]

But the most important element in Garveyism was its emphasis on a
return to Africa (whether in a physical or a spiritual sense), the expulsion
of the European powers from the African continent, and the belief that
once a strong and independent 'African nation' was established,
Negroes would gain automatically in strength and prestige. Although
Garvey did not expect all black Americans to go to Africa, he viewed the
UNIA as representing the vanguard in the struggle for African
liberation.

> The thoughtful and industrious of our race want to go back to Africa,
> because we realize it will be our only hope of permanent
> existence. ... We do not want all the Negroes in Africa. Some are no
> good here, and naturally will be no good there. The no-good Negro will
> naturally die in fifty years. The Negro who is wrangling about and
> fighting for social equality will naturally pass away in fifty years, and
> yield his place to the progressive Negro who wants a society and country
> of his own.[34]

Failing the peaceful resettlement of blacks in colonized Africa, Garvey
advocated the use of force, and the UNIA included such paramilitary
units as the African Legion, the Garvey Militia, the Black Eagle Flying
Corps and the Universal African Motor Corps. At a meeting held in
Carnegie Hall during the 1920 convention, Garvey informed delegates
(and the European colonialist powers in Africa):

> We are striking homeward toward Africa to make her the big black
> republic. And in the making of Africa the big black republic, what is the
> barrier? The barrier is the white man; and we say to the white man who
> dominates Africa that it is to his interest to clear out now, because we
> are coming, not as in the time of Father Abraham, 200,000 strong, but
> we are coming 400,000,000 strong and we mean to retake every square
> inch of the 12,000,000 square miles of African territory belonging to us
> by right Divine.[35]

At the Second International Convention of Negroes in 1921, Garvey
delivered a speech at Liberty Hall which concluded with the ringing
declaration:

> It falls to our lot to tear off the shackles that bind Mother Africa. Can
> you do it? You did it in the Revolutionary War. You did it in the Civil

War. You did at the Battles of the Marne and Verdun. ... You can do it marching up the battle heights of Africa. Let the world know that 400,000,000 Negroes are prepared to live or die as free men. ... Climb ye the heights of liberty and cease not in well doing until you have planted the banner of the Red, the Black and the Green on the hilltops of Africa.[36]

The liberation of Africa from European colonial rule, and the repatriation there of the 'best' Afro-Americans (mulattos, by definition, were excluded), appear as constant – although not always clearly expressed – themes in Garvey's writings and speeches. But the mass appeal exerted by the UNIA transcended the impracticality and fantasy of its 'Back-to-Africa' ideology. The noted black novelist Richard Wright, recalling his encounters with Garveyites in the 1920s, thought that they

> had embraced a totally racialistic outlook which endowed them with a dignity I had never seen before in Negroes. I gave no credence to the ideology of Garveyism; it was, rather, the emotional dynamics of its adherents that evoked my admiration. Those Garveyites I knew could never understand why I liked them but would never follow them, and I pitied them too much to tell them that they would never achieve their goal, that Africa was owned by the imperial powers of Europe, that their lives were alien to the mores of the natives of Africa, that they were people of the West and would forever be so until they either merged with the West or perished. It was when the Garveyites spoke fervently of building their own country, of someday living within the boundaries of a culture of their own making, that I sensed the passionate hunger of their lives.[37]

GARVEY AND HIS BLACK CRITICS

Even more than Booker T. Washington, Garvey aroused conflicting and varying responses from his American black contemporaries. All, however, agreed on Garvey's appeal to the masses, whether for good or ill. E. Franklin Frazier, writing in the *Nation* in 1926, viewed the Garvey movement as 'a crowd movement essentially different from any other social phenomenon among Negroes', and suggested some telling comparisons between Garvey's leadership style and that of Washington and Du Bois. Washington, Franklin asserted, could not be regarded as a mass leader, since his programme had 'commended itself chiefly to those Negroes who prided themselves on their opportunism. There was nothing popularly heroic or inspiring in his programme to capture the imagination of the average Negro.' Du Bois, on the other hand, had shown himself to be 'too intellectual' to attract a popular following.

Even his glorification of the Negro has been in terms which escape the black man. The Pan-African Congress which he has promoted, while supporting to some extent the boasted aims of Garvey, has failed to stir any considerable number of American Negroes. The NAACP, which has fought uncompromisingly for equality of the Negro, has never secured ... the support of the masses. It has lacked the dramatic element.

But Garvey, a West Indian, and an outsider, had offered a new style of aggressive leadership, based on personal magnetism, religiosity, symbolism, a fierce race pride, and ritual. 'A uniformed member of a Negro lodge paled in significance beside a soldier of the Army of Africa. A Negro might be a porter during the day, taking his orders from white men, but he was an officer in the black army when it assembled at night at Liberty Hall.' Although Garvey's schemes for African redemption were flights of fancy, it was 'idle to apply to the schemes that attract crowds the test of reasonableness'.[38] In an assessment of 'The Garvey movement', written for *Opportunity*, the journal of the National Urban League, Frazier offered some additional, incisive suggestions as to the source of Garvey's appeal:

Many American Negroes have belittled the Garvey Movement on the ground that he is a West Indian and has attracted only the support of West Indians. But this very fact made it possible for him to contribute a new phase to the life of the American Negro. The West Indian Negroes have been ruled by a small white majority. In Jamaica, the Negro majority has often revolted and some recognition has been given to the mulattoes. This was responsible for Garvey's attempt, when he first came to this country, to incite the blacks against those of mixed blood. He soon found that there was no such easily discernible social cleavage recognized by the whites in this country. Yet his attempt to draw such a line has not failed to leave its effect. The fact that the West Indian has not been dominated by a white majority is probably responsible for a more secular view of life. The Garvey Movement would find the same response among the Negroes of the South as among the West Indians were it not for the dominating position of the preacher, whose peculiar position is symptomatic of an other-worldly outlook among the masses. ... In his half acknowledged antagonism towards Negro preachers and the soporific religion they served the masses, Garvey did not ignore its powerful influence. In fact he endeavoured to fuse the religious experience of the Negro with his own programme. ... Doubtless the World War with its shibboleths and stirrings of subject minorities offered a volume of suggestion that facilitated the Garvey Movement. Another factor that helped the Movement was the urbanization of the Negro. ... It is in the cities that mass movements are initiated.[39]

In a later essay, Frazier observed that while Garvey had possessed a keen insight into the psyche of the underprivileged black proletariat, he had signally failed to attract support from the black middle classes, who not only regarded his ideas as fantastic, but were also contemptuous of the poor and illiterate blacks – especially the West Indians – attracted by Garvey's rhetoric. Frazier also noted that he had been informed by a wealthy black physician in Chicago that UNIA really stood for 'Ugliest Negroes in America'.[40]

James Weldon Johnson found a little to praise and more to deplore in Garvey and the movement he led. The Jamaican had possessed 'energy and daring and the Napoleonic personality' that attracted followers; he had 'raised more money in a few years than any other Negro organization has ever dreamed of'. But he was also 'a supreme egotist' who had surrounded himself with 'cringing sycophants' and 'cunning knaves'. Garvey's plans for African redemption and the repatriation of black Americans had simply echoed those of the American Colonization Society a century earlier.

> The central idea of Garvey's scheme was absolute abdication and the recognition as facts of the assertions that this is a white man's country in which the Negro has no right, no future, no chance. To that idea the overwhelming majority of thoughtful American Negroes will not subscribe.[41]

T. Thomas Fortune, Booker T. Washington's close associate, and later editor of *The Negro World,* also rejected Garvey's racial separatism and non-engagement in civil rights protest, but found more to admire in Garvey than had Johnson.

> He [Garvey] has constrained the Negro to think Negro, as the Jew thinks Jew, and that is a very great achievement, something no other Negro ever did. To redeem Africa, to unify Negro sentiment and cooperation, to teach the Negro to conserve his social, civil and economic values, under Negro leadership and financed by Negroes – that is a worthwhile programme.[42]

Garvey's fellow West Indian, Claude McKay, applauded his propagandistic skills and the sheer audacity of the BSL, which 'had an electrifying effect upon all the Negro peoples of the world'. Unfortunately, Garvey's revolutionary fervour had not been accompanied by a revolutionary's consciousness. His ignorance of Africa was profound, taking no account of its tribal, political and geographic divisions. His visions of black capitalism had foundered with the collapse of the BSL, while the Negro Factories Corporation had only existed on paper. But, McKay conceded, Garvey's 'five years of stupendous vaudeville' had made him 'the biggest popularizer of the Negro problem, especially among Negroes, since *Uncle Tom's Cabin*'.[43]

To the Reverend Adam Clayton Powell, Sr, pastor of the Abyssinian Baptist Church, and a noted Harlem leader, Garvey's arrival there in 1916:

> was more significant to the Negro than the World War, the Southern exodus and the fluctuation of property values. Garvey with his Black United States, Black President ... Black Cabinet, Black Congress, Black

Army and Black Generals, Black Cross Nurses ... Black Star Line, and a Black Religion with a Black God, had awakened a race consciousness that made Harlem felt around the world. The cotton picker of Alabama ... and the poor ignorant Negro of the Mississippi delta ... lifted their heads and said, 'Let's go to Harlem and see this Black Moses'. During the reign of Garvey there were two places in America – the federation of 48 states, and Harlem, and two million Negroes thought that Harlem was both of them. I am not writing a brief for Marcus Garvey, but it is recording the truth to say that he is the only man that ever made Negroes who are not black ashamed of their colour.[44]

Yet to other Afro-American spokesmen and leaders, there was little that was attractive and much that was ugly in Garvey and the UNIA.

From the time of his arrival in Harlem until his deportation, Garvey faced the bitter opposition of established and aspiring Negro leaders of differing ideological persuasions. To the middle-class, integrationist members of the National Urban League and the NAACP, as well as to black socialists and radicals, Garvey was by turns a visionary, a charlatan, a demagogue and a madman. Unaware of or indifferent to the factions within the American black leadership class, Garvey, as McKay observed, 'stumbled headlong into the hornet's nest of the Northern Negro intelligentsia'. A declared admirer of Booker T. Washington, and a 'partisan of the Tuskegee school of politics', Garvey aroused the bitter animosity of the Talented Tenth within the NAACP.

It accused Garvey of advocating segregation and of pandering to the worst prejudices of Southern whites. This opposition was joined by the small but influential group of Negroes affiliated with the Labour and Radical movements ... it was this powerful combination of Negro intelligentsia, aided by wealthy white supporters, which finally brought about Garvey's downfall.[45]

Certainly the National Urban League, with its vested and known interest in economic opportunity for blacks within the American capitalist system, and its support for racial integration, was less than enthusiastic about Garvey's aims and methods. Charles S. Johnson, writing for *Opportunity* in 1923, characterized Garvey as a 'dynamic, blundering, temerarious visionary' and trickster. Not only were his ideas unrealistic, 'his financial exploits were ridiculously unsound, his plans for the redemption of Africa absurdly visionary, and the grand result, the fleecing of hundreds of thousands of poor and ignorant Negroes'.[46] From the perspective of the Urban League, Garveyism was 'a gigantic swindle', providing a 'dream-world escape for the "illiterati" from the eternal curse of their racial status in this country'. For the urban poor, Garveyism offered 'an opiate for their hopeless helplessness – a fantastic world beyond the grasp of logic and reason in which they might slake cravings never in this social order to be realised'.[47] Spokesmen for the

Urban League welcomed Garvey's prison sentence, and expressed sympathy for those he had duped. His overtures to the Klan were seen as highly dangerous in that they could only bring comfort to white racists. The Leaguers also rejected Garvey's racial separatism, and there were also significant differences between Garvey and the black board members of the League in the 1920s which made for tension.

> Garvey was born in Jamaica; all of the Urban Leaguers were native Americans. ... Garvey dropped out of school at the age of fourteen; two-thirds of the Urban Leaguers had gone to college ... a third had earned degrees. Garvey came from the working class; the Urban Leaguers represented the black bourgeoisie. Half of them were educators, and a quarter were doctors or ministers; only one was a printer.[48]

Similarly, the staff of League chapters across the United States had little in common with Garvey. Board members of the League were also light-skinned, and this fact alone ensured animosity between the League and the UNIA. On all counts, Garvey and the Urban Leaguers were antithetical. Yet, despite its opposition to Garvey, the League was not insensible to his mass appeal, based on the twin pillars of racial pride and the right of self-determination. Charles S. Johnson conceded that Garvey's personal characteristics, deplored by his critics, were precisely those which had made him a charismatic leader.

> His extravagant self-esteem could be taken for dignity, his hard-headedness as self-reliance, his ignorance of law as transcendency, his blunders as persecution, his stupidity as silent deliberation, his churlishness and irascibility as the eccentricity of genius.[49]

On the left wing of the black leadership front, Garvey was to earn the enmity of the socialists A. Philip Randolph and Chandler Owen, joint editors of *The Messenger.* Randolph, the most notable black labour organizer of the 1920s, had helped to form the Brotherhood of Sleeping Car Porters in 1925. In later years, he claimed to have given Garvey his first opportunity of addressing a Harlem street audience. For a time, Randolph and Garvey, despite differences in their racial and political attitudes, enjoyed cordial relations. In 1919, Randolph addressed a UNIA meeting which considered sending a Negro delegate to the Paris Peace Conference. Earlier, Garvey had attended a conference organized by Randolph that led to the formation of the short-lived International League of Darker Peoples, which aimed to secure African liberation by an interracial alliance of radical, liberal and labour movements. As the UNIA grew, however, relations between the two men became strained. Already in competition with Du Bois and the NAACP, Randolph became increasingly critical of the Garveyites because of their economic separatism which contradicted his call for interracial cooperation. Randolph and Owen also differed with Garvey in their economic and political objectives. Garvey's glorification of black capitalism ran counter to the Randolph–Owen belief in democratic socialism, while other aspects of Garveyism earned their disapproval. In a series of articles in *The Messenger,* they attacked Garvey's African schemes as being based on simplistic reasoning, since the oppression of the masses, world-wide, was colour-blind. The UNIA was judged as 'not a promise but a definite menace to Negroes', and Garvey was accused of stirring white prejudice against blacks and between West Indians and Afro-Americans. *The Messenger*'s critiques of Garvey also took on a pronounced anti-West Indian tone. The Reverend Robert W. Bagnall, writing in the magazine in 1923, depicted Garvey as:

> A Jamaican Negro of unmixed stock, squat, fat and sleek, with protruding jaws and heavy jowls, small bright pig-like eyes and ... bull-dog-like face. Boastful, egotistic, tyrannical, intolerant, cunning, shifty, smooth and suave, avaricious ... gifted at self-advertisement, without shame in self-laudation, promising ever, but never fulfilling, without regard for veracity, a lover of pomp and tawdry finery and garish display, a bully with his own folk but servile in the presence of the Klan, a sheer opportunist. ... If he is not insane, he is a demagogic charlatan, but the probability is that the man is insane. Certainly the movement is insane, whether Garvey is or not.[50]

Following Garvey's meeting with the Ku-Klux-Klan, the editors served notice that they were going to campaign for his expulsion from America. *The Messenger* now adopted the slogan 'Garvey Must Go'. The Friends of Negro Freedom, a civil rights propaganda organization, founded by Randolph and Owen (and which also included several NAACP officers) also promoted anti-Garvey meetings. Randolph declared in *The Messenger*: 'I think we are justified in asking the question, that if Mr Garvey is seriously interested in establishing a Negro nation, why doesn't he begin with Jamaica, West Indies?'[51] An editorial in the same issue called Garvey 'A supreme Jamaican jackass'. Randolph also showed his antipathy to Garvey's flamboyant style, UNIA ceremonial and titles. In 1923, eight leaders of the 'Garvey Must Go' campaign, with Owen as secretary, wrote to the US Attorney-General, urging the government to speed up its prosecution case against Garvey for mail fraud. (Garvey charged the committee of eight with offences against race solidarity.) The signatories included Harry H. Pace of the Urban League, William Pickens, field secretary of the NAACP and Owen – Randolph, despite his major role in the campaign, did not sign the letter. During Garvey's imprisonment without bail, *The Messenger* advocated the total destruction of the UNIA, and commended Du Bois' critique of Garvey 'Lunatic or traitor', published in 1924. The 'Garvey Must Go' campaign produced a common front among his opponents; with his deportation, the basis for that unity disappeared.

Randolph and Owen, like other black spokesmen, rejected Garvey's intense black nationalism, and resented his success in leading a movement composed almost entirely of the black working class. Above all, they resented his challenge to the Talented Tenth's claims to the monopoly of race leadership. Garvey himself noted that 'my success as an organizer was more than rival Negro leaders could tolerate'.[52] Nowhere was this resentment more apparent than in the response of W. E. B. Du Bois to the rise (and fall) of Garvey.

DU BOIS AND GARVEY

In his first autobiography, Du Bois recalled that he had first heard of Garvey in 1915 when 'I took a short vacation trip to Jamaica, where I was surprisingly well-received by coloured people and white, because of the wide publicity given me from my participation in the Races Congress of London, in 1911. Garvey and his associates, The United [*sic*] Improvement and Conservation Association, joined in the welcome.'[53] Shortly after Garvey's arrival in America, Du Bois noted in *Crisis*:

> Mr Marcus Garvey, founder and President of the Universal Negro Improvement Association of Jamaica, West Indies, is now on a visit to America. He will deliver a series of lectures on Jamaica in an effort to raise funds for the establishment of an industrial and educational institution for Negroes in Jamaica.[54]

At this time, Du Bois was ambivalent about Garvey. As his critique of Washington had shown, Du Bois was not a wholehearted supporter of industrial education for blacks. Yet four years after Garvey's American activities, Du Bois conceded that he had 'with singular success capitalized and made vocal the great and long suffering grievances and spirit of protest among the West Indian peasantry'. Moreover: 'Thousands of people believe in him. He is able to stir them with singular eloquence and the general run of his thought is on a very high plane. He has become to thousands of people a sort of religion.'[55] But Du Bois' references to Garvey, open or veiled, became increasingly bitter and occasionally shrill. In a cryptic editorial in *Crisis* in 1922, Du Bois was obviously referring to Garvey when he predicted that 'we must expect the Demagogue among Negroes more and more. He will come to lead, inflame, lie and steal. He will gather large followings and then disappear.'[56] Garvey did not let such references pass unchallenged, and the developing feud between the two leaders far surpassed in invective and bitterness the Du Bois–Washington quarrel. Garvey blamed Du Bois and the NAACP for most of his problems, including the thwarting of his Liberia plans, the collapse of the BSL, and his trial and imprisonment. Regarding himself as the successor to Washington in the fight against Du Bois, Garvey frequently compared the two, to Du Bois' detriment, and Garveyism became a formidable challenge to Du Bois and the interracial ideal.

> Adopting what he wanted from Washington's ideas, Garvey carried them further – advocating Negro self-sufficiency in the United States linked ... with the idea of regaining access to the African homeland as a basis for constructing a viable black economy. Whereas Washington had earlier chosen an accommodationist position in the South to achieve his objectives, Garvey added the racial ingredient of black nationalism to Washington's ideas with potent effect. ... Du Bois and the NAACP took a strong stand against the Garvey movement and against revolutionary nationalism. The issues were much deeper than mere rivalry between different factions for the leadership of Negro politics. The rise of Garvey nationalism meant that the NAACP became the accommodationists, and the nationalists became the militants.[57]

Du Bois was also angered because Garvey's African schemes were competing – and were often confused with – his own Pan-African philosophy and activities.

> Often the Pan-African Congress was confounded with the Garvey movement with consequent suspicion and attack. The unfortunate debacle of his over-advertized schemes naturally hurt and made difficult further effective development of the Pan-African Congress idea.[58]

From 1920 onwards, Du Bois began to aim *Crisis* editorials at Garvey's 'very serious defects of temperament'. He was, Du Bois charged, 'dictatorial and domineering, inordinately vain and very suspicious'. Moreover, Garvey had attempted to introduce the black–mulatto schism in the United States where, Du Bois claimed unconvincingly, 'it has never had any substantial footing and where today it is absolutely repudiated by every thinking Negro'. In capitalizing on this division, Garvey had 'aroused more bitter colour enmity inside the race than has ever before existed'.[59] Two weeks before the UNIA 1920 Convention, Garvey wrote to Du Bois inviting him to stand for election as 'the accredited spokesman for the Negro people' at the meeting. Du Bois icily refused the provocative invitation, and sent instead a series of requests to Garvey for information on UNIA membership, finances and activities, for a 'critical estimate' to be published in *Crisis*. At the convention, Garvey told an interviewer that Du Bois represented the 'antebellum' Negro as distinct from the militant, post-war New Negro. Du Bois told the same interviewer that Garvey was insincere, that his followers were 'the lowest type of Negroes', mostly from the British West Indies, and that the UNIA could not be considered an Afro-American movement. In retaliation, Garvey characterized Du Bois as 'the associate of an alien race', and accused him of being 'more of a white man than a Negro ... only a professional Negro at that'. Warming to this theme, Garvey castigated Du Bois' 'aristocratic' pretensions and asked:

> Where does he get this aristocracy from? He picked it up on the streets of Great Barrington, Massachusetts. He just got it into his head that he should be an aristocrat and ever since that time he has been keeping his very beard as an aristocrat; he has been trying to be everything else but a Negro. Sometimes we hear he is a Frenchman and another time he is Dutch and when it is convenient he is a Negro. Now I have no Dutch. I have no French, I have no Anglo-Saxon to imitate; I have but the ancient glories of Ethiopia to imitate. ... Anyone you hear always talking about the kind of blood he has in him other than the blood you can see, he is dissatisfied with something and I feel sure that many of the Negroes of the United States of America know that if there is a man who is most dissatisfied with himself, it is Dr Du Bois.[60]

With relations between the two men worsening rapidly, Du Bois denied that he was envious of Garvey's success. Rather, he insisted, was he fearful of Garvey's failure, as were all 'American Negro leaders ... for his failure would be theirs'.

> He can have all the power and money he can efficiently and honestly use ... if in addition he wants to prance down Broadway in a green shirt – let him – but do not let him foolishly overwhelm with bankruptcy and disaster one of the most interesting spiritual movements in the modern Negro world.[61]

In 1922, Du Bois intensified his campaign against Garvey, and again attempted to secure details on the state of BSL finances. When he failed to receive a financial statement from Garvey on any matters relating to the UNIA, Du Bois concluded: 'When it comes to Mr Garvey's industrial and commercial enterprises there is more ground for doubt and misgiving than in the matter of his character.' With the collapse of the BSL, Du Bois lamented: 'Here then is the collapse of the only thing in the Garvey movement which was original or promising.'[62] The following year, Du Bois claimed that the UNIA had fewer than 18,000 members, and published a long article in *Century* magazine, portraying Garvey as a buffoon. At a UNIA meeting, Du Bois said he had seen:

> A little fat black man, ugly but with intelligent eyes and a big head ... seated on a plank platform beside a 'throne', dressed in a military uniform of the gayest mid-Victorian type. ... Among the lucky recipients of titles was the former private secretary of Booker T. Washington.

Du Bois reiterated his contentions that intraracial prejudice was a West Indies phenomenon, that Garvey was poorly educated, and the leader of peasants. Du Bois also took this opportunity to link Garvey with Washington, and deplored the influence of both the master and his declared follower.

The present generation of Negroes has survived two grave temptations, the greater one fathered by Booker T. Washington, which said, 'Let politics alone, keep your place, work hard, and do not complain,' and which meant perpetual caste status for the coloured folk by their own cooperation and consent, and the consequent inevitable debauchery of the white world; and the lesser, fathered by Marcus Garvey, which said, 'Give up. Surrender! The struggle is useless; back to Africa and fight the white world.'[63]

Garvey's response was immediate and savage. *The Negro World* carried the headline: 'W. E. B. DU BOIS AS A HATER OF DARK PEOPLE', subtitled 'Calls his own race "black and ugly"', judging from the white man's standard of beauty.' Garvey called Du Bois the great Negro 'misleader' and an 'unfortunate mulatto', one who 'bewails every day the drop of Negro blood in his veins, being sorry that it is not Dutch or French ... the great 'I AM' of the Negro race'. On the sensitive issue of physical and personal appearance, Garvey suggested that:

This so-called professor of Harvard and Berlin ought to know by now that the standard of beauty within a race is not arrived at by comparison with another race. ... But ... anything that is black to him is ugly, is hideous, is monstrous, and that is why in 1917 he had but the lightest of coloured people in his [NAACP] office, when one could hardly tell whether it was a white show or a coloured vaudeville he was running at Fifth Avenue.

Garvey alleged that Du Bois actually believed black to be ugly, sought out the company of white people, danced with them, and even slept with them. How, then, could he be a leader of the NAACP? 'In what direction must we expect his advancement ... it is in the direction of losing our black identity and becoming, as nearly as possible, the lowest whites by assimilation and miscegenation.' Again, Du Bois had ridiculed titles conferred on blacks by the UNIA, because he 'can see and regard honours conferred only by their white masters'. Comparing and contrasting their respective backgrounds to his own advantage in terms of self-reliance and achievements, Garvey conceded that Du Bois was highly educated, but if this education 'fits him for no better service than being a lackey for ... white people, then it were better that Negroes were not educated'. Du Bois, Garvey claimed, was the avowed enemy and known saboteur of the UNIA – an all-black organization, based on the common people. But for the support of such white patrons as Mary White Ovington and Oswald Garrison Villard, Du Bois 'would be eating his pork chops from the counter of the cheapest restaurant in Harlem like so many other Negro graduates of Harvard and Fisk'. Garvey concluded his indictment by pointing up the fundamental ideological differences which separated him from Du Bois.

Du Bois cares not for an Empire of Negroes but contents himself with being a secondary part of white civilization. We of the UNIA feel that the greatest service that the Negro can render to the world and himself ... is to make his independent contribution to civilization ... it is only a question of time before coloured men and women everywhere will harken to the voice in the wilderness, even though a Du Bois impugns the idea of Negro liberation.[64]

Despite the acerbity of his reply, Garvey did not answer all of Du Bois' charges. 'He ignored the charge that he was a black Jamaican peasant uninterested in the Afro-American struggle.'[65]

Following Garvey's trial and conviction, Du Bois published his most bitter attack on Garvey in a *Crisis* editorial headed 'A lunatic or a traitor'. It revealed that to Du Bois, the basic principles in conflict were those of racial integration as opposed to separation, and the intraracial colour antagonisms fostered by Garvey's racial chauvinism. Du Bois now believed that Garvey was 'without doubt the most dangerous enemy of the Negro race in America and in the world'. He exposed the 'half-concealed' planks in the UNIA platform as meaning:

> That no person of African descent can ever hope to become an American citizen.
> That forcible separation of the races and the banishment of Negroes to Africa is the only solution to the race problem.
> That race war is sure to follow any attempt to realize the programme of the NAACP.

Garvey, Du Bois insisted, far from attacking white prejudice, was attacking fellow Negroes, for whom he had only contempt. Du Bois refused to accept that Garvey was the victim of white prejudice since 'no Negro in America ever had a fairer and more patient trial'. Rather had Garvey 'convicted himself by his own admissions and swaggering monkey-shines' in court. He had not been refused bail because of his colour, 'but because of the repeated threats and cold-blooded assaults charged against his organization'.

> American Negroes have endured this wretch too long and with fine restraint and every effort at cooperation and understanding. But the end has come. Every man who apologizes for and defends Marcus Garvey from this day forth writes himself down as unworthy of the countenance of decent Americans. As for Garvey himself, this open ally of the Ku Klux Klan should be locked up or sent home.

In a dramatic climax to his piece, Du Bois claimed that he had been advised not to publish it 'lest I be assassinated'. He concluded with a flourish: 'I have been exposing white traitors for a quarter of a century. If the day has come when I cannot tell the truth about black traitors it is high time that I died.'[66]

At the end of the 1924 UNIA Convention, a resolution was passed which declared:

In view of the fact that W. E. B. Du Bois has continually attempted to obstruct the progress of the UNIA to the loss and detriment of the Negro race and that he has on several occasions gone out of his way to try to defeat the cause of Africa's redemption, that he be proclaimed as ostracized from the Negro race as far as the UNIA is concerned, and from henceforward be regarded as an enemy of the black people of the world.[67]

From Atlanta prison in 1925, Garvey continued to castigate the NAACP and Du Bois as 'the greatest enemies the black people have in the world'. After Garvey's release and deportation, Du Bois – with the threat removed – denied that the NAACP had opposed the UNIA, and claimed that *Crisis* had published only five articles on Garvey, ignoring those which had attacked him indirectly.

In later years, Du Bois was more magnanimous towards Garvey. In *The World and Africa* (1947), Du Bois characterized Garveyism as:

a poorly conceived but intensely earnest determination to unite the Negroes of the world, especially in commercial enterprise. It used all of the nationalist and racial paraphernalia of popular agitation, and its strength lay in its backing by the masses of West Indians and by increasing numbers of American Negroes. Its weakness lay in its demagogic leadership, poor finance, intemperate propaganda, and the natural apprehension it aroused among the colonial powers.[68]

Du Bois, in his second autobiography, concerned to disclaim any 'enmity or jealousy' in his feud with Garvey, was prepared to stand by that part of his *Crisis* editorial (following Garvey's deportation) in which he had stated that he had had 'a great and worthy dream. We wish him well. He is free; he has a following; he still has a chance to carry on his work in his own home and among his own people and to accomplish some of his ideas. We will be the first to applaud any success that he might have.'[69] The message was clear; with Garvey's American career at an end, Du Bois could consign him thankfully to the West Indies – and oblivion.

For his part, Garvey refused to come to even partial peace terms with his most influential black American protagonist. In the 1930s, when Du Bois began to espouse the idea of a non-profit, cooperative racial economy, Garvey roundly accused him of stealing the UNIA's clothes and preaching Garveyism. *The Negro World* carried the headline: 'Dr Du Bois agrees with UNIA leader – takes programme over finally – but does not openly confess it.' In a short piece entitled 'Dr Du Bois criticized', published in 1934, Garvey repeated his contention that Du Bois was 'exceptional' only in his admiration for and imitation of white culture.

To us he was never a leader ... just a vain opportunist who held on to the glory and honour showered on him because he was one of the first experiments of Negro higher education. He was never a born leader. He is too selfish to be anything but Du Bois.[70]

Writing from England in 1935, Garvey delivered a final verdict on Du Bois, a man with 'no racial self-respect, no independent ideas, nothing of self-reliance', and was prepared to compose (thirty years before it was required) Du Bois' obituary notice:

> When Du Bois dies he will be remembered as the man who sabotaged the Liberian colonization scheme of the Negro, the man who opposed the American Negro launching steamships on the seas, the man who did everything to handicap the industrial, educational system of Tuskegee, the man who never had a good word to say for any other Negro leaders, but who tried to down every one of them.[71]

Marcus Garvey relished conflict and competition, and this was both a source of his appeal, and a reason for his downfall.

> He denounced practically the whole Negro leadership. They were all bent upon cultural assimilation; they were all looking for white support ... and they were making a compromise between accommodation and protest. Within a short time he succeeded in making enemies of practically all Negro intellectuals. Against him were mobilized most leaders in the Negro schools, the Negro organizations and the Negro press. He heartily responded by naming them opportunists, liars, thieves, traitors and bastards.[72]

REFERENCES

1. Jaques-Garvey, A., *Garvey and Garveyism* (Kingston, Jamaica, 1963), p. 27.
2. Isaacs, H. R., *The New World of Negro Americans* (London, 1964), p. 139.
3. Osofsky, G., *Harlem: the making of a ghetto, 1880–1930* (New York, 1968), p. 120.
4. Weiss, N., *The National Urban League: 1910–1940* (Oxford U.P.; New York, 1974), pp. 66–7.
5. Meier, A. and Rudwick, E. M., *From Plantation to Ghetto* (1970), p. 218.
6. Hellwig, D. J., 'Black meets black: Afro-American reactions to West Indian immigrants in the 1920s', *SAQ,* 77 (1978), 212–14.
7. McKay, C., *Harlem: Negro metropolis* (New York, 1940), p. 143.
8. Jaques-Garvey, A. (ed.), *Philosophy and Opinions of Marcus Garvey* (New York, 1969), p. 124.
9. Jaques-Garvey (ed.), op. cit., (1969), p. 125.
10. Jaques-Garvey (ed.), op. cit., (1969), p. 8.
11. Jaques-Garvey (ed.), op. cit., (1969), p. 126.
12. Martin, T., *Race First: the ideological and organizational struggles of Marcus Garvey and the UNIA* (Westport, Connecticut, 1976), p. 281.

13.   Harlan, L. R., *Booker T. Washington: the wizard of Tuskegee, 1901–1915* (Oxford U.P.; New York, 1983), p. 281.

14.   Martin, op. cit., pp. 281–3.

15.   Jaques-Garvey (ed.), op. cit., (1969), p. 56.

16.   Vincent, T., *Black Power and the Garvey Movement* (San Francisco, 1972), p. 26.

17.   Jaques-Garvey (ed.), op. cit., (1969), pp. 127–8.

18.   James, C. L. R., *Black Jacobins* (1938, 1980), p. 396.

19.   James, op. cit., p. 396.

20.   Jaques-Garvey, op. cit., (1963), p. 31.

21.   Jaques-Garvey, op. cit., (1963), p. 91.

22.   Vincent, op. cit., p. 103.

23.   Jaques-Garvey, op. cit., (1963), p. 86.

24.   Ottley, R., *'New World A-Coming'* (New York, 1943, 1969), p. 75.

25.   *Opportunity,* I, Aug. 1923, p. 21.

26.   Martin, op. cit., p. 346.

27.   Vincent, op. cit., p. 191.

28.   Weisbord, R. G., *Ebony Kinship: Africa, Africans, and the Afro-American* (Westport, Connecticut, 1973), p. 55.

29.   Jaques-Garvey (ed.), op. cit., (1969), p. 44.

30.   Mays, B. E., *The Negro's God as Reflected in his Literature* (1938), pp. 184–5.

31.   Nielsen, D. G., *Black Ethos: Northern urban Negro life and thought, 1890–1930* (London, 1977), p. 108.

32.   Myrdal, G., *An American Dilemma* (New York, 1944), pp. 750–1.

33.   Vincent, op. cit., p. 25.

34.   Jaques-Garvey (ed.), op. cit., (1969), p. 122.

35.   Johnson, J. W., *Black Manhattan* (New York, 1930, 1968), p. 254.

36.   Jaques-Garvey (ed.), op. cit., (1969), p. 97.

37.   Wright, R., *American Hunger* (New York, 1944, 1977), pp. 28–9.

38.   Frazier, E. F., 'Garvey a mass leader', *Nation,* CXXIII, 18 Aug. 1926, pp. 147–8.

39.   Frazier, E. F., 'The Garvey movement', *Opportunity,* IV, Nov. 1926, pp. 346–8.

40.   Frazier, E. F., *Black Bourgeoisie* (1957), p. 250.

41.   Johnson op. cit., pp. 256–7.

42.   Thornbrough, E. L., *T. Thomas Fortune: militant journalist* (London, 1972), pp. 361–2.

43.   McKay, C., 'Garvey as a Negro Moses', in W. Cooper (ed.) *The Passion of Claude McKay* (New York, 1922), pp. 65–9.

44.   Powell, A. C., *Against the Tide* (New York, 1938), pp. 70–1.

45.   McKay, op. cit., (1940), p. 158.

46.   Johnson, C. S., *Opportunity,* I, Aug. 1923, p. 231–3

47.   Weiss, op. cit., pp. 148–9.

48.   Weiss, op. cit., p. 150.

49.   Johnson, op. cit., (1923), p. 232.

50.   Bagnall, R. W., *The Messenger,* March 1923, p. 368.

51.   Kornweibel, T., *No Crystal Stair: black life and The Messenger, 1917–1928* (Westport, Connecticut, 1975), p. 148.

52.   Kornweibel, op. cit., p. 170.

53. Du Bois, W. E. B., *Dusk of Dawn* (1940), p. 277.
54. Martin, op. cit., p. 284.
55. *Crisis,* Dec. 1920, in J. Lester (ed.), *The Seventh Son: the thought and writings of W. E. B. Du Bois,* vol. II (New York, 1971), pp. 175–6.
56. Rampersad, A. *The Art and Imagination of W. E. B. Du Bois* (London, 1976), p. 149.
57. Cruse, H., *Rebellion or Revolution* (New York, 1968), p. 86.
58. Du Bois, op. cit., (1940), pp. 277–8.
59. Lester, op. cit., pp. 175, 183.
60. Rudwick, E., *W. E. B. Du Bois: propagandist of the Negro protest* (New York, 1969), p. 219.
61. Lester, op. cit., p. 183.
62. Rudwick, op. cit., pp. 217–29.
63. Martin, op. cit., pp. 297–9.
64. Jaques-Garvey (ed.), op. cit., (1969), pp. 310–20.
65. Martin, op. cit., p. 301.
66. Lester, op. cit., pp. 184–6.
67. Martin, op. cit., pp. 306–7.
68. Du Bois, W. E. B., *The World and Africa* (1947), p. 236.
69. Du Bois, W. E. B., *The Autobiography of W. E. B. Du Bois: a soliloquy on viewing my life from the last decade of its first century* (1968), pp. 273–4.
70. Essien-Udom, E. U. and Jaques-Garvey (eds), *More Philosophy and Opinions of Marcus Garvey* (London, 1977), p. 124.
71. Martin, op. cit., p. 311.
72. Myrdal, op. cit., p. 746.

MALCOLM X (1925–1965): SINNER AND CONVERT

If Malcolm X were not a Negro, his *Autobiography* would be little more than a journal of abnormal psychology, the story of a burglar, dope pusher, addict and jailbird – with a family history of insanity – who acquires messianic delusions and sets forth to preach an up-side down religion of 'brotherly' hatred.

(*The Saturday Evening Post*)[1]

It does not promote the cause of responsible leadership to deny the importance of Malcolm X to the particular segment of people whose political and/or ideological leader he was, or sought to be, and this despite the threat he represented to the acceptance of more traditional procedures advanced by more traditional leaders. Malcolm X made an impact on the minds of the black masses irrespective of his criminal past or his strong pro-black ideology.

(C. Eric Lincoln, 'The Meaning of Malcolm X')[2]

BLACK NATIONALISM AFTER GARVEY: THE SEPARATIST IMPULSE, 1930–1966

Marcus Garvey's deportation in 1927 and the onset of the Great Depression effectively ended black American support for UNIA. Negro organizations and leaders, concerned with ensuring the sheer survival of blacks, stressed interracial cooperation, integration, and the political and economic advancement of Afro-Americans within the United States. From the advent of the New Deal in 1932 to the climax of the civil rights coalition in the mid 1960s, integration remained the overwhelmingly dominant ideology of the Negro protest movement. The goals of integration and equal rights coincided with the aspirations of a growing black middle class, reflected in the increased membership of the National Urban League and the NAACP. During the period of the Second World War, for example, NAACP branches increased from

335 in 1940 to 1,073 in 1946, and its membership rose from 50,000 to 450,000. The publication of Gunnar Myrdal's monumental *An American Dilemma* in 1944, with its deprecation of separatist action by blacks, and its acceptance of racial integration as the proper goal of protest activity, also helped to set the ideological tone accepted by most black and white theoreticians and civil rights activists. Not until the mid 1960s, with the emergence of the Black Power slogan, growing disillusionment on the part of many younger blacks with the 'tokenism' of civil rights legislation, and their rejection of non-violent strategy, did black nationalist theories and organizations enjoy the currency (and publicity) which had attended Garvey and the UNIA.

But even in the 1930s and 1940s, not all black spokesmen or leaders subscribed to the integrationist ethic. W. E. B. Du Bois, as has been seen (Ch. 4), because of his ardent advocacy of a separate black collective economy, clashed with the NAACP's traditional opposition to any form of racial separatism. The American Communist Party, founded in 1919, made some converts among black intellectuals with its Stalinist-derived call for 'self-determination' for Afro-Americans, including a proposal to create an all-black '49th state' out of the heart of the Southern Black Belt. But the Communist appeal to the black masses was minimal and by 1935, operating on the mistaken assumption that the proletarian revolution was at hand, American Communists reversed their nationalistic stand in favour of a policy of equal rights for blacks in America. During the 1930s, some blacks did engage in a variant of Garvey-type bourgeois economic nationalism in 'Don't Buy Where You Can't Work' campaigns – pickets and boycotts to secure jobs for Negroes in white-owned stores in the black ghettos. A. Philip Randolph's March on Washington Movement (see Ch. 7) was an avowedly all-Negro protest movement which consciously drew on the power of the urban black populations. Religious nationalism was represented by such separatist and exotic sects as Noble Drew Ali's Moorish-American Science Temple, founded in Newark, New Jersey, in 1913, which gained in membership from the influx of a large number of Garveyites in the late 1920s.

> Noble Drew Ali taught his followers that they were descendants of the once-proud Moorish Empire of North Africa, an Islamic state, and gave them Moorish names to replace the slave names given by the white man. Like Garvey, he insisted the black American must have a nation, but Ali held that North America was but an extension of the true African homeland, Morocco, and that a Moorish nation should be built in America. As his movement grew, a contest for leadership developed, and on March 15, 1929, Noble Drew Ali's chief rival was shot and stabbed in the organization's offices. Ali was arrested and charged with murder but released on bond. A few weeks later he died mysteriously – some claimed he died of injuries inflicted by police, others that he had been killed by partisans of the slain contender.[3]

Black religious separatism also took a more restrained form in Father Divine's Peace Movement, established on Long Island in 1919, which instituted a collectivist economy among its followers – who also included ex-Garveyites, and functioned as much as a social as a religious black nationalist movement. From 1931 to 1936, Father Divine's Peace Mission grew from a handful to over a million followers. Wages and benefits acquired by followers were used to purchase the movement's missions and houses ('Heavens'), which were turned into sexually segregated communal living quarters. Members were employed in Father Divine's laundries, restaurants or communal farms in New Jersey and New York. During their heyday, the Peace Missions provided sumptuous banquets and meals at minimal prices. The faithful were granted personal communion with God – Father Divine himself. (In 1931, following complaints by local residents that meetings of the movement were creating a public nuisance, Father Divine was sentenced by Justice Lewis J. Smith, on 16 November, to six months in jail, and a $500 fine. Four days later, the justice died of a heart attack. Father Divine was quoted as saying: 'I hated to do it!') A believer in economic communalism, opposed to trade unions and New Deal legislation which 'deprives the individual of the right to sell his goods for little or nothing if he chooses', Father Divine, through the collective efforts of his followers, was able to provide food, accommodation and work for large numbers of blacks untouched by the welfare agencies and programmes of the New Deal. In terms of religious nationalism, as his biographer suggests, Father Divine:

> went a step beyond even what Marcus Garvey, the most aggressive Negro chauvinist of recent years, had ever dared to say. Where Garvey said that black was basically superior and white basically inferior, the Messenger Father Divine exemplified that statement. He said I am a Negro and God dwells in me. You are a Negro and you are like unto me. Therefore, you are superior to white.[4]

Father Divine died in 1965, in a mansion on his Peace Mission's seventy-three-acre estate outside Philadelphia. But of greater significance for the separatist movements of the 1950s and 1960s, was the Nation of Islam, founded by W. D. Fard in 1930 (see below). Emigrationist/repatriation sentiment and territorialist ideas were confined during the 1930s to such organizations as the Ethiopian Pacific Movement, established in Chicago in 1932 by Mittie Gordon, a former president of the Chicago division of the UNIA. In 1939, 300 members of the movement set out for Washington, DC, to lobby the federal government in support of Senator Theodore Bilbo's proposal to allocate government funds to blacks who wished to live in Africa. Most never arrived in Washington, as their transportation began breaking down even before they had left the Chicago city limits. (In 1941, Miss Gordon appeared before federal authorities, charged with inciting blacks to avoid conscription.)

The civil rights movement which emerged in the post Second-World-War period scored some notable victories in improving the citizenship rights of black Americans. 'The political impact of the heavy black migration to northern and western cities now became evident. The growing black vote made civil rights a major issue in national elections, was a crucial factor in the re-election of Truman in 1948, and the subsequent desegregation of the armed forces, and ultimately led to the establishment of a federal Civil Rights Commission in 1957.'[5] The civil rights coalition made notable gains in moving Congress to improve the citizenship status of blacks – the Civil Rights Act of 1964 and the Voting Rights Act of 1965 – which abolished legal segregation and discrimination, and also served to heighten the political consciousness and expectancies of Negroes. Yet in 1966, the unemployment rate for blacks was 7.8 per cent, or twice the national average, with 40 per cent of black families earning less than $3,000 a year. Again, ten years after the Supreme Court's historic decision on school desegregation (see Ch. 7), the United States Commissioner of Education reported that the majority of American children still attended racially segregated schools.

The disillusioned mood of urban black Americans was most frighteningly revealed in the wave of 'civil disorders' which swept over the country's major cities in the 1960s: Harlem (1964), Watts, Los Angeles (1965), Newark, New Jersey; Detroit, Michigan and Cleveland, Ohio (1967–68), suffered major racial disturbances which resulted in over 200 deaths (mostly of blacks), with at least 10,000 injured and 60,000 arrested, and the widespread destruction of property. Opinion polls indicated that while most blacks agreed that rioters and looters were guilty of criminal acts, many also regarded rioting as a justifiable form of political protest against police brutality, persistent white racism, and the appalling conditions within the black ghettos. President Lyndon Johnson's National Advisory Commission on Civil Disorders reported:

> What white Americans have never fully understood – but what the Negro can never forget – is that white society is deeply implicated in the ghetto. White institutions created it, white institutions maintain it, and white society condones it. ... Our nation is moving toward two societies, one black, one white – separate and unequal.

It was in this atmosphere that the slogan 'Black Power', popularized (but not coined) by Stokely Carmichael, the West Indian-born chairman of the Student Non-Violent Coordinating Committee (SNCC), and Floyd McKissick of the Congress of racial Equality (CORE), signalled a resurgence of black nationalist and separatist sentiments as direct challenges to the integrationism and legalism of the NAACP and other elements of the civil rights coalition. At its annual convention in 1966, CORE passed a resolution which dismissed integration as a failure and urged that 'Black Power replace assimilation and moral suasion as the dominant philosophy, theme, and method of the civil rights movement'. To achieve (and utilize) Black Power, CORE advocated working within the Democratic Party and forming alliances with other groups, sanctioned the use of violence in self-defence, and called for black economic boycotts and all-black business and financial institutions based on and located in the ghettos. In contrast, SNCC endorsed independent black political action outside the established parties, questioned the value of alliances with whites, and appeared to support the idea of guerilla warfare against American racists. The Black Panther Party, founded in Oakland, California, by Huey P. Newton and Bobby Seale in 1966, was the most extreme example of Black Power in action. Its ten-point programme 'What We Want' asserted[6]:

1. We want power to determine the destiny of our black community.
2. We want full employment for our people.
3. We want an end to the robbery by the white man of our black community.
4. We want decent housing, fit for shelter of human beings.
5. We want education for our people that exposes the true nature of this decadent American society.
6. We want all black men to be exempt from military service.
7. We want an immediate end to police brutality and murder of black people.
8. We want freedom for all black men held in federal, state, country, and city prisons and jails.
9. We want all black people when brought to trial to be tried in court by a jury of their peer group or people from their black communities, as defined by the Constitution of the United States.
10. We want land, bread, housing, education, clothing, justice and peace.

With their firearms, black berets, and menacing Black Panther emblem, the new party (membership of which spread rapidly across the country) seemed a direct threat to 'law and order'. The Black Panthers, within two years of formation, moved beyond defence of the black community against police brutality and the espousal of black liberation to the creation of a Marxist–Leninist party advocating a 'socialist revolution to free the oppressed people of America, regardless of race'. By the close of the 1960s, as a consequence of police and FBI infiltration and harassment, the leading Black Panthers were either dead, imprisoned, or – as in the case of Eldridge Cleaver, the theorist of the party – in exile abroad.

But one separatist organization, the Nation of Islam, persisted and grew in strength throughout the 1950s and 1960s. Its most notable convert, later to become its most famous apostate, was to challenge the aims and methods of the civil rights movement with devastating logic, and emerge as the most important spokesman for black nationalist separatism since the demise of Marcus Garvey.

MALCOLM LITTLE AND MALCOLM X

Malcolm Little was born in Omaha, Nebraska, the son of a West Indian mother and a black American father, a Baptist minister and follower of Marcus Garvey.

> My father, the Reverend Earl Little, was ... a dedicated organizer for Marcus Garvey's UNIA. With the help of such disciples as my father, Garvey, from his headquarters in Harlem, was raising the banner of black-race purity and exhorting the Negro masses to return to their ancestral African homeland – a cause which made Garvey the most controversial black man on earth.[7]

When Malcolm was very young, the family, following warnings by the Ku-Klux-Klan that the Reverend Little's UNIA activities were unwelcome, moved to Lansing, Michigan. When Malcolm was six, his father was beaten and thrown to death under a tramcar by members of a local white supremacist group, the Black Legion – who had earlier burned the Little family home. These childhood experiences (his mother became insane and entered a mental hospital) had a profound effect on Malcolm, who later recalled that he had, as a child, accompanied his father on UNIA business around Lansing, and 'the image of him that made me proudest was his crusading and militant campaigning with the words of Marcus Garvey'. At the meetings held in private houses, Malcolm remembered seeing 'big shiny photographs of Marcus Garvey that were passed from hand to hand', and his father exhorting the gatherings: 'Up you mighty race, you can accomplish what you will.'

> The pictures showed what seemed to me millions of Negroes thronged in parade behind Garvey riding in a fine car, a big black man dressed in a dazzling uniform with gold braid on it ... wearing a thrilling hat with tall plumes. I remember hearing that he had black followers not only in the United States but all around the world.[8]

An intelligent and promising high school student, Malcolm hoped to become a lawyer, an ambition that was summarily dismissed by his teacher as being unrealistic for a Negro (she suggested that he become a carpenter), and the episode increased Malcolm's sense of alienation from an unremittingly hostile white society. In 1941, he left school, and went to live with his older half-sister in Roxbury, Massachusetts, the black ghetto of Boston. Employed as a shoeshine boy at the Roseland Ballroom (where he met such famous black jazzmen as Lionel Hampton and Johnny Hodges), and a dining-car porter on the Boston–New York route, Malcolm became a small-time criminal, known as 'Detroit Red', operating for a time in Harlem. As he later recalled:

> I was a true hustler, uneducated, unskilled at anything honourable, and I considered myself nervy and cunning enough to live by my wits, exploiting my prey. I would risk just about anything.[9]

Returning to Boston in 1945, he was soon arrested for burglary, and sentenced to seven years in prison. He was not yet twenty-one years old.

During his first year in prison, in Charlestown, Malcolm continued to behave as a delinquent, baiting the guards, sniffing nutmeg and other semi-drugs and, by his own account, raging against God and the Bible – earning himself the nickname 'Satan' from the other inmates. But he met and came to respect a fellow prisoner, Bimbi, who was literate and highly articulate. With his encouragement, Malcolm began a correspondence course in English, laboriously copied out an entire dictionary, and read so voraciously in his cell after lights out that he permanently impaired his vision. In 1948, after his transfer to Concord prison, Malcolm received a letter from his brother, Philbert, who informed him that he had discovered 'the natural religion for the black man', and had joined the Nation of Islam. When his brother Reginald also wrote to him from Detroit, instructing him not to eat pork or smoke cigarettes, adding that 'I'll show you how to get out of prison', Malcolm's curiosity was aroused. Further correspondence and visits from his family, together with his own reading, introduced Malcolm to the Black Muslim theology and life-style as preached (if not practised) by the sect's leader, Elijah Muhammad. Malcolm embraced the new creed with all the enthusiasm of the convert.

THE NATION OF ISLAM

The Nation of Islam, an offshoot of the Moorish-American Science Temple, was founded in Detroit in 1930 by a mysterious pedlar, Wallace D. Fard. Presenting himself as a Muslim prophet, Fard preached a message of black redemption within Islam. Whites were castigated as 'devils', and mankind itself was said to have begun with the black race which brought civilization to earth. The white race, a degenerate mutation of the original inhabitants of the earth – the 'Asiatic Black Man' – had been given 6,000 years of domination by God to test the capacity and strength of the Black Nation. But the day of judgement was at hand, when the Caucasians and their religion, white Christianity, would be destroyed.

Within three years, Fard had developed an organization so effective that he was able to withdraw almost entirely from active leadership. He had not only set up the Temple of Islam and established its ritual and worship but also founded a University of Islam (actually, a combined elementary and secondary school), dedicated to 'higher mathematics', astronomy, and the 'ending of spook civilization'. He had created the Muslim Girls Training Class, which taught young Muslim women the principles of home economics and how to be a proper wife and mother. Finally, fear of trouble with unbelievers, especially with the police, led to the founding of the Fruit of Islam – a military organization for the men who were drilled by captains and taught tactics and the use of firearms. A Minister of Islam was now appointed to run the entire organization, aided by a staff of assistant ministers. Each of these men was selected and trained personally by Fard, who gradually stopped his public appearances and eventually disappeared from view.[10]

In 1933, leadership of the movement (which had gained about 33,000 followers) was taken up by Elijah Poole, the son of Georgia tenant farmers and former slaves, and a former Garveyite. Poole changed his name to Elijah Muhammad, and asserted that he was 'Allah's Prophet'. During the 1930s and 1940s, the Nation of Islam grew slowly, drawing support mainly from the black lower classes. Muhammad organized temples in Chicago, Milwaukee and Washington, DC, and refined and amplified the precepts of the faith. According to Elijah Muhammad, the black race originally inhabited the moon, and at one time the earth and the moon were one planet. But following an explosion – caused by a black scientist named Yakub – the two were separated. 'Original Man' – the first people to inhabit the earth – were black people, members of the tribe of Shabazz. Under Muhammad, the Black Muslims advocated racial separatism, self-determination and the setting up of an independent black republic within the borders of the United States – or a return to Africa.

Black Muslims published their own newspaper, *Muhammad Speaks*, and history books stressing the glories of the African past. They rejected the term 'Negro' as derogatory and favoured the term 'Afro-American', and discarded black surnames as marks of the slave past, substituting instead the suffix 'X'. Converts were enjoined to follow a strict code of personal conduct which included a prohibition on the eating of pork, extramarital sexual relations, and the uses of alcohol, tobacco or narcotics. Muslims were not allowed to vote in national or local elections, to serve in the armed forces or to engage in any kind of political activity. Indolence and laziness were sternly deprecated, and habits of thrift, personal cleanliness and economic self-help were extolled as positive virtues. The Nation of Islam, under Muhammad, was the most significant black nationalist movement since the UNIA, carrying the idea of racial separatism to its extreme. Until the government would grant them a separate state, the Muslims elected to avoid any social, religious or political contacts with whites. 'During the

Depression and New Deal, Muslims refused relief checks, WPA or other government-sponsored employment, and even social security numbers.'[11] In 1942, Muhammad and sixty-two of his followers were convicted of draft evasion and jailed for three years.

In several respects, the Black Muslims represented a latter-day version of Garveyism. The separatism of the Nation of Islam was motivated by very similar forces to those which had prompted Garveyites to discover their individual and group identity in racial separation. The Fruit of Islam, the Nation's police force, was analogous to Garvey's African Legions. More significantly, the group economy practised by the Muslims – dry cleaners, grocery stores, restaurants, dairy farms and bakeries – duplicated Garvey's collective black economy. And in its commitment to racial uplift and redemption, the Nation of Islam retailed fundamental tenets of Garveyism, which itself had drawn selectively on Booker T. Washington's economic nationalism and racial separatism. Under Elijah Muhammad, the Nation of Islam

> was nothing but a form of Booker T. Washington's philosophy of economic self-help, black unity, bourgeois hard work, law-abiding, vocational training, stay-out-of-the-civil-rights-struggle agitation, separate from the white man etc., morality. The only difference was that Elijah Muhammad added the potent factor of the Muslim religion to a race, economic, and social philosophy of which the first prophet was none other than Booker T. Washington.[12]

Where Washington was a moderate, 'accommodationist' separatist, Elijah Muhammad, given the integrationist climate of American Negro thought after 1945, preached a militant, assertive separatism. Muslim demands and beliefs, as stated by Elijah Muhammad, included the following:

> We want our people in America whose parents or grandparents were descendants from slaves, to be allowed to establish a separate state or territory of their own – either on this continent or elsewhere.
> We want the government of the United States to exempt our people from ALL taxation as long as we are deprived of equal justice under the laws of the land.
> We believe that intermarriage or race mixing should be prohibited. We want the religion of Islam taught without hindrance or suppression.
> We believe that the offer of integration is hypocritical and is made by those who are trying to deceive the black peoples into believing that their 400-year-old open enemies of freedom, justice and equality are, all of a sudden, their 'friends'. Furthermore, we believe that such deception is intended to prevent black people from realizing that the time in history has arrived for the separation from the whites of this nation.
> We believe that Allah (God) appeared in the Person of Master W. Fard Muhammad, July, 1930; the long-awaited 'Messiah' of the Christians and the 'Mahdi' of the Muslims.[13]

Malcolm X (as he became after his conversion to the Nation of Islam) was following in the footsteps of his father, a disciple of Marcus Garvey, who in turn, was an admirer of Booker T. Washington.

MALCOLM X: BLACK MUSLIM

Released from prison in 1952, Malcolm went directly to Detroit to meet Elijah Muhammad, was made a formal member of the Nation, took the surname X, and rapidly advanced within the Muslim hierarchy to become assistant minister of Temple No. 1 in Detroit. He also became the movement's most effective preacher and proselytizer. In 1954, he was given the ministry of Temple No. 7 at Lennox Avenue and 116th Street in Harlem, and quickly built a following in New York. As the trusted disciple and minister of Elijah Muhammad, Malcolm X at first preached the orthodox Black Muslim message:

> The Western World today faces a great catastrophe. It stands on the brink of disaster. Mr Muhammad says the only way our people can avoid the fiery destruction that God Himself will soon unleash upon this wicked world, is for our people to come together among themselves in unity and practice true brotherhood. Mr Muhammad says God is with us to Unite our people into one brotherhood. ... The Western World is filled with drunkenness, dope addiction, lying, stealing, gambling, adultery, fornication, prostitution and hosts of other evils. ... The God of Peace and Righteousness is about to set up His Kingdom of Peace and Righteousness here on this earth. ... Mr Muhammad is trying to clean up our morals and qualify us to enter into this new Righteous Nation of God. The American so-called Negroes must recognize each other as Brothers and Sisters ... stop carrying guns and knives to hurt each other, stop drinking whiskey, taking dope, reefers, and even cigarettes. No more gambling! Save your money. ... Elevate the Black woman; respect her and protect her. ... We want only an equal chance on this earth, but to have an equal chance we must have the same thing that the white man himself needed before he could get this nation started ... WE MUST HAVE SOME LAND OF OUR OWN. ... How else can 20 million Black people who now constitute a nation in our own right, A NATION WITHIN A NATION, expect to survive forever in a land where we are the last ones hired and the first ones fired? ... We Muslims don't want to be a burden on America any longer. God has given Mr Muhammad a Divine Message, Program, and Solution. WE MUST HAVE SOME LAND. ... We will then set up our own farms, factories, businesses and schools ... to become self-sustaining, economically and otherwise.[14]

Yet, despite Malcolm's eloquence and dedication, the Black Muslim appeal was limited, and recruitment to the Nation was slow.

Their discipline was very strict. ... Their moral and sexual codes were puritanical. The members had many obligations and few rights; no pretence was made that the organization was democratic. Their religion seemed exotic to Negroes still under the influence of Christianity and bogus to the few attracted to orthodox Islam, and it was an obstacle to those who had learned from sad experience to be wary of rackets disguising themselves as churches. Their solution – 'separation' – was couched in vague terms, hard to pin down concretely and understand at a non-emotional level.[15]

As an effective orator and inspired evangelist, Malcolm X began to attract attention and support from lower-class blacks from the ghetto, less for his exegesis of Black Muslim tenets than for his blistering condemnations of white racism, advocacy of retaliatory violence, and critiques of the civil rights movement's stress on non-violent resistance. Some of his most stinging comments were reserved for Martin Luther King's philosophy of redemptive black suffering. Drawing an analogy with slavery, Malcolm X asserted that the two classes of slaves were the 'House Negro', loyal to the master, and the 'Field Negro', who hated both the master and slavery. Their modern counterparts were the 'Uncle Toms', accommodating, peaceable and self-serving, and the 'New Negro' who had a pride in blackness and demanded racial separation. Martin Luther King (see Ch. 7) belonged firmly in the first category, an Uncle Tom whose

primary concern is in defending the white man, and if he can elevate the black man's condition at the same time, then the black man will be elevated. But if it takes a condemnation of the white man in order to elevate the black man, you'll find that Martin Luther King will get out of the struggle. Martin Luther King isn't preaching love – he's preaching love the white man.[16]

When asked by the social psychologist, Kenneth Clark, if his strictures against 'Negroes you see running around here talking about "love everybody" [when] they don't have any love whatsoever for their own kind' was an oblique reference to King, Malcolm replied:

You don't have to criticize Reverend Martin Luther King. His actions criticize him. ... Any Negro who teaches other Negroes to turn the other cheek is disarming that Negro ... of his God-given right ... his moral right ... his natural right ... his intelligent right to defend himself. Everything in nature can defend itself except the American Negro. And men like King – their job is to go among Negroes and teach Negroes, 'Don't fight back.' He doesn't tell them, 'Don't fight each other.' 'Don't fight the white man' is what he's saying ... because the followers of Martin Luther King will cut each other from head to foot, but they will not do anything to defend themselves against the attacks of the white man. ... *White* people follow King. ... *White* people subsidize King. *White* people support King ... the masses of black people don't support ... King. King's the best weapon that the white man, who wants to brutalize Negroes, has ever gotten in this country, because he is setting up a situation where, when the white man wants to attack Negroes, they can't defend themselves, because King has put this foolish philosophy out – you're not supposed to fight, or you're not supposed to defend yourself.[17]

Malcolm gave a similar assessment of King to the black journalist Louis Lomax, adding on this occasion that:

... the goal of Dr Martin Luther King is to give Negroes a chance to sit in a segregated restaurant beside the same white man who has brutalized them for years ... to get Negroes to forgive the people who have brutalized them for 400 years ... but the masses of black people today don't go for what Martin Luther King is putting down.[18]

That Malcolm was prepared to act directly against white provocation was dramatically shown in 1957, when he led a squad of followers and surrounded a Harlem police station, following a beating of a Black Muslim by police. Malcolm demanded the victim's release and hospitalization, and filed a $70,000 claim for damages against the New York City police department. This widely publicized action caught the attention of blacks throughout the country, and membership of the Nation increased rapidly. According to one estimate, by 1959 the annual income of the Nation was $3,000,000; by 1961, the eight temples founded by Malcolm in the Eastern states had completed payment of nearly $39,000 to the Nation's headquarters in Chicago. Malcolm's own New York Temple No. 7 contributed over $23,000.

The Nation's best-known spokesman, Malcolm X, by 1964 was the second most requested speaker on college campuses – the first being the ultra-conservative Republican, Barry Goldwater. In numerous public addresses, and in articles in *Muhammad Speaks*, Malcolm, gaining in confidence and sophistication, pointed up the major issues confronting blacks: inadequate housing and high rents, inferior welfare and educational facilities, and political powerlessness. He was also increasingly disenchanted with the conservatism of Elijah Muhammad, and his refusal to allow the Nation to join the civil rights movement. 'In fact, he came – before he was fully conscious of it himself – to identify with the black masses more than with the Nation of Islam; under the impact of the Negro upsurge of the 1960s, he began to put their needs ahead of the interests of the Black Muslim hierarchy.'[19] Moreover, the exclusiveness of the Muslims, and their theological mysticism, no longer satisfied the intellectually mature Malcolm X. Recalling this period, Malcolm reflected:

If I harboured any personal disappointment ... it was that privately I was convinced that our Nation of Islam could be an even greater force in the American black man's overall struggle – if we engaged in more *action*. By that I mean I thought privately that we could have amended or relaxed our general non-engagement policy. I felt that, wherever black people committed themselves, in the Little Rocks and Birminghams ... militantly disciplined Muslims should also be there – for all the world to see, and respect, and discuss. It could be heard increasingly in the Negro communities: 'Those Muslims *talk* tough, but they never *do* anything, unless somebody bothers Muslims.'[20]

At the height of his popularity, Malcolm was to split decisively with the Nation. The occasion of the break was provided by John F. Kennedy's assassination in November 1963. Disregarding Elijah Muhammad's directive that Muslim spokesmen should refuse to comment on the assassination, Malcolm X, when asked for his thoughts (at the end of an address prepared a week before the murder in Dallas, entitled 'God's Judgement of White America'), remarked that it was simply a matter of 'chickens coming home to roost'.

I said that the hate in white men had not stopped with the killing of defenceless black people, but that hate, allowed to spread unchecked, finally had struck down this country's Chief of State.[21]

Malcolm's comment was widely reported, and Elijah Muhammad suspended him from the Nation for a ninety-day period, during which he was forbidden to speak as a minister. Malcolm correctly sensed that his suspension (he was not to be reinstated) was an attempt to curb his influence within the movement, as it also reflected the growing divergence between his ideas and those of Elijah Muhammad. (Malcolm's suspicion that Muhammad had not adhered to the Nation's strict sexual code, also weakened his respect for the man and the movement.)

MALCOLM X: MUSLIM

In 1964, Malcolm resigned from the Nation, and in a 'Declaration of Independence' announced that he would continue as a Muslim, but not as a member of the Nation, because of the ongoing civil rights struggle. Although he still publicly endorsed Muhammad's solution to the race problem – separation and an ultimate return to Africa – Malcolm conceded that the theology of the Nation did not appeal to the black youth of the ghettos. He announced his intention of forming a new mosque in New York City, the Muslim Mosque, Incorporated, membership of which would be 'organized in such a manner to provide for the active participation of all Negroes in our political, economic, and social programme'.[22] The new organization would provide both a spiritual and an activist base for Muslims and non-Muslims, and would adopt a black nationalist, direct-action approach to the racial problem.

Malcolm reiterated his belief that blacks should and would retaliate in self-defence when provoked.

> Concerning nonviolence: it is criminal to teach a man not to defend himself when he is the constant victim of brutal attacks. It is legal ... to own a shotgun or rifle. When our people are being bitten by dogs, they are within their rights to kill those dogs. We should be peaceful ... but the time has come for the American Negro to fight back in self-defence whenever and wherever he is being unjustly and unlawfully attacked.[23]

From its inception, the Muslim Mosque, Inc., was weak, poorly organized and without sufficient funding. The radical wing of the civil rights coalition – SNCC and CORE – rejected Malcolm's overtures to form a working alliance. Despite his breach with the Black Muslims, Malcolm was regarded by the younger black militants as too extremist, a potential (if not an actual) rival for leadership, and certainly out of step with the prevailing integrationist sentiments of the black majority. At the other end of the ideological spectrum, Elijah Muhammad never forgave Malcolm's apostasy, and *Muhammad Speaks* published weekly diatribes comparing him with such notable traitors as Judas, Brutus and Benedict Arnold. In fact, Malcolm was now in an ambivalent position: a confirmed Black Muslim and an aspiring black protest leader, a religious and a secular black nationalist, who was beginning to view the plight of black Americans in a world-wide perspective.

In 1964, Malcolm made a tour of the Middle East and Africa, where he was well received by heads of state, politicians and students. The turning point on this tour was his pilgrimage to Mecca, where his exposure to Islam broke his remaining ties with the doctrinal and political narrowness of the Black Muslims. In particular, he was impressed by the fraternal relations between multiracial pilgrims at Mecca, and the interest expressed in the American racial situation by African and Arab leaders.

> Malcolm was now persuaded that it was time for all Afro-Americans to become an integral part of the world's Pan-Africanists, and even though they might remain in America physically ... they must return to Africa philosophically and culturally to develop a working unity within the framework of Pan-Africanism. The Malcolm who returned from Africa as El-Hadj Malik El-Shabazz (although he continued to be known as Malcolm X) was far different from the one who left. He returned with a sense of his African heritage and a broadened perspective on world forces affecting Afro-Americans.[24]

On his return from Africa, Malcolm informed a reporter:

> Every time you see another nation on the African continent become independent, you know that Marcus Garvey is alive. All the freedom movement that is taking place right here in America today was initiated by the philosophy and teachings of Garvey. The entire Black Nationalist

philosophy here in America is fed upon the seeds that were planted by Marcus Garvey.

In June 1964, Malcolm announced the formation of the Organization of Afro-American Unity (OAAU), based on the Organization for African Unity. With distinct overtones of Garvey's UNIA, the OAAU declared itself:

> *Dedicated* to the unification of all peoples of African descent in this hemisphere and to the utilization of that unity to bring into being the organizational structure that will project the black people's contribution to the world.

It would include 'all people of African descent in the Western hemisphere, as well as our brothers and sisters on the African continent'. Among its other objectives, the OAAU asserted 'the Afro-American's right of self-defence' against 'mass murderers, bombers, lynchers, floggers, brutalizers and exploiters', complete independence for black peoples, and the formulation of a manifesto to be presented to the United Nations Human Rights Commission, calling for the prosecution of the United States government on the grounds that the deteriorating condition of Afro-Americans constituted a threat to world peace. It also demanded educational and welfare facilities geared specifically to the needs of blacks, the running of independent black candidates for political office, and a voter registration drive 'to make every unregistered voter in the Afro-American community an independent voter'. The prospectus of the OAAU read

> like a Black Power manifesto two years ahead of its time – a declaration of the controlling importance of colour and of black control of every aspect of the black community. . . . Its agenda was to include . . . school boycotts, rent strikes, housing rehabilitation, programmes for addicts, unwed mothers, a war on organized crime, a black cultural revolution 'to unbrainwash an entire people' – more activities . . . than an organization with eight or nine hundred active members at its peak could possibly have undertaken.[25]

In effect, the OAAU was the institutional embodiment of Malcolm's changing and developing views on the racial situation, at home and abroad. The OAAU rallies were not membership meetings, but rather public relations and educational events during which Malcolm explained his thoughts and strategies on a variety of issues.

Indeed, in both his Black Muslim and post-Black Muslim periods, Malcolm was most effective as a speaker and propagandist. Although he was a recognized black leader, Malcolm X never commanded a broadly based organization like Garvey. 'He was not a scholar in the formal tradition of W. E. B. Du Bois, and he did not command the respect of poor blacks in the rural South and whites throughout the country as did

Martin Luther King. ... Like Garvey, Malcolm X was primarily a speaker, and one of exceptional ability.'[26] Malcolm's most attractive theme for black audiences was his exposition of the history of racial discrimination in America, generally with references to the 'legacy of slavery'. Like Washington and Garvey, Malcolm made frequent allusions to the debilitating effects of enslavement on the black psyche. But, after his break with the Nation of Islam, Malcolm 'no longer drew the analogy between Hebrew slavery and Negro slavery. God would not deliver the Negro from bondage through heavenly intervention as Elijah Muhammad had promised. The Negro masses had better free themselves.'[27] With the emergence of independent African nations in the 1960s, Malcolm advocated a 'psychological' and not a physical return to Africa, which black Americans would achieve when they gained 'independence' from white domination at home. Following his second visit to African capitals in 1964, the purpose of which was to lobby the Organization for African Unity, meeting in Cairo, to support his moves to indict the American government before the United Nations, Malcolm began to appeal to non-racist whites for support in the civil rights struggle.

> We will work with anyone, with any group, no matter what their colour is, as long as they are genuinely interested in taking the type of steps necessary to bring an end to the injustices that black people in this country are afflicted by. No matter what their colour is, no matter what their political, economic, or social philosophy is, as long as their aims and objectives are in the direction of destroying the vulturous system that has been sucking the blood of the black people in this country, they're all right with me.[28]

In his last speeches, Malcolm also made favourable references to socialism. At an OAAU meeting in Harlem, in December 1964, he declared that:

> Almost every one of the countries that has gotten independence has devised some kind of socialistic system, and this is no accident. ... You can't operate a capitalistic system unless you are vulturistic; you have to have someone's blood to suck to be a capitalist. You show me a capitalist, and I'll show you a blood sucker.[29]

But Malcolm never moved beyond a vague critique of capitalism, and never endorsed Marxism. As one confidant remarked: 'He had no use for Marxism. He considered Marxism as another political ideology invented by white men for white men, to shift the seat of power from one group of white men to another group of white men. He thought it had no relevance to the black man.'[30] Fundamentally an inspired agitator, not an original thinker or political theorist, Malcolm, unlike Martin Luther King, did not even envisage a coalition of the underprivileged across racial lines. As he informed an interviewer:

The history of America is that working class whites have been just as much against not only working Negroes, but *all* Negroes, because all Negroes are working class within the caste system. The richest Negro is treated like a working class Negro. There never has been any good relationship between the working class Negro and the working class whites ... there can be no worker solidarity until there is first some black solidarity. We have got to get our problems solved first and then if there's anything left to work on the white man's problems, good, but I think one of the mistakes Negroes make is this worker solidarity thing. There's no such thing – it didn't even work in Russia.[31]

To the end of his life, Malcolm remained a black nationalist, committed to the spiritual and material elevation of black Americans through the affirmation of his own faith in the redemption of the individual. Like Booker T. Washington, Malcolm produced an authorized, inspirational account of his own life, completed shortly before his assassination by three members of the Nation of Islam, in New York City, on 21 February 1965. Published after his death, it became a sacred text of the emerging Black Power Movement, and presented Malcolm's search for identity (as well as his claims to leadership) to a wider audience that had been either unaware of, or actively opposed to, him during his comparatively short career. It is possible to regard it as his greatest achievement.

THE AUTOBIOGRAPHY OF MALCOLM X

Like *Up From Slavery*, Malcolm's autobiography (dictated in instalments to the then struggling black writer, Alex Haley), is a black success story, but one profoundly different in content and tone. In many respects, it belongs to the genre of spiritual conversion autobiography – 'that of the sinner who becomes a saint, and the saint, like his Christian parallels is a preacher'.[32] It contains graphic descriptions of Malcolm's criminal activities, his prison experiences, conversion to the Nation of Islam, relationships with Elijah Muhammad, and the discovery of 'true' Islam on his journey to Mecca. It is, in effect, a black *Pilgrim's Progress*, and Malcolm retails the episodes of his life as though they were moral parables. Incidents are described, and then the appropriate morals are drawn. Thus Malcolm recounts how, as a ghetto youth, he allowed his friend Shorty to straighten his hair at home, with a mixture of lye, eggs and other ingredients. In every respect, the experience was hair-raising.

The congolene just felt warm when Shorty started combing it in. But then my head caught fire. I gritted my teeth and tried to pull the sides of the kitchen table together. The comb felt as if it was raking my skin off.

My eyes watered, my nose was running. I couldn't stand it any longer; I bolted to the washbasin. I was cursing Shorty with every name I could think of when he got the spray going and started soap-lathering my head.

When the operation was completed, 'my first view in the mirror blotted out the hurting ... on top of my head was this thick, smooth sheen of shining red hair – real red – as straight as any white man's'. To the mature Malcolm, the episode was revealing and cautionary:

> This was my first really big step toward self-degradation: when I endured all that pain, literally burning my flesh with lye, in order to cook my natural hair until it was limp, to have it look like a white man's hair. I had joined that multitude of Negro men and women in America who are brainwashed into believing that the black people are 'inferior' – and white people 'superior' – that they will even mutilate their God-created bodies to try to look 'pretty'.[33]

Throughout the book, Malcolm shrewdly adjusts his language to parallel the particular stages of his life. Recounting his career as a hustler, he informs the reader:

> Shorty would take me to groovy, frantic scenes in different chicks' and cats' pads, where with the lights and the juke down mellow, everybody blew gage and juiced back and jumped. I met chicks who were as fine as May wine, and cats who were hip to all happenings.

And then adds:

> That paragraph is a bit deliberate of course; it's just to display a bit more of the slang that was used by everyone I respected as 'hip' in those days.[34]

Malcolm could also employ parody and satire in an attempt to convey the world of unreality inhabited by the aspiring black bourgeoisie. Those blacks living in the Roxbury section of Boston who affected white middle-class ways, drew Malcolm's derisory scorn.

> I'd guess that eight out of ten of the Hill Negroes of Roxbury, despite the impressive-sounding job titles they affected, actually worked as menials and servants. 'He's in banking,' or 'He's in securities.' It sounded as though they were discussing a Rockefeller or a Mellon – and not some grey-headed, dignity-posturing bank janitor or bond-house messenger. 'I'm with an old family,' was the euphemism used to dignify the professions of white folks' cooks and maids who talked so affectedly among their own kind in Roxbury that you couldn't even understand them. I don't know how many forty and fifty-year old errand boys went down the Hill dressed like ambassadors in black suits, to down-town jobs in 'government', 'in finance', or 'in law'. It has never ceased to amaze me how so many Negroes, now and then, could stand the indignity of that kind of self-delusion.[35]

Yet, as he is also prepared to admit, as a teenager, Malcolm had himself conformed to current trends and fashions, as when he went to buy a suit.

> I was measured, and the young salesman picked off a rack a suit that was just wild; sky-blue pants thirty inches in the knees and angle-narrowed down to twelve inches at the bottom, and a long coat that pinched my waist and flared out below my knees. As a give, the salesman said, the store would give me a narrow belt with my initial 'L' on it. Then he said I ought to buy a hat, and I did – blue, with a feather in the four-inch brim. Then the store gave me another present: a long, thick, gold-plated chain that swung down lower than my coat hem.

'I was', Malcolm recalls ironically, 'sold forever on credit.'[36]

After encountering Elijah Muhammad, Malcolm's dictated life-story takes on a more formal, sober and dignified form.

> Never in prison had I studied and absorbed so intensely as I did now under Mr Muhammad's guidance. ... I went to bed every night ever more awed. If not Allah, who else could have put such wisdom into that little humble lamb of a man from the Georgia fourth grade and sawmills and cotton patches. The 'lamb of a man' analogy I drew for myself from the prophecy in the Book of Revelations of a symbolic lamb with a two-edged sword in its mouth. Mr Muhammad's two-edged sword was his teachings, which cut back and forth to free the black man's mind from the white man. My adoration of Mr Muhammad grew, in the sense of the Latin root and word *adorare*.[37]

After his break with the Nation of Islam, Malcolm, a convert to the true Muslim faith, reflected (during his visit to Mecca) on his ingenuousness in having followed his mentor without question.

> I guess it would be impossible for anyone ever to realize fully how complete was my belief in Elijah Muhammad. I believed in him not only as a leader in the ordinary *human* sense, but I also believed in him as a *divine* leader. I believed he had no human weaknesses or faults, and that, therefore, he could make no mistakes and that he could do no wrong. There on a Holy World hilltop, I realized how very dangerous it is for people to hold any human being in such esteem, especially to consider anyone some sort of 'divinely guided' or 'protected' person.[38]

'One difficulty in assessing what Malcolm X stood for is that, ideologically, there were at least two Malcolm X's – one the orthodox, faithful follower of Elijah Muhammad, the other an independent leader of his own movement after his break with Muhammad. Malcolm was a follower for twelve years, a leader in his own right for only one. His autobiography was largely written – or told to his collaborator, Alex Haley – in his first phase.'[39] Yet in retailing the story of his life, Malcolm was skilfully presenting his claims to leadership. During every period of his life – petty criminal, autodidact, Muslim minister, emerging independent black leader – Malcolm presents himself as eminently successful. He relates his reception in Saudi Arabia with ostensible modesty, but also with obvious relish.

> Never have I been so highly honoured. ... Who would believe the blessings that have been heaped upon an *American Negro*? A few nights ago, a man who would be called in America a 'white' man, a United Nations diplomat, an ambassador, a companion of kings, gave me *his* hotel suite, *his* bed. ... His Holiness Sheikh Muhammad Harkon himself okayed my visit to Mecca ... he told me that he hoped I would be a successful preacher of Islam in America. A car, a driver, and a guide have been placed at my disposal. ... Never would I have thought of dreaming that I would ever be a recipient of such honours – honours that in America would be bestowed upon a King – not a Negro.[40]

Embracing his new faith with enthusiasm and obvious sincerity, Malcolm also displayed the self-confidence and boosterism of the archetypal American abroad:

> Behind my nods and smiles ... I was doing some American-type thinking and reflection. I saw that Islam's conversions around the world could double and triple if the colourfulness and the true spiritualness of the Hajj pilgrimage were properly advertized and communicated to the outside world. ... The Arabs said 'insha Allah' ('God willing') – then they waited for converts. Even by this means, Islam was on the march, but I knew that with improved public relations the number of new converts turning to Allah could be turned into millions.[41]

Malcolm, as this passage reveals, 'had become a Hajj but remained in some ways a Babitt, the salesman, archetype of ... American society. A creed was something to *sell*. Allah, the Merciful, needed better merchandising.'[42] *The Autobiography of Malcolm X* presents a man in constant motion, who only came to rest – physically and metaphysically – at the Holy City of Mecca. His sense of spiritual kinship with fellow pilgrims is movingly conveyed in the following passage:

> ... the Muslim world's customs no longer seemed strange to me. My hands now readily plucked up food from a common dish shared with brother Muslims; I was drinking without hesitation from the same glass as others; I was washing from the same little pitcher of water; and sleeping with eight or ten others on a mat in the open. I remember one night at Muzdalfia ... I lay awake amid sleeping Muslim brothers and I learned that pilgrims from every land – every colour, and class, and rank; high officials and beggar alike – all snored in the same language.[43]

'Paradoxically, it was his experience in feudal Saudi Arabia rather than in democratic America, that tended to erase Malcolm's racist feelings.'[44]

Malcolm X designed his remarkable autobiography in order to influence his readers; his purpose was to create a type or character, that of the emerging black leader, and to 'convert the reader from the fiction of him as a threat to society, operating on the fringes of the black world, to the fiction (or suggestion) of him as a central figure of major stature and integrity'.[45]

MALCOLM X AND HIS BLACK CRITICS

During his lifetime, Malcolm X had considerably less appeal for the majority of black and white Americans than did Martin Luther King. At the end of his life, Malcolm had only a few active followers, and also had to face constant harassment from the Nation of Islam. He was killed at a time when his racial philosophy appeared to be undergoing a profound change. But during his career as a Black Muslim and an independent minister, Malcolm X faced the distrust, fear and outright condemnation of most black leaders and spokesmen. Only after his death, in the mood of intense disillusionment felt by blacks in the late 1960s, the outbreak of 'civil disorders' in American cities, and the resurgence of black nationalist sentiment, did Malcolm X join Marcus Garvey, W. E. B. Du Bois and Martin Luther King as a recognized Negro leader.

The tone of much black criticism of Malcolm X echoed that of an earlier generation's assessment of Du Bois and Garvey. Malcolm, it was conceded, had been the voice of urban black protest, calling on Negroes to reassert their racial pride, and to resist the forces of white oppression. But he was also seen as a confused and uncertain figure. Bayard Rustin, one of the elder statesmen of the civil rights movement, told an interviewer in October 1964:

> I think there's every indication that Malcolm X doesn't know where he's going, and I think he's somewhat frightened of coming back here [from the Near East]. I feel he's just lost. He has very little in the way of an organization – practically nothing. They're a few frustrated youngsters and a few confused writers ... but even before he left here, these Sunday meetings which he was having got smaller and smaller, because he doesn't have any real answers to the immediate problems which Negroes want an answer to.[46]

To Roy Wilkins of the NAACP, Malcolm's greatest limitation was that 'the only way you could judge things was whether you did the thing that was *manly*, no matter if it was suicidal or not'.[47] Other black spokesmen asserted that Malcolm X was the creation of the white-controlled media, and not a representative or authentic black leader. Whitney M. Young, of the National Urban League, asserted that despite his frequent appearances in the headlines,

> ... there aren't ten Negroes who would follow Malcolm X to a separate state. The only appeal he has is to give a Negro who's been beaten down all day a chance to get a vicarious pleasure out of hearing someone cuss out the white people.[48]

James Farmer of CORE informed Robert Penn Warren: 'Malcolm has done nothing but verbalize – his militancy is a matter of posture, there has been no action.'[49]

If Malcolm X, in his Black Muslim phase, was unacceptable to the older civil rights leadership, his independent ministry and expressed wish to engage in some kind of concerted black-and-white protest action, was seen by others as a promise unfulfilled. Although he rejected Malcolm's racial separatism and advocacy of retaliatory violence, Martin Luther King, his widow believed, had agreed with some aspects of Malcolm's thought:

> ... he shared with Malcolm the fierce desire that the black American
> reclaim his racial pride, his joy in himself and his race – in a physical, a
> cultural, and a spiritual rebirth. He shared with the nationalists the sure
> knowledge that 'black is beautiful' and that, in so many respects, the
> quality of the black people's scale of values was far superior to that of
> the white culture which attempted to enslave us. Martin too had a close
> attachment to our African brothers and to our common heritage. Martin
> too believed that *white* Christianity had failed to act in accordance with
> its teachings. Martin also believed in non-violent Black Power. He
> believed that we must have our share of the economy, of education, of
> jobs, of free choice.[50]

Where Malcolm X's claims to recognition – by whites and blacks – as a leader of American Negroes were not generally acknowledged during his lifetime, those of Martin Luther King, Jr, were beyond dispute.

REFERENCES

1. *The Saturday Evening Post*, 12 Sept. 1964, quoted in *The Autobiography of Malcolm X*, (Penguin, Harmondsworth, 1980), p. 44.
2. Lincoln, C. E., 'The meaning of Malcolm X', in J. H. Clarke (ed.) *Malcolm X: the man and his times* (New York, 1969), p. 10.
3. Vincent, T., *Black Power and the Garvey Movement* (San Francisco, 1972), p. 223.
4. Harris, S., *Father Divine: holy husband* (New York, 1953), p. 27.
5. Meier, A., Rudwick, E. and Broderick, F. L., *Black Protest Thought in the Twentieth Century* (New York, 1971), p. xxxvii.
6. Bracey, J. H., Meier, A. and Rudwick, E., *Black Nationalism in America* (New York, 1970), pp. 531–2.
7. Malcolm X., *The Autobiography of Malcolm X.* (Penguin, Harmondsworth, 1980), p. 79.
8. Malcolm X, op. cit., p. 85.
9. Malcolm X, op. cit., p. 197.
10. Lincoln, C. E., *The Black Muslims in America* (Boston, 1973), p. 16.
11. Vincent, op. cit., p. 223.

12. Cruse, H., *Rebellion or Revolution* (New York, 1968), p. 211.
13. Muhammad, E., 'The Muslim program', in Bracey *et al.*, op cit., pp. 404–7.
14. Malcolm X, Speech at Harlem Unit Rally, in Bracey *et al.*, op. cit., pp. 413–20.
15. Breitman, G., *The Last Year of Malcolm X* (New York, 1970), p. 13.
16. Goldman, P., *The Death and Life of Malcolm X* (London, 1974), p. 75.
17. Clark, K. B., *The Negro Protest* (1963), pp. 26–7.
18. Lomax, L. E., *When the Word is Given: a report on Elijah Muhammad, and the Black Muslim world* (New York, 1964), p. 174.
19. Breitman, op. cit., (1970), p. 21.
20. Malcolm X, op. cit., p. 397.
21. Malcolm X, op. cit., p. 411.
22. Breitman, G. *Malcolm X Speaks* (1965), p. 22.
23. Breitman, op. cit., (1965), p. 22.
24. Blair, T. L., *Retreat to the Ghetto: the end of a dream* (London, 1977), p. 42.
25. Goldman, op. cit., p. 190.
26. Pinkney, A., *Red, Black, and Green: black nationalism in the United States* (Cambridge U.P., 1976), p. 65.
27. Epps, A. (ed.), *The Speeches of Malcolm X at Harvard* (New York, 1969), p. 71.
28. Breitman, op. cit., (1970), p. 48.
29. Blair, op. cit., p. 46.
30. Goldman, op. cit., p. 234.
31. Breitman, op. cit., (1970), p. 46.
32. Mandell, B. J., 'The didactic achievement of Malcolm X's autobiography', *AAS* 2 (1972), 270.
33. Malcolm X, op. cit., pp. 137–8.
34. Malcolm X, op. cit., p. 140.
35. Malcolm X, op. cit., p. 123.
36. Malcolm X, op. cit., p. 135
37. Malcolm X, op. cit., pp. 310–11.
38. Malcolm X, op. cit., pp. 482–3.
39. Draper, T., *The Rediscovery of Black Nationalism* (New York, 1969), p. 89.
40. Malcolm X, op. cit., pp. 455–6.
41. Malcolm X, op. cit., p. 469.
42. Stone, I. F., *In a Time of Torment* (New York, 1967), p. 117.
43. Malcolm X, op. cit., pp. 343–4.
44. Margolies, E., *Native Sons: a critical study of twentieth century black American authors* (New York, 1968), p. 152.
45. Mandell, op. cit., p. 271.
46. Warren, R. P., *Who Speaks for the Negro?* (New York, 1965), p. 244.
47. Goldman, op. cit., p. 385.
48. Warren, op. cit., p. 161.
49. Warren, op. cit., p. 197.
50. King, C. S., *My Life with Martin Luther King, Jr* (New York, 1970), pp. 256–7.

Chapter seven

MARTIN LUTHER KING, JR (1929–1968): APOSTLE FOR NON-VIOLENCE

> Early on I decided that if I was going to shoot craps on anyone's philosophy, I was putting my money on Martin Luther King, Jr. From the start I had respect for Martin. He reminded me of Jackie Robinson. These were the first cats to break down barriers made of iron and steel. Both guys took punishment for a whole race of people. I figured that if I was going to pick up my cross and follow someone, it could only be a cat like King. Yet I couldn't see me doing any marching. First, I wouldn't have known when to duck when they started throwing broken beer bottles at my head. And secondly, I'd just defeat Martin's purpose. My temperament just wouldn't stand certain treatment. I can take abuse. But if you touch me ... man, that's another story. I hit back.
>
> (Ray Charles and David Ritz, *Brother Ray: Ray Charles' own story*)[1]

> It was not that King was a bad man, except in the sense that all men of overweening ambition are bad. It was simply that he was an inopportune man ... his primary service to the black struggle in America was an attempt to substitute righteousness for effectiveness.
>
> (Frank Hercules, *American Society and Black Revolution*)[2]

A NEW DEAL FOR BLACKS? CIVIL RIGHTS AND NEGRO PROTEST, 1932–1954

For most black Americans, the collapse of the United States economy after 1929 simply aggravated an already desperate situation. An Urban League report of 1933 indicates that over 17 per cent of the entire Negro population was on relief. Conditions were equally bad in the North and South, but in the Southern states, private charity organizations often refused to aid blacks. In the Southern farm belts, black tenant farmers and share-croppers went increasingly into debt. Those organizations traditionally concerned with black welfare – the NAACP and the National Urban League – were unable to cope with the conditions produced by the Depression. But the election of the Democrat Franklin D. Roosevelt in 1932, with his promise of a 'New Deal', raised black hopes, and marked a turning point in American race relations. (Yet even the Depression had not shaken the traditional Republican loyalties of blacks. In the 1932 presidential election, Negroes in Detroit, Cleveland, Philadelphia and other major cities voted for Herbert Hoover.) By 1934, the Negro vote began switching to the Democrats; in 1936, according to one estimate, 84.7 per cent of blacks favoured Roosevelt's re-election. Although New Deal reform policies were not free of racial discrimination (and no major piece of civil rights legislation was adopted during Roosevelt's four terms of office), blacks shared in the relief measures instituted by the administration. Despite or perhaps because of Roosevelt's uncertain commitment to blacks (FDR displayed a keen awareness of Southern sensibilities on race issues because of his dependence on Southern votes in Congress for the passage of New Deal legislation), the New Deal radicalized the strategies of the NAACP and Urban League as they attempted to bring pressure on the government to make the new policies and programmes more responsive to black needs. In 1933, following an NAACP initiative, various race advancement organizations established the Joint Committee on National Recovery to fight discriminatory practices in federal relief agencies. (One black writer commented bitterly that NRA – the National Recovery Administration – stood for 'Negroes Ruined Again'.) The emergence of the Congress of Industrial Organizations (CIO) saw an attempt by the American Federation of Labour, under the leadership of John L. Lewis of the United Mine Workers, to organize black skilled and unskilled workers into industrial unions, with the establishment of a Committee to Abolish Racial Discrimination and a Political Action Committee. The NAACP, in response, reversed its critical stance towards organized labour, and worked to build an alliance with the CIO. In the election of 1940, Negro voters overwhelmingly supported Roosevelt for a third term.

The NAACP, in a *Crisis* editorial of November 1940, conceded that Roosevelt, despite Southern white opposition, had 'managed to include Negro citizens in practically every phase of his administrative programme', and allowed that 'no matter how far behind the ideal he may be, he is far ahead of any other Democratic president, and of recent Republican ones'. But it condemned Roosevelt's failure to support a federal anti-lynching bill, and the persistence of racial discrimination in civilian life and in the armed services.

THE SECOND WORLD WAR

On the event of American involvement in the Second World War, Negro protest organizations were united in demanding full and equal participation in the armed forces, and an end to discrimination in the defence industries – which offered new employment opportunities for blacks. While some sections of the Negro press came to adopt a more conservative and conciliatory tone on racial issues, arguing that the national crisis demanded that civil rights agitation should be suspended or muted for the duration of the war, A. Philip Randolph, president of the Brotherhood of Sleeping Car Porters, threatened a mass march on Washington, DC, in 1941, to lobby for equal opportunities in employment and racial integration in the armed forces. The March on Washington Movement, an all-black protest, based its strategy on Gandhi's example of non-violent protest in India, appealed directly to the Negro working class, and anticipated the post-war forms and objectives of the civil rights movement. In his 'Call to the March', Randolph declared:

> Negroes can build a mammoth machine of mass action with a terrific and tremendous driving and striking power that can shatter and crush the evil fortress of race prejudice and hate. .... However, we sternly counsel against violence and ill-considered and intemperate action and the abuse of power. .... We summon you to mass action that is orderly and lawful, but aggressive and militant, for justice, equality and freedom. .... Nat Turner, Denmark Vesey, Gabriel Prosser ... and Frederick Douglass fought, bled and died for the emancipation of American slaves and the preservation of American democracy. Abraham Lincoln, in times of the grave emergency of the Civil War, issued the Proclamation of Emancipation for the freedom of Negro slaves and the preservation of American democracy ... we call upon President Roosevelt, a great humanitarian and idealist, to follow in the footsteps of his noble and illustrious predecessor and take the second decisive step in this world and national emergency and free American Negro citizens of the stigma, humiliation and insult of discrimination and Jim Crowism in Government departments and national defence.[3]

In the event, the March on Washington did not take place; Roosevelt issued Executive Order 8802 in June 1941. It stipulated that 'there shall be no discrimination in the employment of workers in defence industries or Government because of race, creed, or national origin ... it is the duty of employers and labour organizations to provide for the full and equitable participation of all workers in defence industries without discrimination because of race, creed or national origin'. Although a clause to this effect was inserted in all war contracts, defence jobs only opened slowly for blacks, and the Executive Order did not pronounce on segregation and discrimination in the armed forces.

CORE

Gandhi's philosophy and techniques were also reflected in the formation of the Congress of Racial Equality (CORE) in 1942. Founded by James Farmer, a Louisiana Negro, and members of the Fellowship of Reconciliation (FOR), a Quaker pacifist social-action organization, CORE was chiefly responsible for pioneering the use of non-violent protest as a civil rights strategy. Its 'Statement of Purpose' declared:

> CORE has one purpose – to eliminate racial discrimination.
> CORE has one method – inter-racial, non-violent direct action.
> CORE asks its members to commit themselves to work as an integrated, disciplined group:
> by renouncing overt violence in opposing racial discrimination and using the method of non-violent direct action;
> which refuses to cooperate with racial injustice;
> which seeks to change existing practices by using such techniques as negotiation, mediation, demonstration, and picketing;
> which develops a spirit of understanding rather than antagonism.[4]

In 1943 CORE engaged in its first 'sit-in', when Farmer and an interracial group of members employed the tactic against a Chicago restaurant which had refused to serve blacks; CORE was to remain active in the direct-action protests of the 1950s and 1960s, concentrating its efforts on voter-registration drives in the South. (In 1964, two CORE staff members, James Chaney and Michael Schwerner, along with Andrew Goodman, were abducted and murdered in Philadelphia, Mississippi.)

In the post-war period, heightened expectations on the part of black Americans, the growing significance of the black vote, and the continuing mass migration of Negroes out of the South, combined to produce some improvements in the condition of Afro-Americans. Roosevelt's successor, Harry Truman, created the President's committee on Civil Rights in 1946, and urged a variety of civil rights measures on a Congress controlled by Southern Democrats and conservative Republicans. In response to the wartime complaints of black troops who had faced discriminatory and segregationist practices, Truman issued Executive Order 9981, in 1948, which called for 'equality of opportunity for all persons in the armed forces, without regard to race, colour, or national origin'. Although sections of the military were slow to implement the policy, by the time of the Korean War there was a substantial measure of racial integration in the armed forces.

In the presidential election of 1948, Truman's espousal of civil rights measures and reforms provoked Southerners to leave the Democratic Party and form the 'Dixiecrat' Party, which carried four Southern states for its candidate, Strom Thurmond. With the aid of the mass of black votes in the electorally important states of the North, Truman beat his opponent Thomas Dewey, but continued to face a recalcitrant Congress on civil rights issues. But a series of Supreme Court decisions of the 1950s, striking down discrimination and segregation, buoyed black optimism for peaceful racial progress. In this period also, the NAACP continued to work for the rights of due process of law, equal protection of the laws, and the voting rights set forth in the Fourteenth and Fifteenth Amendments. At the state and local levels from the early 1950s, there were distinct signs of increased militancy among black leaders. As a younger generation of black activists began to challenge racial discrimination and segregation in the South, they faced not only the opposition of whites, but also of black 'conservatives' – the older-established leadership class which had practised the politics of restraint and caution in their dealings with the white power structure. In 1957, CORE, in cooperation with FOR, staged a 'Journey of Reconciliation' – what came to be called a 'Freedom Ride' – in the states of the Upper South, to test compliance with a Supreme Court ruling of the previous year which had declared segregation in interstate transportation unconstitutional.

The Supreme Court's most notable civil rights decision was, however, its 1954 ruling that 'in the field of public education the doctrine of "separate but equal" has no place. Separate educational facilities are inherently unequal.' *Brown* v. *Board of Education* marked the triumphant conclusion of the NAACP's long campaign against educational segregation, and overturned the *Plessy* v. *Ferguson* decision of 1896. The *Brown* decision was immediately recognized – by its supporters and opponents – as a landmark step in American race relations. Blacks were encouraged to press their protests against all forms of racial proscription to a successful conclusion.

Southern whites, in particular, resolved not to comply with the Supreme Court's 1955 request for implementation of its 1954 ruling 'with all deliberate speed'. President Dwight D. Eisenhower, although forced to nationalize the state militia and to send United States army units to Little Rock, Arkansas, in 1957, when Governor Orville Faubus refused to allow black students to enter Little Rock High School, did not otherwise provide executive leadership on the civil rights front. His disinterest, and the inaction of Congress, certainly encouraged Southern whites to defy the 1954 Supreme Court ruling. Segregationist governors, white citizens' councils, and vigilante mobs expressed the South's determination to resist even the minimal implications of the Court's decision. For their part, however, Southern blacks engaged in a wide range of direct-action protests – boycotts of stores and restaurants which practised racial discrimination, and a series of bus boycotts across the South, protesting against continuing 'separate but unequal' policies applied to blacks in local transport systems. This renewed black militancy was to be most notably demonstrated in Montgomery, Alabama, in 1955–56.

MARTIN LUTHER KING, JR: MILITANT CLERGYMAN

On 1 December 1955, Mrs Rosa L. Parks, a forty-three-year-old black seamstress in a downtown Montgomery store, refused a bus driver's order to vacate her seat to a white man. The secretary of the local chapter of the NAACP, Mrs Parks had been ejected from Montgomery buses on several occasions for refusing to obey the Alabama segregation ordinance which required Negroes to give up their bus seats for whites, if ordered to do so by (white) drivers. On this occasion, however, she was arrested, charged with breaking a city segregation law and fined $14.00. The Reverend E. D. Nixon, head of the local chapters of both the NAACP and the Brotherhood of Sleeping Car Porters, conceived of a bus boycott as a direct-action black protest against the treatment of Mrs Parks, and on behalf of all Southern blacks exposed to the ritual humiliations of Jim Crow. Under Nixon's leadership, a group of black ministers formed the Montgomery Improvement Association (MIA) to direct and coordinate what became a 382-day boycott of the bus company. The modest demands of the MIA were that black passengers receive courteous treatment from white bus drivers; that black drivers be hired on predominantly black routes; the seating of Negro passengers on a first-come-first-served basis, with blacks seated from the back to the front of the bus, and whites from the front to the back.

Martin Luther King, Jr, a twenty-six-year-old Negro minister, who had arrived in Montgomery from Atlanta only a year before, was unanimously elected to preside over the MIA. Nixon agreed to serve as treasurer, but refused to run for the presidency of the new organization because he would be away from Montgomery for long periods on railroad business. By all accounts, including his own, King was surprised to gain leadership of the MIA. During his first year in Montgomery, he had concentrated his energies on his pastorate of the Dexter Avenue Baptist Church, a black middle-class parish, and on completing his doctoral dissertation. King later recalled that his election as MIA president 'caught me unawares. It happened so quickly I did not even have time to think it through. It is probable that if I had, I would have declined the nomination.'[5] In fact, a month before his nomination, King had refused the presidency of the city chapter of the NAACP, and had not engaged in any organized civil rights protests. Moreover, he had not yet met Mrs Parks. But on several counts, King was an ideal choice for the MIA presidency. As a relative newcomer, he was not involved in the factionalism of local black politics, and had not been compromised by his dealings with the white community. In addition, as Nixon recognized, King possessed the personal and educational qualities necessary in a leader who would have to conduct negotiations at a high level. In other respects, however, Martin Luther King was an unknown quantity. The Montgomery bus boycott was to bring him American and international recognition and fame.

Martin Luther King, Jr, was born in Atlanta, Georgia, the son of a share-cropper who attended Morehouse College, and became a Baptist minister. King's maternal grandfather, the Reverend Alfred Daniel Williams, had founded the Ebenezer Baptist Church, and Martin Luther King, Sr, a forceful preacher, active Republican and member of the NAACP, was a strong personality. Martin Luther King, Jr, grew up in a close-knit, middle-class, religious family, and seemed himself destined for the ministry. At the age of fifteen, he entered Morehouse College, where he was influenced by its president, Benjamin E. Mays, a leading black theologian and church historian. May's attacks on racial injustice, and his beliefs in Christian social responsibility and political engagement, greatly impressed King (who had considered studying law or medicine), and he elected to continue the family tradition and become a Baptist minister. At Morehouse, King read Henry David Thoreau's classic essay *Civil Disobedience*, and accepted its central assertion that the individual should refuse to cooperate with an evil system and is entitled to disobey unjust laws.

In 1948, King graduated from Morehouse with a degree in sociology, and enrolled at Crozer Theological Seminary in Chester, Pennsylvania, to study for the ministry. At Crozer, he discovered the writings of the Social Gospel theologian Walter Rauschenbusch, and endorsed his contention that the church should concern itself with social conditions, as well as with the salvation of souls. King later asserted:

> It has been my conviction ever since reading Rauschenbusch, that any religion which professes to be concerned about the souls of men and is not concerned about the social and economic conditions that scar that soul, is a spiritually moribund religion, only waiting for the day to be buried.[6]

Already a declared pacifist, King added Gandhi's philosophy of non-violent resistance to injustice to his intellectual system, and came to celebrate the redemptive power of love and suffering as forces for social change.

> Gandhi was probably the first person in history to lift the love ethic of Jesus above mere interaction between individuals to a powerful and effective force on a large scale. It was in this Gandhian emphasis on love and non-violence that I discovered the method for social reform that I had been seeking. I came to feel that this was the only morally and practically sound method open to oppressed people in their struggle for freedom. ... My study of Gandhi convinced me that true pacifism is not non-resistance to evil, but non-violent resistance to evil.[7]

At Crozer King also encountered the theologian Reinhold Niebuhr's concept of 'collective evil' (but rejected Niebuhr's break with pacifism), and rejected Marxism as atheistic and materialistic, although he welcomed its social concerns, and noted that 'Communism grew as a protest against the hardships of the underprivileged'.[8]

After a distinguished career at Crozer, King entered the doctoral programme at Boston University, in 1951. Here he met and married Coretta Scott, from Alabama, then a student at the New England Conservatory of Music. Before completing his Ph.D. thesis on the opposing theological views of Paul Tillich and Henry Nelson Wieman, King was offered and accepted a pastorship at the Dexter Avenue Baptist Church in Montgomery. In addition to his intellectual abilities and credentials, King brought to his first appointment a love for the South, a supportive wife and a social philosophy based on a belief in Christian activism and Gandhian non-violent resistance to evil. As pastor and then as leader of the MIA, he came to display considerable powers as an orator and public performer, qualities which were to distinguish his career as the prophet and practitioner of civil disobedience in the cause of civil rights.

As chairman of the MIA, which included twenty black ministers in its membership, King united and inspired the boycott movement. The MIA's proposed seating arrangements for the Montgomery buses did not at first challenge the 'separate but equal' doctrine, and might easily have been adapted to existing segregation ordinances. King himself was aware that the demands of the boycott did not meet the NAACP's minimum standard for racial integration, but hoped that the original demands could be negotiated with the city fathers. When Montgomery blacks followed the call not to ride on the city's buses, the MIA created and maintained a car pool, which gave more affluent Negroes an opportunity to participate in the boycott. When Montgomery whites put pressure on the insurance companies to cancel insurance on the MIA car pool, the organizers turned to Lloyd's of London for coverage. An attempt to divide the black community into its traditional factions failed, and the mayor and city fathers resorted to other tactics. King was arrested for an alleged speeding offence, and jailed (for the first time in his life).

On 30 January 1956, King's house was bombed; on 21 February a Montgomery Grand Jury indicted 115 Negroes for breaking a 1921 anti-labour law which held that it was illegal to injure a legitimate business enterprise without 'just cause or legal excuse'. Faced with such provocations, King continued to preach a message of non-violent resistance, but it was the visit to Montgomery of the Gandhian disciple and scholar Ranganath Diwakar that convinced him that he should also set an example of personal suffering. The Montgomery boycott began to attract national support and received financial donations from various sources, including the NAACP, the United Auto Workers and donations from overseas. During this period, King developed a close working relationship with Ralph Abernathy, Negro pastor of the First Baptist Church, and an activist preacher. Following the attack on his home, King was visited by Bayard Rustin, the respected theorist of the civil rights movement, a pacifist and member of FOR.

It was a white woman, Miss Juliette Morgan, in a letter to the *Montgomery Advertizer*, who alerted King to the parallels between the bus boycott and Gandhi's strategy in India:

> The Negroes of Montgomery seem to have taken a lesson from Gandhi – and our own Thoreau, who influenced Gandhi. Their own task is greater than Gandhi's, however, for they have greater prejudice to overcome. One feels that history is being made in Montgomery these days. ... It is hard to imagine a soul so dead, a heart so hard, a vision so blinded and provincial as not to be moved with admiration at the quiet dignity, discipline and dedication with which the Negroes have conducted their boycott.

King remembered that Miss Morgan

> sensitive and frail, did not long survive the rejection and condemnation of the white community, but long before she died in the summer of 1957, the name of Mahatma Gandhi was well-known in Montgomery. ... Non-violent resistance had emerged as the technique of the movement, while love stood as the regulating ideal. ... Christ furnished the spirit and motivation, while Gandhi furnished the method. This philosophy was disseminated mainly through the regular mass meetings which were held in the various Negro churches of the city.[9]

Despite a Supreme Court ruling against segregation in intrastate buses in South Carolina, the Montgomery city government obtained a local court injunction ordering it to continue the practice. On 4 June 1956, a federal district court ruled that the city ordinance violated the United States Constitution, but the city appealed, and the boycott continued. However, as King and his associates were awaiting a court decision regarding the continuing operation of the car pool, news came of the United States Supreme Court decision declaring Alabama's state and local laws upholding segregation on the buses to be unconstitutional. King and the MIA now worked to prepare the black community for the arrival of the desegregation order, and urged blacks to behave courteously when they went back on the buses. Negroes were instructed to 'read, study and memorize' a listing of 'Integrated Bus Suggestions' which included the following:

> Pray for guidance and commit yourself to complete non-violence as you enter the bus.
> Be quiet but friendly; proud, but not arrogant; joyous, but not boisterous. If cursed, do not curse back. If pushed, do not push back. If struck, do not strike back, but evidence love and goodwill at all times.[10]

Montgomery's buses were desegregated, but there was further violence against blacks, and Negro churches in the city were firebombed. But for King, the boycott was the decisive point in his career, and one which 'did more to clarify my thinking on the question of non-violence than all the books which I have read'. While the boycott was still in progress, he declared:

> ... our non-violent protest in Montgomery is important because it is demonstrating to the Negro, North and South, that many of the stereotypes he has held about himself and other Negroes are not valid. Montgomery has broken the spell and is ushering in concrete manifestations of the thinking and action of the new Negro. ... We now know that the Southern Negro has become of age, politically and morally. Montgomery has demonstrated that we will not run from the struggle, and will support the battle for equality. ... This is a protest – a *nonviolent* protest against injustice. We are depending on moral and spiritual forces. To put it another way, this is a movement of passive resistance, and the great instrument is the instrument of love ... no matter what sacrifices we have to make, we will not let anybody drag us down so low as to hate them.[11]

King's great contribution to the Montgomery boycott was his oratory and his passionately expressed belief in the power of moral suasion to effect social change. In his first (hastily prepared) speech as leader of the boycott, his concern was to 'make a speech that would be militant enough to keep my people aroused to positive action and yet moderate enough to keep this fervour within controllable and Christian bounds'. He advised his black audience that despite the mistreatment and abuse they had already suffered, they must not become embittered. King quoted Booker T. Washington directly and to good effect: 'Let no man pull you so low as to make you hate him.' The reference to Washington was apposite, since King was to emerge from the boycott as a black leader with a national reputation similar to that gained by Washington after his Atlanta Exposition Address. Unlike Washington, King had been chosen by blacks themselves as their spokesman and leader.

During a 'Prayer Pilgrimage' to Washington, DC in May 1957, King, in the company of Roy Wilkins, executive secretary of the NAACP, and A. Philip Randolph, received the greatest ovation after an address in which he demanded that blacks now be given the ballot to enforce politically their legal rights. The editor of the black newspaper, the New York *Amsterdam News,* asserted that King had 'emerged from the Prayer Pilgrimage to Washington as the number one leader of 16 million Negroes in the United States. ... At this point in his career, the people will follow him anywhere.' For the next three years, however, King appeared uncertain as to the direction he should take. In retrospect, it is clear that the Montgomery boycott was a dress rehearsal for the civil rights movement of the 1960s. Yet the boycott itself did not touch off a national Negro revolt. 'The genius of the boycott was also its major weakness. People could refuse to ride the bus without directly and individually placing themselves at risk. The boycott was an act of omission, not commission.'[12] What was needed were new organizations and strategies.

In 1957, King and other black clergymen formed the Southern Christian Leadership Conference (SCLC) to spread and coordinate the idea of non-violent civil rights protest across the South. The philosophy of the SCLC was derived from a religious amalgam:

> The basic tenets of the Hebraic–Christian tradition coupled with the Gandhian concept of *satyagraha* – is at the heart of SCLC's philosophy. Christian nonviolence actively resists evil in any form. It never seeks to humiliate the opponent, only to win him. ... At the centre of nonviolence is redemptive love. Creatively used, the philosophy of nonviolence can restore the broken community in America. ... SCLC believes that the American dilemma in race relations can best and most quickly be resolved through the actions of thousands of people, committed to the philosophy of nonviolence, who will physically identify themselves in a just and moral struggle. ... SCLC is firmly opposed to segregation in any form ... and pledges itself to work unrelentingly to rid every vestige of its scars from our nation through nonviolent means. ... Our ultimate goal is genuine intergroup and interpersonal living – *integration.*[13]

A loosely organized and unorthodox organization, SCLC was remarkable in that its clerical leadership (traditionally dedicated to the preservation of the status quo) was uniquely equipped to communicate at the grass-roots level. 'SCLC's leaders clothed political ideas in a religious phraseology that blacks readily understood, and used Christian tenets to give the civil rights movement a divine sanction.'[14]

For the remainder of his life and career, King was to be identified with the SCLC, which was increasingly to come into competition with both the older and younger black protest organizations. The declared aim of SCLC was to promote non-violent direct action, but for the first three years of its existence it engaged in an unsuccessful effort to double the number of registered black voters in the South, in a 'Crusade for Citizenship'. Unlike the NAACP, however, SCLC did not possess the resources to mount effective organizational campaigns at the local level. Ella Baker, the temporary executive director of SCLC, believed that it was simply an extension of King's unformulated ideas on civil rights, and needed collective and expert leadership. 'The fame that King had garnered from the Montgomery bus boycott gave an exaggerated impression of his leadership abilities. In fact, King had neither instigated the boycott nor sought its leadership, and the protests' success owed as much to the collective efforts of the MIA as it did to King himself.'[15] Certainly before 1960, SCLC was without a clearly defined purpose and strategy, undecided whether to instigate its own protests or simply to assist in local actions.

131

In 1959, after surviving a stabbing by a deranged black woman as he was signing copies of *Stride Toward Freedom* in a New York bookstore, King (who had earlier visited Ghana, Nigeria and several European capitals, including London), made a spiritual pilgrimage to India, and went to Gandhi's shrine. The Indian visit was a significant event in King's intellectual and political development. In particular, he was impressed by Nehru's explanation that under the Indian Constitution, caste discrimination was punishable by imprisonment, and concluded that India had made greater progress against caste untouchability than had the United States against racial discrimination. Flattered by the attentions paid to him by the Indians, King returned to America with the renewed conviction 'that nonviolent resistance is the most potent weapon available to the oppressed people in their struggle for freedom. It was a marvellous thing to see the results of a nonviolent campaign.'[16]

In November 1959, King resigned as pastor of Dexter church, and moved to Atlanta, Georgia, to concentrate his energies on the SCLC. Its strategy for the election year 1960 was to continue its voter registration drive, together with direct-action protests against segregation. With many of Atlanta's established black leaders hostile to civil rights agitation (and with his father resident in the city as well), King diplomatically agreed that he would not undertake any SCLC campaigns there. When Ella Baker called the founding conference at Raleigh, North Carolina, in April 1960, of the Student Nonviolent Coordinating Committee (SNCC), King agreed to serve on its Adult Advisory Committee. Aware of the extent of student activity against segregated lunch counters in the South, and concerned to unify direct-action protests, King attempted to mould the new organization in the image of SCLC.

> In addition to suggesting a nationwide campaign of 'selective buying',
> King advised the students to establish a permanent organization, collect
> a group of volunteers willing to go to jail rather than pay fines, and take
> the 'freedom struggle' into all parts of the South to compel the
> intervention of the federal government. He also urged the students to
> learn more about the philosophy of nonviolence.[17]

Although it was soon to move beyond what it came to regard as King's cautious and conciliatory approach to civil rights, SNCC, at its inception, accepted his philosophy in its statement of purpose.

> We affirm the philosophical or religious ideal of non-violence as the
> foundation of our purpose, the presupposition of our faith, and the
> manner of our action. Non-violence as it grows from the
> Judaic–Christian tradition seeks a social order of justice permeated by
> love. ... Love is the central motif of non-violence. ... It matches the
> capacity of evil to inflict suffering with an even more enduring capacity
> to absorb evil, all the while persisting in love.[18]

MLK AND JFK

Whereas King had been unhappy with the record of the Eisenhower administration on civil rights – apart from the president's stand on the 1957 Little Rock, Arkansas, school integration crisis – he entertained greater hopes for the Democratic challenger in 1960, Senator John F. Kennedy. When King was given a four-month prison sentence for an alleged driving offence in Georgia, he was released following Kennedy's intervention, an action which proved decisive in the presidential election since it gained Kennedy crucial black votes. 'Had whites only gone to the polls in 1960, Nixon would have taken 52 percent of the vote.'[19] Writing in the *Nation,* shortly after Kennedy's inauguration, King ascribed the 'intolerably' slow progress of civil rights not only to the opposition of white segregationists, but also 'to the limits which the federal government has imposed on its own action'.

> In the legislative area, he demanded that the President fight for a 'really far-reaching' civil rights programme with particular emphasis on the right to vote. In the area of executive action, he called on the President to 'give segregation its death blow through a stroke of the pen' – especially by stopping the use of federal funds to support housing, hospital and airport construction in which discrimination was open and notorious. 'We must face the fact ... that the federal government is the nation's highest investor in segregation.'[20]

Although he declared his commitment to civil rights, and appointed blacks to federal offices, Kennedy was also aware of opposition in Congress to the passage of a civil rights bill. His naming of three 'strict constructionists' to federal judgeships in the South came as a disappointment to King, who came to believe that neither the president nor his brother, Attorney-General Robert Kennedy, were sufficiently aware of the urgency of the racial problem. As events were to prove, King's relations with both John and Robert Kennedy were to be, on both sides, ambivalent and ambiguous. In 1963, Kennedy warned King that the FBI, under J. Edgar Hoover's directive, had begun to keep the SCLC under close surveillance because of alleged Communist infiltration of the organization. Robert Kennedy, convinced that King's close associate and adviser, Stanley Levison, a white lawyer from New York City, was an active member of the American Communist Party, authorized FBI wiretaps on King. Yet President Kennedy, as King observed after the assassination in Dallas in November 1963, had after his first two years in office, emerged as 'a strong figure', actively involved in the cause of civil rights.

> History will record that he vacillated like Lincoln, but he lifted the cause far above the political level. ... No other American President has written with such compassion and resolution to make clear that our nation's

destiny was unfulfilled so long as the scar of racial prejudice disfigured it.[21]

That Kennedy was moved to exercise stronger executive leadership on behalf of black Americans was, in large measure, due to the unremitting activities of the civil rights coalition from 1961 to 1963.

SCLC IN ACTION

As the civil rights movement gathered momentum in the early 1960s, King lent his prestige to various forms of direct-action protest, with varying degrees of success and failure. In 1961 he supported the CORE-sponsored Freedom Riders who were met by white violence (and federal military intervention) in their attempts to gain compliance by Alabama and Mississippi with Supreme Court and Interstate Commerce Commission rulings nullifying segregation in interstate travel. King realized that the intensive press coverage of Southern attacks on the Freedom Riders should be utilized by the SCLC and its allies, since the strongest force promoting non-violent black protest was the disgraceful behaviour of white Southerners themselves.

From December 1961 to the summer of 1962, King and the SCLC led a mass direct-action campaign in Albany, Georgia, demanding not only integrated facilities, but employment for Albany's Negroes in the city's police force, and other municipal jobs. The Albany campaign failed, partly because on this occasion, the police force did not over-react. Instead, police chief Laurie Pritchett simply closed down municipal facilities, rather than integrate them. But the chief factor in the failure of King's Albany venture was his inability to control or direct a diverse and heterogeneous group of protesters. As King later conceded, SCLC had gone to Albany without proper planning or preparation. Although King and 2,000 of his followers went to jail during the demonstrations – King himself was arrested three times – because of police 'restraint', national consciousness was not aroused, and the federal government did not intervene. 'Albany, by any standards, was a staggering defeat for King [who] ... allowed himself to be pushed into action, without adequate preparation, on a battlefield he did not choose, with a faction-ridden army he never completely commanded.'[22]

The lessons of Albany were well learned, and SCLC's next target was carefully chosen, and its strategy meticulously planned. New staff members, with direct experience of voter registration campaigns and Freedom Rides, made SCLC, after 1961, a more efficient and effective organization. King privately conceded that the success of non-violent resistance depended on the existence or fostering of 'creative tension' – attacks by whites on non-violent demonstrators, full coverage of these events by the media, consequent national outrage, and subsequent government intervention. All of these ingredients were to be present in the Birmingham, Alabama, campaign of 1962–63. The South's major industrial city, Birmingham was also a stronghold of racial oppression, fully fledged segregation and intimidation. From 1957 to 1963, there were seventeen 'unsolved' bombings of Negro churches and the homes of black civil rights leaders. Inspired by the Montgomery boycott, the Reverend Fred Shuttlesworth, pastor of Baptist Bethel Church, had formed the Alabama Christian Movement for Human Rights (later an affiliate of SCLC). With the support of Negro college students, Shuttlesworth had led a boycott of Birmingham stores in an effort to desegregate lunch counters and open up jobs for blacks. His home had been bombed, his church destroyed, and he had been imprisoned eight times as reprisals for his agitation. Shuttlesworth asked King to come to Birmingham to focus and direct a campaign directed against the business community. King readily agreed.

> Along with Fred Shuttlesworth, we believed that while a campaign in Birmingham would surely be the toughest fight of our civil rights careers, it could, if successful, break the back of segregation all over the nation.[23]

He decided to confront the business community with three demands:
1. The desegregation of lunch counters, fitting rooms, rest rooms and drinking fountains in department stores.
2. The upgrading and hiring of blacks on a non-discriminatory basis in business and industry.
3. The creation of a biracial committee to work out a timetable for desegregation in other areas of Birmingham life.

'The dispersal of energies that had characterized the Albany demonstrations was not to be repeated.'[24] Demonstrations were twice postponed; once to allow for (abortive) negotiations with business leaders, and a second time, to await the outcome of a mayoralty election between the white supremacist police commissioner, Eugene 'Bull' Connor, and a racial moderate, Albert Boutwell. Despite criticisms from some Birmingham blacks, as well as whites, that King was not giving the new mayor a fair chance, demonstrations were ordered to begin. When Connor obtained a court order enjoining all demonstrations pending a court decision, King deliberately defied the order, and marched on city hall – wearing the denim overalls that had become the uniform of the SCLC. He was arrested and held for two days in prison, without being allowed to communicate with his wife, lawyers or the SCLC. The intervention of President Kennedy, for a second time, on King's behalf, restored contact with his wife and attorneys.

When King's activities in Birmingham were criticized by eight white clergymen in the city, who described him as an outside agitator and extremist, and urged blacks to end their demonstrations, his response was to produce a classic statement on civil rights and non-violence, 'Letter from a Birmingham jail'. King asserted that he had been invited to Birmingham by the Alabama Christian Movement for Human Rights, and claimed that no one could be an 'outsider' to injustice. He responded to the charge that the demonstration had been ill-timed with the statement that:

> Frankly, I have yet to engage in a direct-action campaign that was 'well-timed' in the view of those who have not suffered unduly from the disease of segregation. For years now I have heard the word 'Wait!' It rings in the ear of every Negro with a piercing familiarity. This 'Wait!' has almost always meant 'Never'.[25]

He also claimed that direct action must necessarily precede negotiation, and reasserted his belief in resistance to unjust laws. King also expressed disappointment that 'fellow clergymen would see my nonviolent efforts as those of an extremist', and warned that black disaffection had already produced the Black Muslim Movement made up of people who have lost faith in America, who have absolutely repudiated Christianity, and who have concluded that the white man is an incurable "devil" '. In contrast, King presented himself as having 'tried to stand between these two forces saying that we need not follow the "do-nothingism" of the complacent or the hatred and despair of the black nationalist'.

Released on bond after eight days in prison, King now brought the demonstrations to a well-orchestrated climax, sending hundreds of black schoolchildren into direct confrontation with the white authorities. Bull Connor met the marchers with fire hoses, police dogs and clubs, and 2,500 were arrested and jailed. (Malcolm X's comment on these tactics was: 'Martin Luther King is a chump not a champ. Any man who puts his women and children on the front line is a chump, not a champ.')[26] Press and television coverage of the events in Birmingham outraged the rest of the United States and shocked the world. Eventually, the Justice Department opened negotiations between the SCLC and the city government, and an agreement was signed which promised to meet the limited demands of the demonstrators within ninety days, and the setting up of a biracial committee within two weeks.

> Yet, despite the modest scope of the agreement itself, it had far-reaching implications for the city and its leaders. Since 1950 ... white business leaders in Birmingham had been involved in an unsuccessful quest for racial harmony. Before 1963, they had always been restrained by the limitations imposed by segregation. But the negotiations to end the demonstrations in that spring of 1963 finally freed them from the bonds of segregation, and thus liberated their search for racial order. ... King's demonstrations ... provided the catalyst both for change and for restoration of harmony. Although the groundwork had already been laid by the change in government and the previous biracial bargaining, the end of segregation in Birmingham was dramatically

hastened because King and his demonstrators threatened chaos in a city whose leaders were now desperate for order. When the settlement was finally reached, both blacks and whites could claim some measure of victory. The blacks had won pledges of desegregation in the most segregated city in the South, and the white leaders had won what they had really been seeking all along – racial harmony.[27]

Yet the Birmingham agreement left untouched the issue of school desegregation, and was disowned by Alabama's segregationist governor, George Wallace. Some black critics accused King of negotiating a surrender when total victory was in sight, but he claimed the outcome of the campaign as a victory for direct-action and massive non-violent resistance. A *Newsweek* opinion poll of Negroes indicated that 95 per cent now regarded King as their most successful black spokesman. Moreover, the Birmingham campaign moved Kennedy to 'ask Congress for a major civil rights bill that would not only solve the public accommodations problem, but would attempt to protect the Southern blacks' political rights and provide national legislative sanction for fair-employment practices'.[28] His successor, Lyndon Johnson, was finally to secure congressional agreement which resulted in the passage of the Civil Rights Act of 1964 which not only included Kennedy's proposals but also gave the executive the power to withdraw federal funds from state and local governments that practised racial discrimination. The Birmingham protest also atoned for the miscalculations of SCLC's Albany campaign, and propelled King into leadership of the civil rights coalition. At the March on Washington in August 1963, when a quarter of a million people, about 20 per cent of them white, converged on the capital in an effort to obtain passage of the Civil Rights Bill, King delivered his 'I have a dream' oration from the steps of the Lincoln Memorial, one of the great speeches of the twentieth century.

I have a dream that one day this nation will rise up and live out the true meaning of its creed: 'We hold these truths to be self-evident; that all men are created equal.' I have a dream that one day on the red hills of Georgia the sons of former slaves and the sons of former slave owners will be able to sit down together at the table of brotherhood. I have a dream that one day even the state of Mississippi, a desert state sweltering with the heat of injustice and oppression, will be transformed into an oasis of freedom and justice. I have a dream that my four little children will one day live in a nation where they will not be judged by the colour of their skin but by the content of their character. I have a dream today. I have a dream that one day the state of Alabama, whose governor's lips are presently dripping with the words of interposition and nullification, will be transformed into a situation where little black boys and black girls will be able to join hands with little white boys and white girls and walk together as sisters and brothers. I have a dream today. I have a dream that one day every valley shall be exalted, every hill and mountain shall be made low, the rough places will be made plain, and the crooked places will be made straight, and the glory of the Lord shall be revealed, and all flesh shall see it together.[29]

In 1964, King appeared on the cover of *Time* magazine, in which he was credited with 'an indescribable capacity for empathy that is the touchstone of leadership'. In the same year, he was awarded the Nobel Peace Prize. Significantly, in his acceptance speech, King linked the civil rights movement with the larger cause of world peace and human rights.

At the height of his power and influence within the civil rights movement, King joined forces with SNCC and CORE in a voter registration drive focused on Selma, Alabama, in 1965. The SNCC field-workers were ambivalent about the project, and interorganizational tensions soon became evident. In Alabama, SNCC's members 'knew that King's effort would aid their own voter registration work by attracting national publicity and perhaps prompting federal intervention against white Alabama authorities'. But they also feared that King's involvement 'would undermine their long-standing efforts to develop black leadership. They agreed not to hamper SCLC's campaign and even offered the use of their equipment and facilities to SCLC representatives, but expected to remain on the sidelines, hoping that local blacks would recognize the deficiencies of SCLC's leader-centered approach to organizing.'[30] Many SNCC members also disliked the excessive religiosity of King's style and his tendency to compromise at critical junctures. When King, leading a march from Selma to Montgomery, refused to break through a police barricade, led the marchers in prayer, and then turned back to Selma (with many of the marchers singing 'Ain't Gonna Let Nobody Turn Me 'Round'), SNCC workers were openly contemptuous. King had, in fact, after discussions with the United States Attorney-General, decided against a confrontation with the Alabama police, but had not informed the SNCC workers of his resolve.

But again, King had dramatized an already violent situation. Demonstrators had earlier been gassed and beaten in Selma, and the killing of a white Unitarian minister from Boston, James J. Reeb, by Alabama whites, produced a highly charged atmosphere which moved President Lyndon Johnson to call Congress into special session and call for new voting rights legislation. On 17 March 1965, a federal court approved the Selma-to-Montgomery march, Johnson mobilized the state militia to protect the marchers (who were also accompanied by Justice Department Officials), and on 25 March King spoke to 25,000 people from the capitol steps in Montgomery. 'The march from Selma had brought the Negro protest full circle, since it had all begun with the Montgomery bus boycott a decade before.'[31] Urging his audience on to 'the realization of the American Dream', King indicated a shift in his thinking when he advocated a 'march on poverty' as well as a continuing assault on segregation and racism, as the unrealized goals of black protest. In retrospect, the Selma campaign was King's finest hour. He had masterminded a massive demonstration, and as the *Washington Post* declared, had revealed 'the plight of the Negro in the South as had never been done before. ... Dr King brought Alabama dramatically into the homes of Americans. He made racism in the South come alive.'

CHICAGO AND VIETNAM

After the Selma campaign, King began to suggest to his colleagues in SCLC that they should direct their attentions to the problem of urban poverty, and in particular, to that of the Northern ghettos. Concurrently, he was also coming to express concern over the course and implications of the escalating American presence in Vietnam. These two issues – which King believed were intimately related – were to dominate his thoughts and actions for the remaining three years of his life. Together, they offer convincing evidence to support the contention that King became increasingly radical (and less reformist) in his last years. His positions on these issues were to alienate him from most of the established black civil rights leadership, and, in the case of the Vietnam War, earned him the enmity of Lyndon Johnson, and the renewed attentions of the FBI. Although King's position on Vietnam allied him with the younger elements of the civil rights coalition – CORE and SNCC – his opposition to the concept of Black Power and its spokesmen exacerbated the growing rift within the black protest movement. King's final years, then, were marked by change and controversy. They revealed his strengths and weaknesses as a leader in more heightened forms than had been apparent earlier in his career.

In 1966, against the advice of Bayard Rustin, King decided to move to Chicago to lead a non-violent direct-action campaign against segregated slum housing, *de facto* segregated schools, unemployment and job discrimination. In effect, as he was aware, King was taking on the formidable Richard J. Daley, mayor of Chicago, a consummate politician and power broker in the Democratic Party. As the Reverend Arthur Brazier, leader of the South Side's Woodlawn Association, observed:

> King decided to come to Chicago because he thought Chicago was
> unique in that there was one man, one source of power, who you had to
> deal with. He knew this wasn't the case in New York or any other city.
> He thought if Daley could be persuaded on the rightness of open
> housing and integrated schools that things would be done.[32]

As events in Chicago were to prove, SCLC tactics did not transpose easily from the rural South to the urban North. In Chicago SCLC workers soon discovered 'that the black preacher lacked the prestige he enjoyed in the South and that the church alone was an inadequate organizing tool. SCLC thrived on spontaneity and dramatic confrontations; it had little experience of the tedious job of community organizing. The sheer size of the task overwhelmed SCLC resources.'[33] (SCLC workers did not even possess adequate clothing for Chicago winters.) Although Daley treated King outwardly with respect, the considerable resources of the city government were used to frustrate the campaign. Thus when King, in a move to dramatize the housing crisis, moved into a rat-infested apartment, Daley sent in building inspectors with slum violation notices. When SCLC marched through the blue-collar suburb of Cicero (under police protection), they faced the bitter opposition of working-class whites, and King himself was assaulted. (He commented later: 'I've never seen anything like it in my life. I think the people from Mississippi ought to come to Chicago to learn how to hate.') Although Daley was forced to the negotiating table, and appeared to concede an open housing agreement with the city's banking, real estate and political interests, it achieved little in practice. Chicago was King's first, and last, campaign outside the South.

The growing rift between SCLC and SNCC increased during the civil rights continuation of James Meredith's one-man 'March Against Fear' of 1966. In 1962, James Meredith had become the first Negro to enrol at the University of Mississippi, but only after a confrontation between President Kennedy and the state's segregationist governor, Ross Barnett, the deployment of 600 United States marshals and 15,000 federalized National Guardsmen, and riots which resulted in the loss of two lives and the injury of 375 people. When Meredith was shot and wounded by a white sniper in Mississippi, King joined with Stokely Carmichael of SNCC and Floyd McKissick of CORE in a march through the state. In the course of the march, McKissick and Carmichael stressed the need for greater black militancy, and criticized the federal government for its continuing indifference to the plight of Southern blacks. Carmichael's use of the emotive slogan 'Black Power' became the central controversy of the march. King, opposed to the phrase because of its connotations of racial separatism and apparent acceptance of violence, threatened to withdraw from the march unless it made a commitment to non-violence.

> I pleaded with the group to abandon the Black Power slogan. It was my contention that a leader has to be concerned about the problem of semantics. Each word, I said, has a denotative meaning – its explicit and recognized sense – and a connotative meaning – its suggestive sense. While the concept of legitimate Black Power might be denotatively sound, the slogan 'Black Power' carried the wrong connotations. I mentioned the implications of violence that the press had already attached to the phrase.[34]

While agreement was reached between King and McKissick and Carmichael not to use the competing slogans of 'Black Power' and 'Freedom Now' for the remainder of the march, the dispute was indicative of the approaching demise of the civil rights coalition.

> For King, the Meredith March Against Fear was a terrible blunder. He had undertaken it to unify the civil rights movement and confront white Mississippi under the banner of nonviolence. Instead, the march had unleashed a combustible slogan that embarrassed and bewildered him.[35]

When King began publicly to denounce United States involvement in Vietnam, he gained the support of SNCC and CORE, but the hostility of the NAACP and National Urban League, both of which declared their opposition to the conjunction of the war with the civil rights movement. Since 1965, King had questioned the morality of the war in South-East Asia, but did not join the anti-war lobby until early in 1967, when he appeared in demonstrations with Dr Benjamin Spock. Coretta King, an ardent pacifist and a member of Women Strike for Peace, supported her husband's position. However, as he continued to protest against the war, King aroused critical press comment; *Newsweek* magazine accused him of being 'in over his head', and of displaying 'simplistic political judgment'. King's response was to assert that there was a connection between racism, poverty, American militarism and imperialism, and that Lyndon Johnson's projected Great Society had 'been shot down on the battlefields of Vietnam'. The FBI kept Johnson informed of King's anti-war activities, and intensified its surveillance of the SCLC.

In an effort to bridge the divisions within the civil rights movement, King, by the end of 1967, had conceived of a Poor People's March on Washington – a reassertion of the principle of non-violence that would unite a coalition of the poor and disaffected along class rather than racial lines. In an article published after his assassination, King explained the rationale of the projected march (which was to take place after his death).

> The time has come for a return to mass non-violent protest. . . . We believe that if this campaign succeeds, non-violence will once again be the dominant instrument for social change – and jobs and income will be put in the hands of the tormented poor. . . . Our Washington demonstration will resemble Birmingham and Selma in duration. . . . Just as we dealt with the social problem of segregation through massive demonstrations, and we dealt with the political problem – the denial of the right to vote – through massive demonstrations, we are now trying to deal with the economic problems – the right to live, to have a job and income – through massive protest. It will be a Selma-like movement on economic issues. We hope that the sight and sound of a growing mass of poor people walking slowly toward Washington will have a positive, dramatic effect on Congress. . . . Our idea is to dramatize the whole economic problem of the poor. . . . We'll focus on domestic problems, but it's inevitable that we've got to bring out the question of the tragic mix-

up in priorities. We are spending all of this money for death and destruction, and not nearly enough money for life and constructive development. We've seen no changes in Watts, no structural changes have taken place as the results of riots. ... We plan to build a shantytown in Washington, patterned after the bonus marches of the thirties, to dramatize how many people have to live in slums. ... But essentially, this will be just like our other non-violent demonstrations. We welcome help from all civil rights organizations. There must be a diversified approach to the problem, and I think that both the NAACP and the Urban League play a significant role. I also feel that CORE and SNCC have played very significant roles. I think SNCC's recent conclusions are unfortunate. We have not given up on integration. ... Some of the Black Power groups have temporarily given up on integration. We have not. So maybe we are the bridge in the middle, reaching across and connecting both sides.[36]

The planned march also revealed King's growing belief that American society needed a fundamental redistribution of wealth and economic power. He informed an interviewer:

America is deeply racist and its democracy is flawed both economically and socially ... the black revolution is much more than a struggle for the rights of Negroes. It is forcing America to face all its interrelated flaws – racism, poverty, militarism, and materialism. It is exposing evils that are deeply rooted in the whole structure of our society.[37]

In February 1968, Negro sanitation workers in Memphis, Tennessee, went on strike to win union recognition and improved wages and working conditions. King accepted an invitation from James Lawson, an old friend and pastor of the Centenary Methodist Church, to lead a protest march in Memphis. The demonstration (which King regarded as a dress rehearsal for the Poor People's March on Washington) ended in tragedy, when police shot a black youth during a pitched battle with Negro teenagers. King admitted that he had gone to Memphis without adequate preparation or knowledge of the local situation, and left abruptly. The *Memphis Commercial Appeal* commented on the episode: 'Dr King's pose as a leader of a non-violent movement has been shattered. He now has the entire nation doubting his word when he insists that his April project (the Poor People's March) can be peaceful. In short, Dr King is suffering from one of those credibility gaps. Furthermore, he wrecked his reputation as a leader when he took off at high speed when violence occurred, instead of trying to use his persuasive prestige to stop it.' Other newspapers – taking their cues from FBI informants – predicted that the violence in Memphis would be repeated on a larger scale on the Washington march. King was deeply disturbed by the events in Memphis, and press comment on his own culpability. But Lyndon Johnson's unexpected announcement that he would not seek re-election in 1968, appeared to offer some hope that the anti-war and anti-poverty movements might achieve unified victory under a new Democratic president. In the event, Richard M. Nixon won the election.

King returned to Memphis in a more optimistic mood to lead a new (and carefully planned) march. Addressing an enthusiastic audience at Mason Temple, he referred to the increasing number of threats on his life, but asserted:

> ... it really doesn't matter with me now, because I've been to the mountaintop, and I don't mind. Like anybody, I would like to live a long life; longevity has its grace. But I'm not concerned about that now. I just want to do God's will. And He's allowed me to go up to the mountain. And I've looked over, and I've seen the promised land of justice and freedom.

The next day, Martin Luther King, Jr was shot and killed by a white sniper as he stood on the balcony of the Lorraine Motel.

King's death touched off a wave of black violence across the United States, in which more than twenty people died. Stokely Carmichael, an acerbic critic of King's commitment to non-violence, mourned the murder of 'the one man of our race that this country's older generations, the militants and the revolutionaries and the masses of black people would listen to'.[38] *Newsweek* commented that:

> King's martyrdom on a motel balcony did far more than rob Negroes of their most compelling spokesman, and whites of their most effective bridge to black America. His murder, for too many blacks, could only be read as a judgment upon his nonviolent philosophy – and a license for retaliatory violence.[39]

Floyd McKissick announced simply: 'Dr Martin Luther King was the last prince of nonviolence. Nonviolence is a dead philosophy and it was not black people that killed it.'[40] For Eldridge Cleaver, King's assassination was a 'requiem for nonviolence'.

> ... here was a man who refused to abandon the principle of nonviolence in the face of the hostile and racist nation which has made it clear that it has no intention and no desire to grant a redress of the grievances of the black colonial subjects who are held in bondage.[41]

KING'S REFLECTIONS ON FOUR BLACK LEADERS

In his writings and speeches, King expressed his not always consistent assessments of the triumvirate of black leaders – Washington, Du Bois and Garvey – who had preceded him, and of his contemporary rival,

Malcolm X. Not surprisingly, none received his unequivocal endorsement. Washington's message, King asserted, was: 'Be content with doing well what the times permit you to do at all.' But many Negroes had come to believe that Washington's programme 'had too little freedom in its present and too little promise in its future'.[42] Four years later, King offered a more judicious estimate of Washington.

> I do not share the notion that he was an Uncle Tom who compromised for the sake of keeping the peace. Washington sincerely believed that if the South was not pushed too hard ... it would voluntarily rally to the Negro's cause. Washington's error was that he underestimated the structures of evil; as a consequence his philosophy of pressureless persuasion only served as a springboard for racist Southerners to dive into deeper and more ruthless oppression of the Negro.

King drew the appropriate moral from his judgement of Washington's 'failure', which was that 'every ethical appeal to the conscience of the white man must be accompanied by non-violent pressure'.[43] Yet King also frequently expressed admiration for the Washingtonian virtues of self-help, thrift, personal cleanliness, and a detestation of black irresponsibility and failure to conform to middle-class standards of morality.

> Negroes must be honest enough to admit that our standards do often fall short. .... We must not let the fact that we are victims of injustice lull us into abrogating responsibility for our own lives. Our crime rate is far too high. Our level of cleanliness is frequently far too low. ... We are often too loud and boisterous, and spend far too much on drink. Even the most poverty-stricken among us can purchase a ten-cent bar of soap; even the most uneducated among us can have high morals.[44]

King expressed greater respect for Du Bois because his concept of the 'Talented Tenth' had 'served somewhat to counteract the apparent resignation of Washington's philosophy'. But Du Bois was also an unabashed élitist – 'in the very nature of Du Bois' outlook there was no role for the whole people'. Rather was he the effective propagandist for 'an aristocratic élite who would themselves be benefited while leaving behind the "untalented" 90 per cent'.[45] But in the last major address before his assassination, delivered at Carnegie Hall on the occasion of the centennial of Du Bois' birth, King softened and broadened his verdict. Du Bois was 'one of the most remarkable men of our time ... unsurpassed as an intellect ... passionately proud to be black'. He was also a 'tireless explorer and gifted discoverer of social truths ... a man possessed of priceless dedication to his people'. A man of many parts, 'it was never possible to know where the scholar Du Bois ended and the organizer Du Bois began. The two qualities in him were a single unified force. .... He exemplified black power in achievement and he organized black power in action.' On the eve of an anti-Vietnam war rally in Washington, DC, King also used the occasion to claim Du Bois as a supporter of non-violent direct action.

We have to go to Washington because they have declared an armistice in the war on poverty while squandering millions to expand a senseless, cruel, unjust war in Vietnam. ... Dr Du Bois would be in the front ranks of the peace movement today. He would readily see the parallel between American support of the corrupt and despised Thieu–Ky regime and Northern support to the Southern slaveholders in 1876.

Having pressed Du Bois into the ranks of the peace movement, King concluded that his greatest virtue 'was his committed empathy with all the oppressed and his divine dissatisfaction with all forms of injustice'.[46] Coretta King, recalling this address, believed that in praising Du Bois' achievements, King wished to demonstrate to 'the black nationalists, with whom he hoped to find reconciliation, that Du Bois was as much our hero as theirs'.[47]

As with Du Bois, so too, with Garvey; King measured his estimates of the man and the movement to suit particular audiences. Garvey's appeal to blacks, King asserted in 1963:

had the virtue of rejecting concepts of inferiority. He called for a return to Africa and a resurgence of race pride. His movement attained mass dimensions, and released a powerful emotional response because it touched a truth which had long been dormant in the mind of the Negro. There was reason to be proud of their heritage as well as of their bitterly won achievements in America.

But King concluded – echoing a familiar criticism – Garvey's 'plan was doomed because an exodus to Africa in the twentieth century by a people who had struck roots for three and a half centuries in the New World did not have the ring of progress'.[48] But on a visit to Jamaica in 1965, when he placed a wreath on Garvey's memorial, King informed Jamaicans only that:

Marcus Garvey was the first man of colour in the history of the United States to lead and develop a mass movement. He was the first man on a mass scale and level to give millions of Negroes a sense of dignity and destiny, and make the Negro feel he is somebody. You gave Marcus Garvey to the United States of America, and gave to millions of Negroes in the United States a sense of personhood, a sense of manhood, and a sense of somebodiness.[49]

Two years later, in an assessment of the Black Power concept, King reverted to a negative appraisal of one element in Garveyism. Black Power in the 1960s, he argued, was very similar to Garveyism in the 1920s – 'it represents a dashing of hope, a conviction of the inability of the Negro to win and a belief in the infinitude of the ghetto'.[50]

Frustrated in his attempt to adapt SCLC techniques and philosophy to the problems of the Northern ghettos, King also faced competing claims for leadership. Most notably, he encountered in Malcolm X (also the son of a black preacher), a direct challenge to (and rejection of) the goal of racial integration based on non-violent resistance to the forces of white supremacy. Although he once remarked to a friend: 'I just saw Malcolm X on television. I can't deny it. When he starts talking about all that's been done to us, I get a twinge of hate, of identification with him', and conceded that he had a genuine concern for the problems faced by blacks, King deplored Malcolm's apparent preoccupation with violence.[51]

> ... violence is not going to solve our problem ... in his litany of articulating the despair of the Negro without offering any positive, creative alternative, I feel that Malcolm has done himself and our people a great disservice. Fiery, demagogic oratory in the black ghettos, urging Negroes to arm themselves and prepare to engage in violence, as he has done, can reap nothing but grief.[52]

Yet, like other black spokesmen, King deplored Malcolm's untimely and violent death. When a young white student informed him that his grandmother had just read *The Autobiography of Malcolm X* and thought 'it was marvellous, a book of love', King replied:

> It was tragic that Malcolm was killed, he was really coming around, moving away from racism. He had such a sweet spirit. You know, right before he was killed he came down to Selma and said some pretty passionate things against me, and that surprised me because after all it was my own territory down there. But afterwards he took my wife aside, and said he thought he could help me more by attacking me than praising me. He thought it would make it easier for me in the long run.[53]

James Baldwin, writing seven years after Malcolm's assassination, offered a similar assessment of his true relationship to King and the civil rights movement:

> Malcolm considered himself to be the spiritual property of the people who produced him. He did not consider himself to be their saviour; he was far too modest for that, and gave that role to another. ... Malcolm was not a racist, even when he thought he was. His intelligence was more complex than that. ... What made him unfamiliar and dangerous was not his hatred for white people but his love for blacks, his apprehension of the horror of the black condition, and the reasons for it, and his determination so to work on their hearts and minds that they would be enabled to see their condition and change it themselves.[54]

REFERENCES

1. Charles, R. and Ritz, D., *Brother Ray: Ray Charles' own story* (London, 1980), pp. 272–3.
2. Hercules, F., *American Society and Black Revolution* (New York, 1972), pp. 207–8.
3. Meier, A., Rudwick, E. and Broderick, F. L., *Black Protest Thought in the Twentieth Century* (New York, 1971), pp. 222–4.
4. Meier *et al.*, op. cit., pp. 239–40.
5. King, M. L. Jr, *Stride Toward Freedom: the Montgomery story* (London, 1959), p. 54.
6. King, op. cit., (1959), p. 91.
7. King, op. cit., (1959), pp. 91–2.
8. King, op. cit., (1959), p. 93.
9. King, op. cit., (1959), p. 79.
10. King, op. cit., (1959), p. 158.
11. Meier *et al.*, op. cit., pp. 293–300.
12. Chafe, W. H., 'The civil rights revolution, 1945–1960', in R. H. Bremner and G. W. Reichard (eds) *Reshaping America: society and institutions 1945–1960* (Columbus, Ohio, 1982), p. 93.
13. Meier *et al.*, op. cit., pp. 303–6.
14. Fairclough, A., 'The SCLC and the second Reconstruction, 1957–1973', *SAQ* 80(1981), 179.
15. Fairclough, op. cit., p. 179.
16. Lewis, D. L., *King: a critical biography* (London, 1970), p. 105.
17. Carson, C., *In Struggle: SNCC and the black awakening of the 1960s* (London, 1981), pp. 22–3.
18. Meier *et al.*, op. cit., pp. 307–8.
19. Schlesinger, A. M. Jr, *A Thousand Days: John F. Kennedy in the White House* (London, 1965), p. 793.
20. Schlesinger, op. cit., p. 793.
21. Oates, S. B., *Let the Trumpet Sound: the life of Martin Luther King, Jr* (London, 1982), p. 272.
22. Bennett, L. Jr, *What Manner of Man: a biography of Martin Luther King, Jr* (New York, 1968), pp. 100–1.
23. King, M. L. Jr *Why We Can't Wait* (New York, 1964), p. 54.
24. Lewis, op. cit., p. 174.
25. King, op. cit., (1964), pp. 79–80.
26. Lomax, L. E., *When the Word is Given: a report on Elijah Muhammad, and the Black Muslim world* (New York, 1964), p. 74.
27. Corley, R., 'Birmingham business leaders and desegregation, 1950–1963', in E. Jacoway and D. R. Colburn (eds) *Southern Businessmen and Desegregation* (Louisiana State U.P., 1982), pp. 189–90.
28. Meier, A. and Rudwick, E., *From Plantation to Ghetto* (1970), pp. 268–9.
29. Meier *et al.*, op. cit., pp. 49–50.
30. Carson, op. cit., p. 158.
31. Oates, op. cit., p. 362.
32. Royko, M., *Boss, Mayor Richard J. Daley of Chicago* (London, 1972), p. 141.

33. Fairclough, op. cit., p. 187.
34. King, M. L. Jr, *Where do We Go from Here. Chaos or Community?* (London, 1967), p. 30.
35. Oates, op. cit., p. 405.
36. Meier *et al.*, op. cit., pp. 586–93.
37. Garrow, D. J., *The FBI and Martin Luther King, Jr: from 'Solo' to Memphis* (London, 1981), p. 214.
38. Carson, op. cit., p. 288.
39. *Newsweek,* 15 April 1968.
40. *Newsweek,* 15 April 1968.
41. Cleaver, E., *Post-Prison Writings and Speeches* (New York, 1969), pp. 73–4.
42. King, op. cit., (1964), p. 33.
43. King, op. cit., (1967), p. 129.
44. King, op. cit., (1959), p. 213.
45. King, op. cit., (1964), p. 33.
46. Foner, P. S. (ed.), *W. E. B. Du Bois Speaks* (1970), pp. 12–19.
47. King, C. S., *My Life with Martin Luther King, Jr* (New York, 1969), p. 305.
48. King, op. cit., (1964), p. 33.
49. Barrett, L. E., *Soul Force: African heritage in Afro-American Religion* (New York, 1974), p. 151.
50. King, op. cit., (1967), p. 47.
51. Warren, R. P., *Who Speaks for the Negro?* (New York, 1966), p. 266.
52. Oates, op. cit., p. 253.
53. Halberstam, D., 'When "civil rights" and "peace" join forces', in C. E. Lincoln (ed.) *Martin Luther King, Jr: a profile* (New York, 1970), p. 211.
54. Baldwin, J., *No Name in the Street* (London, 1972), pp. 66–7.

Chapter eight

CONCLUSION: THE LIMITS OF BLACK LEADERSHIP SINCE 1968

I grew up in the generation that had the privilege to operate in the shadows of Dr King. . . . But it was only when I began to get closer with Dr King personally and philosophically that I began to deal with what all black people in America face at one level or another. You just don't say certain things in the South and live. You just don't say certain things and get a job.

(Rev. Jesse Jackson: American TV interview, 1970)

'We can move from the slave ship to the championship! From the guttermost to the uppermost! From the outhouse to the courthouse! From the state house to the White House!'

(Rev. Jesse Jackson: Los Angeles Rally, August 1983)

Malcolm X, a year before his assassination, remarked that the civil rights movement, and the legal victories of the 1960s, were making blacks 'more politically assertive'. Certainly in the 1970s and 1980s, many blacks came to believe that political activity and political power were the most effective means to realize racial advancement. The strategies employed by black leaders and organizations increasingly turned away from demonstrations, confrontations and boycotts, towards more use of the ballot gained by the 1965 Voting Rights Act. In 1967, Carl Stokes, a black Democrat, and the great-grandson of a slave, defeated Seth Taft, grandson of the twenty-seventh President of the United States, in the Cleveland, Ohio, mayoralty election. The Democratic Party responded to this upsurge in political activity by significantly increasing the number of Negro delegates to the 1972 Democratic National Convention, and a black congresswoman, Shirley Chisholm, unsuccessfully campaigned for the party's presidential nomination. In 1971, William Clay, spokesman for the 'Black Caucus' in Congress, asserted:

Black people in this country have no permanent friends, no permanent
enemies, only permanent interests. I think we've reached the point in
black America where we've completely given up on mass demonstrations,
sit-ins and boycotts. We've come to the conclusion that America has no
conscience. ... The only possible avenue for the achievement of equal
rights for all in this country is through the exertion of political power.
We have actual power, and even greater potential power, more than
we've ever had in history.

By 1975, there were 3,503 blacks in elective offices, with more than
200 in 37 state legislatures, and 17 in Congress (the only black
Republican being Senator Edward Brooke of Massachusetts). In 1979,
blacks held 4,607 elected offices (66% of which were in the South), and
there were 191 black mayors and 313 state legislators. Yet even by the
early 1980s, elected black officials constituted less than 1 per cent of all
elected officials nationally. One forecast estimated that at this rate of
change, blacks would hold only 3 per cent of all elective offices by the
year 2000 – far below the nearly 12 per cent of blacks in the national
population. Again, blacks gained power in large urban areas precisely
when the migration of impoverished groups to the large cities, and the
continued exodus of affluent whites to the suburbs and the 'sunbelt'
states made the inner cities as bases of political power less significant
than they had been in the past. Average black family income
consistently remained about 55 per cent of white income, and the
economic gains of the late 1960s eroded as a consequence of recession,
inflation and large-scale unemployment. Black leaders, following the
leads of Martin Luther King and Malcolm X, also began, in the 1970s, to
concern themselves more directly with economic issues.

If nothing else, the ghetto riots of the late 1960s helped to shift the
philosophy of the black protest movement. People who had been active
in the civil rights movement began to focus on ways to erase the cycle of
poverty, unemployment, and poor education. ... With the increased
politicization of the black lower class, black middle class politicians
found it necessary to articulate in a more forceful manner the particular
needs and problems of their constituencies. This resulted in a shift from
middle-class-based politics to a lower-class-based politics, a shift from a
politics whose issues emerged from the concerns of professional civil
rights organizations and which focused primarily on problems of race
discrimination, to a politics whose issues were defined in response to the
urban unrest of the 1960s and which focused on problems of de facto
segregation, class subordination, welfare state measures and human
survival in the ghetto.[1]

Similarly, after the death of Elijah Muhammad in 1975, the Black
Muslims, under the leadership of his son, Wallace D. Muhammad,
began to modify their tenets. The Nation of Islam – now called the
World Community of Al-Islam – became less concerned with
traditional black nationalist goals, and began to direct its efforts

towards the establishment of a collectivist capitalism. Whites were even invited to join a movement which had previously castigated them as 'devils'.

> The official weekly newspaper (*Muhammad Speaks*) was assuming a 'third world' as opposed to a traditional black nationalist stance even before the death of Elijah Muhammad. By the mid-1970s, it had supported such disparate movements as Pan-Africanism, Pan-Islam, Puerto Rican nationalism, and international socialism. Elijah Muhammad's much emphasized goal of an all-black homeland for Afro-Americans was being downplayed considerably. The Black Muslims seemed to be abandoning, at least temporarily, territorial black nationalism for a more broadly conceived and conventional variety of Pan-Islamism.[2]

(But not all Black Muslims accepted the move towards integration and increased business enterprise. Black Muslim minister Louis Farrakhan attempted to return the Nation of Islam to the precepts and practices of Elijah Muhammad.) In 1984 Farrakhan threatened to 'punish' one of Jesse Jackson's black critics, Milton Coleman of the *Washington Post*, for reporting that Jackson privately disparaged Jews.

Where Presidents Nixon and Ford showed little awareness of, or sympathy for, black aspirations, Jimmy Carter made some conspicuous black appointments to high office, most notably, that of Andrew Young, a follower of Martin Luther King and member of the SCLC, as US Ambassador to the United Nations. But black leaders of the 1970s and early 1980s were no more united than had been their predecessors. Andrew Young was forced to resign after disregarding the government's prohibition of meetings with the Palestine Liberation Organization (PLO), and when members of the SCLC, including Jesse Jackson, visited Yassir Arafat and the PLO in the Lebanon, they were criticized by Vernon Jordan of the National Urban League for their pro-Arab and anti-Israeli attitudes.

After the assassinations of Malcolm X and Martin Luther King, no black leader with their charisma or glamour emerged to bridge the divisions within the civil rights movement. The Reverend Ralph Abernathy, King's successor as head of the SCLC, not only lacked King's remarkable abilities, but also faced opposition and competition within the organization.

As 'mayor' of Resurrection City, the tent encampment set up on the Washington Mall, during the 1968 Poor People's Campaign, Jesse Jackson preached to the campers: 'Say I am somebody. I may be poor but I am somebody. I may be hungry but I am somebody.' By 1970, Jackson had begun to advocate the use of black economic power to force white-owned businesses to provide more jobs for blacks. As head of SCLC's Operation Breadbasket, he effectively coerced companies in Chicago's predominantly black South Side into employing Negroes, but left after an internal dispute over accounting practices. He then formed Operation PUSH (People United to Serve Humanity), with the objective of negotiating 'trade covenants' with major corporations, designed to secure employment for blacks, and support for black business enterprises.

Espousing a familiar self-help philosophy, Jackson, by the early 1980s, had become the most prominent black American leader, and a contender for the 1984 Democratic presidential nomination, hoping to form a 'rainbow coalition' of blacks, other ethnic minorities, women, peace activists and the white poor. Although Jackson entertained no real hope of gaining the nomination, his campaign revealed a new turn in black leadership strategy. The idea of promoting a black presidential candidate was first given serious consideration by a group of black mayors, congressmen and civil rights leaders, formally known as the Coalition for 1984 Election Strategy (and informally called the 'black leadership family'). Despite the criticisms of some black leaders that Jackson's candidacy would split the Democratic vote, and produce a white backlash, Jackson (over the opposition of Andrew Young and Coretta Scott King) declared:

> Part of our problem now is that some of our leaders do not seize opportunities. I was trained by Martin to be an opportunist.[3]

Given the persistence of caste, racial discrimination and economic inequality, all black American leaders have, of necessity, been opportunists.

REFERENCES

1. Wilson, W. J., *The Declining Significance of Race: blacks and changing American institutions* (University of Chicago Press, 1978), p. 138.
2. Moses, W. J., *Black Messiahs and Uncle Toms: social and literary manipulations of a religious myth* (London, 1982), pp. 187–8.
3. *Time,* 22 Aug. 1983, p. 36.

Chapter nine

EPILOGUE: BLACK LEADERSHIP: CONTINUITIES AND CONTRASTS

Negro leaders should be viewed from the standpoints of the two castes and their interests. The white caste has an interest in supporting those Negro leaders who can transfer their influence upon the lower caste. The Negro caste has two interests: one, to express the Negro protest as far as it does not damage its immediate welfare; two, to get as much as possible from the whites. The partly contradictory interests of the Negro community can be taken care of by the same individual leaders or by several different leaders in a division of responsibility.

(Myrdal, *An American Dilemma*)[1]

'It seems to me,' said Booker T.,
'That all you folks have missed the boat
who shout about the right to vote,
And spend vain days and sleepless nights
In uproar over civil rights.
Just keep your mouths shut, do not grouse,
But work, and save, and buy a house.'
'I don't agree,' said W.E.B.,
'For what can property avail
If dignity and justice fail?
Unless you help to make the laws,
They'll steal your house with trumped-up clause.
A rope's as tight, a fire as hot,
No matter how much cash you've got.
Speak soft, and try your little plan,
But as for me, I'll be a man.'
'It seems to me,' said Booker T. –

'I don't agree,'
Said W.E.B.

(Dudley Randall, 'Booker T. and W.E.B.')[2]

Booker T. Washington, W. E. B. Du Bois, Marcus Garvey, Malcolm X and Martin Luther King developed and utilized distinctive personal appeals in their attempts to eliminate (or improve) the inferior caste status of Afro-Americans. Collectively, however, they displayed ideological similarities – as well as significant differences – in a shared concern to improve the condition of blacks through economic, educational, cultural, political and psychological advancement. All displayed and sought to build on some form of racial pride among their followers, and encouraged the self-help ethic. With the exception of King, they all, at some stage in their careers, endorsed some kind of racial separatism. Again, all owed their elevation, at least in part, to the support (or opposition) of whites. Lines of ideological continuity also link these five black leaders. Washington, himself an admirer of Frederick Douglass's ideas on industrial education for Negroes, was the source of Marcus Garvey's racial and economic philosophy. Malcolm X acknowledged an early (and continuing) enthusiasm for Garvey. Martin Luther King paid tributes to Washington, Du Bois and Garvey, and had at least a grudging respect for his contemporary rival, Malcolm X.

Before the publication of *The Souls of Black Folk,* Du Bois and Washington shared some basic convictions. Both urged a programme of racial advancement which stressed economic achievement and the emulation of white middle-class virtues – thrift, sobriety and capital accumulation. Until the late 1890s

> both tended to blame Negroes largely for their condition, and both
> placed more emphasis on self-help and duties than on rights ... both
> placed economic advancement before universal manhood suffrage, and
> both were willing to accept franchise restrictions based not upon race but
> on education and/or property qualifications equitably applied.[3]

In time, Du Bois was equally opposed to Washington's apparent acceptance of disfranchisement and segregation, and Garvey's Washington-derived vision of a black economy as well as his rejection of the possibility of an egalitarian biracial society in the United States. Ironically, Du Bois came to agree with both Washington and Garvey 'on the necessity of the "black economy" which was Booker T. Washington's original idea, and then on the "Back to Africa" possibility which was Garvey's main platform – which, in turn was a further elaboration of the black economy theme'.[4]

In assessing the contributions of these five black leaders to the causes which they represented, a historical perspective reveals the changing connotations of such concepts as 'integration', 'segregation', 'accommodation' and 'civil rights'. Moreover, such a perspective also suggests that the adjectives 'radical' and 'conservative' when applied to black leaders and the policies they espoused, reflect particular conditions and circumstances. To his contemporary critics, Washington's deprecation of political action and support for social separation of the races, smacked of supine surrender to white supremacy. The NAACP, which institutionalized Negro opposition to Washington and the Tuskegee Machine, was at its inception a radical organization, pledged to securing political participation and racial integration. With the advent of the Nation of Islam, and the rise of Black Power in the 1960s, separatism was seen as a 'radical' response to the dilemma of Afro-Americans, while integration, the agreed goal of the older elements within the civil rights coalition, was regarded as 'conservative' by a younger generation of blacks who rejected integration as 'assimilationism'. They advocated instead, a form of cultural pluralism – a 'Negro nation within a nation' – without sufficient awareness of earlier formulations of the concept.

As in the 1960s, when Malcolm X and Martin Luther King appeared as the polar extremes of black leadership, so too, in the early twentieth century, Washington and Du Bois (and later, Du Bois and Garvey) represented conflicting philosophies of racial advancement. Their respective personal rivalries also reflected a constant problem facing black leaders in America: the inability of any one programme of racial protest to encompass the varieties and changes in the black experience. Writing in 1937, the social psychologist John Dollard observed:

> It will be noted that the official attitude of southern Negro leaders, like Booker T. Washington, has been conciliatory and accommodative, whereas the most active hostility to caste has come from the northern Negroes and their various associations, of which perhaps Dr W. E. B. Du Bois and the National Association for the Advancement of Coloured People are representative. One might say that the difference between Washington and Du Bois is due to a difference in regional culture; Washington wanted to do something in the South, while Du Bois wished to mobilize hostile sentiment against the caste institution and make clear the contradiction between the formal American definition of the status of the Negro and actualities of his situation.[5]

From the end of Reconstruction to the Second World War, Southern black leadership was forced to operate within the 'separate but equal' framework of race relations. Whatever influence Southern black leaders possessed was (as in the case of Booker T. Washington), exercised through white intermediaries. Blacks generally accepted these leaders because they had no other choice. But during the 1950s and 1960s, more assertive Southern black leaders began to emphasize aspirations which ran counter to white customs and mores. Next to racial intermarriage and sexual relations between black men and white women, the South's 'rank order of discriminations' encompassed:

> ... dancing, bathing, eating, drinking together and social intercourse generally ... the segregations and discriminations in use of public facilities such as schools, churches and means of conveyance ... discriminations in law courts, by the police, and by other public servants. Finally came the discriminations in securing land, credit, jobs, or other means of earning a living, and discriminations in public relief and other social welfare facilities.[6]

From the 1950s onwards (as in the case of Martin Luther King), Southern black leaders – with the growing support of Northern sympathizers – began to challenge the traditional list of racial proscriptions. 'The crusade for civil rights specifically aimed at the relatively limited (and ultimately practical) goal of abolishing legal segregation; it was widely (and wrongly) believed that other barriers to racial equality would speedily fall. That they ... failed to do so should not be made a reason for condemning the crusade.'[7]

With these considerations in mind, the claims of Booker T. Washington, W. E. B. Du Bois, Marcus Garvey, Malcolm X and Martin Luther King, Jr, to be regarded as the five outstanding Afro-American leaders of the period from 1895 to 1968 can be given more objective assessment.

BOOKER T. WASHINGTON

In the circumstances of his time and place, Washington evolved a programme and strategy designed to secure the acquiescence of Southern and Northern whites in the educational and economic elevation of a rural black peasantry and an aspiring black bourgeoisie. 'One of Washington's chief concerns as a black leader was to undermine the old otherworldly ethic of the plantation, and to replace it with an ethic of achievement.'[8] Aware that slavery had brought manual labour into disrepute, Washington (in tune with his age) preached a gospel of hard work, self-help and self-reliance. His advocacy of industrial education reflected this belief, as it also reconciled Southern whites to the idea of *any* form of education for blacks. Tuskegee Institute, the Tuskegee Machine and the carefully crafted phrases of the Atlanta Compromise Address, made Washington's position as the outstanding Southern black leader of his day virtually unassailable. Above all, Washington was the master tactician, interracial diplomat and archetypal 'trickster'. In many respects, he bears a striking (and intentional) resemblance to the black college principal, Dr A. Herbert Bledsoe, in Ralph Ellison's novel, *Invisible Man.* Describing his methods and rise to power in the South to the ingenuous narrator, Bledsoe could well have been retailing Washington's personal success formula:

> Negroes don't control this school or much of anything else. True they support it, but I control it. I's big and black and I say 'Yes, suh,' as loudly as any burrhead, when it's convenient. ... The only ones I even *pretend* to please are big white folk, and even those I control more than they control me. I tell them; that's my life, telling white folks how to think about the things I know about. ... It's a nasty deal and I don't like it myself. But I didn't make it and I know that I can't change it. I had to

be strong and purposeful to get where I am. I had to wait and lick around. I had to act the nigger. I don't even insist that it was worth it, but now I'm here and I mean to stay – after you win the game you take the prize and keep it and protect it; there's nothing else to do.[9]

Despite repeated invitations to move to the North, Washington realized that his work lay in the South, although the growing threat from Northern black critics forced him, in later years, to sharpen his condemnations of racial inequalities. In a period of worsening race relations, Washington continued to build up the reputation and resources of Tuskegee (and thereby his own reputation), and secured philanthropic funds for Southern black schools and colleges. Unable to prevent such developments as the loss of black voting rights, racial violence and economic exploitation, Washington attempted (both publicly and privately) to contain them. As Gunnar Myrdal noted perceptively, Washington, his critics to the contrary, was never a totally 'accommodating' race leader, and looked to complete equality as the 'ultimate goal' of black leadership.

> It is a political axiom that Negroes can never, in any period, hope to attain more *in the short term power bargain* than the most benevolent white groups are prepared to give them. With shrewd insight, Washington took exactly as much off the Negro protest – and it had to be a big reduction – as was needed to get the maximum cooperation from the only two white groups in America who in this era of ideological reaction cared anything at all about the Negroes: the Northern humanitarians and philanthropists and the Southern upper class school of 'parallel civilizations'. . . . Remembering the grim reaction of the period, it is difficult to study his various moves without increasingly feeling that he was a truly great politician. . . . For his time, and for the region where he worked and where then nine-tenths of all Negroes lived, his policy of abstaining from talk of rights and of 'casting down your buckets where you are' was entirely realistic.[10]

Washington's faults were glaring – his astigmatism on the intensity of white racial prejudice, his unquestioning acceptance of the normative values of white America, his materialism and philistinism. Yet despite (or because of) these failings, he was, a *representative* black leader. Frank Hercules is correct in his assertion that it is impossible to understand the ethos of Afro-Americans in the main, 'not that of the dissentient minority', unless it is understood that 'they are closer in their thinking to Booker T. Washington – and the governing rules of their behaviour are in more intimate consonance with the standards he described – than they are to any other representative figure in American history. The blacks of America are conservative – like Booker T. Washington; Christian – like Booker T. Washington; profoundly conscious – like Washington – of being, with their former white owners, archetypal Americans.'[11] Moreover, during the years of Washington's ascendancy, militant black protest and agitation in the South would have been a warrant for genocide. Washington recognized and respected the reality of the South's commitment to white supremacy; his evaluation of the situation was realistic and far-sighted. The last black leader to emerge from slavery, Washington not only led Southern Negroes, but preserved them from racial catastrophe. But he also lived dangerously, forced, in Langston's Hughes' phrase, to spend most of his life with his head 'in the lion's mouth'.

Not only was Washington attacked by Negro 'radicals', he also failed to satisfy Southern white extremists. Thomas Dixon, Jr, author of *The Clansman: an historical romance of the Ku Klux Klan* (1905), alleged that Washington, precisely because of his skill in disguising his real aims, was 'the greatest diplomat his race has ever produced'. In fact, Dixon claimed, Washington was quietly preparing the way for the amalgamation of the races, or, and equally dangerous, the building of a separate Negro nation within a nation. Dixon was in no doubt as to the consequences of Washington's educational and economic strategy: education would inevitably polarize the races since 'if there is one thing a Southern white man cannot endure it is an educated Negro'. By the same token, Washington's efforts to make the Negro intò a potential competitor with the white man could only end in bloodshed.

> Does any sane man believe that when the negro [*sic*] ceases to work under the direction of the Southern white man this race will allow the negro to master his industrial system, take the bread from his mouth, crowd him to the wall and place a mortgage on his house. Could fatuity reach a sublimer height than the idea that the white man will stand idly by and see this performance. What *will* he do when put to the test? He will do exactly what his white neighbour in the North does when the negro threatens his bread – *kill* him.[12]

Booker T. Washington, one of his biographers contends, has not been given fair evaluation 'partly because his methods were too compromising and unheroic to win him a place in the black pantheon, but also because he was too complex and enigmatic for historians to know what to make of him'.[13] Yet, as J. R. Pole suggests:

> Washington's role playing, though devious, was not essentially mysterious. Like many people of his basic disposition, he was instinctively supple towards his masters while revealing his authoritarian personality towards subordinates. ... In many ways he emerges as a type remarkable for its familiarity among the operators of American interest groups – that familiarity being disguised by skin pigmentation. He worked assiduously within the system, to whose economic and political conventions he faithfully subscribed; he took conservative views of larger social causes while showing great tactical skill in maintaining his own personal power base.[14]

On all counts Washington was, and remains, a black leader to be reckoned with.

W. E. B. DU BOIS

Intellectually superior to Washington, Du Bois through all his ideological shifts and turns, attempted to resolve what he regarded (and personally experienced) as being the fundamental dilemma of the Afro-American: 'One ever feels his two-ness'. Unlike Washington, Du Bois always felt himself to be apart from the mass of Negroes and for long periods of his life was defiantly out of step with orthodox black responses to such issues as segregation, socialism, Marxism and Pan-Africanism. An inferior (and disinterested) administrator, Du Bois, as editor of *Crisis,* was the outstanding agitator and propagandist of the Negro protest movement which arose in opposition to Washington's power and policies. 'Where Washington wanted to make Negroes entrepreneurs and captains of industry in accordance with the American economic dream, Du Bois stressed the role of the college educated elite ... and later developed a vision of a world largely dominated by the coloured races which would combine with the white workers in overthrowing the domination of white capital and thus secure social justice under socialism.'[15]

More than any other black leader, Du Bois influenced the Negro intelligentsia (the Talented Tenth), and contributed to the formation of that black consciousness which had its flowering in the Harlem Renaissance, and the growing awareness of black peoples throughout the world of their relationship to Africa, to each other and to whites. Du Bois himself admired but was rejected by white society, and out of this rejection came his reasoned but impassioned hatred of racial discrimination. As Frank Hercules suggests, had Du Bois been a British colonial subject, his abilities would have been recognized and rewarded. 'They would have knighted him, and as Sir Burghardt Du Bois, he would have been intellectually estimable, politically reliable, and ideologically harmless. But the Americans, with their crude oversimplification of racial categories, could only make an enemy of him.'[16]

From the formation of the Niagara Movement to his resignation from the NAACP, Du Bois (who would have preferred a life of historical and sociological research bent to the cause of black advancement) was the singularly gifted spokesman for Negro economic and political rights, and for racial integration. With the death of Booker T. Washington in 1915, the continuing black exodus from the South and the rising expectations of the educated black middle class, Du Bois finally achieved leadership of the Talented Tenth. Simultaneously, he also waged a bitter internal campaign against what he regarded as the élitism, conservatism and narrowness of the organization which had elected him as its major propagandist. The NAACP rejected Du Bois' call for voluntary segregation (which he had first articulated in the 1890s), and did not share his Pan-African or collectivist enthusiasms. He had to live with the irony that to his black critics, such a programme, with its materialist bias, resembled nothing so much as the philosophy of the despised Booker T. Washington. Yet Du Bois, on the eve of his departure from the NAACP, was firmly opposed to any deprivation of black political, civil, social or economic rights, and to enforced segregation. 'He did not wish to shut whites out of black organizations; he wanted interracial organizations such as the faculties of black colleges or the NAACP to assert the centrality of black power as a goal and to make the furthering of black pride and black economic advance their main interest. Du Bois could hardly have hoped to convince the NAACP of 1934 to adopt such a programme.'[17] By this date, leadership of the association had passed to racial conservatives, who were 'radical' only on the issue of segregation, and to whom Du Bois had become an embarrassment, if not a liability.

Du Bois, however, had multiple careers, which spanned the lifetimes of Booker T. Washington, Marcus Garvey, Malcolm X and Martin Luther King. In comparison with these leaders, Du Bois' 'longevity and productivity have given him a quantitative claim hard to match'. As one of his biographers suggests:

> Du Bois' significance will emerge more clearly if the extravagant claims made by him and for him are scuttled. ... Du Bois' importance to the history of the Negro in American society lies in two achievements: First, for thirty years he made himself the loudest voice in demanding equal rights for the Negro and in turning Negro opinion away from the acceptance of anything else. ... Du Bois' second achievement lies in his service to the Negro's morale. When Booker T. Washington was training Negro youth for manual work, Du Bois held high the ideal of liberal education. When Washington measured civilization in material terms, Du Bois reminded his people of Socrates and St Francis. ... His monthly editorials held up the strong, recharged the weak, and flayed the compromisers. *Crisis* became the record of Negro achievement. ... In this context, even Du Bois' aloofness became an asset; it removed him in Negro eyes from everyday life and, by giving him a transcendent quality, it raised the goal of aspiration.[18]

In the course of his long, distinguished and eventful life, Du Bois was inspired by a vision of reasoned, ordered and dynamic racial change. This vision was perhaps best expressed in the 'Postlude' to his second autobiography:

> ... this is a beautiful world; this is a wonderful America, which the founding fathers dreamed until their sons drowned it in the blood of slavery and devoured it in greed. Our children must rebuild it. Let then the Dreams of the Dead rebuke the Blind who think that what is will be forever and teach them that what was worth living for must live again.[19]

MARCUS GARVEY

Where Du Bois failed to reach a mass black audience, Marcus Garvey, his bitter rival in the 1920s, was able to build a popular movement and following for his programme of racial uplift and the redemption of Africa. Garvey's greatest achievement was to arouse in poor and lower-class blacks, unaffected by or unaware of the Harlem Renaissance and the 'New Negro', a fierce pride in their colour.

> Garvey, singlehanded, transformed the racial consciousness of black people in America into a potent instrument of racial uplift. He moved large numbers of blacks from a defensive to an aggressive position on the subject of race. The slogan 'Black is Beautiful' was not minted, except perhaps in the literal sense, by Stokely Carmichael. It was Garvey's distinctive coinage. . . . No one since Frederick Douglass and before Malcolm X had so aroused and rallied the pride of Negroes in the sheer fact of being black. . . . Garvey possessed remarkable powers of oratory, and, like Martin Luther King, he had a dream. In his case, it was the dream of returning to Africa. That it was a dream largely impracticable of realization never seemed to occur to him; or if it did, he concealed it from his followers. He spoke as though the then colonial powers in Africa did not exist. . . . He sought, in effect, to make Zionists of black Americans and . . . of blacks everywhere.[20]

More important as a phenomenon than as a social movement, Garveyism struck a responsive chord in the black masses of the 1920s because it exalted all things black and inverted white standards while retaining, in large part, the values of the surrounding white society. For every white institution and belief, Garveyism offered a black counterpart: the Black Star Line, Black Cross Nurses, *The Negro World,* the Black Legion and the Black Eagle Flying Corps. Both a religious – a black God and a black Christ – and a secular impulse, Garveyism linked its constituent elements to the concept of blackness. Moreover, the programme of the UNIA, with its stress on economic nationalism and African liberation, permitted Afro-Americans to identify with 'primitive' Africans from a position of technological and material superiority.

As a West Indian, however, Garvey was not finely attuned to the peculiarities and nuances of either the Negro or Negro–white situation in America. 'He tried to transplant to the United States the West Indian distinction between blacks and mulattoes, thereby alienating many American mulattoes.'[21] Again, in scorning the established black American leadership and appearing to share the racist assumptions and objectives of white supremacists, Garvey succeeded in arousing the bitter opposition of Negro radicals and conservatives, and the suspicions of white liberals.

... the Garvey movement illustrates – as the slave insurrections did a century earlier – that a Negro movement in America is doomed to ultimate dissolution and collapse if it cannot gain white support. ... For white support will be denied to emotional Negro chauvinism when it takes organizational and political form.[22]

Garvey's appeal, then, was limited to those blacks for whom the promised land of the American city had proved to be the squalid ghetto. The UNIA and its flamboyant leader offered compensatory dreams for the dispossessed. But the bulk of Garvey's followers (in common with most black Americans) were never seriously attracted by the prospect of going 'back to Africa'.

Regardless of how dissatisfied Negroes were with conditions in the United States they were unwilling in the 1920s, as their forebears had been ... to undertake the uncertain task of redeeming Africa. The widespread interest in Garvey's programme was more a protest against the anti-Negro reaction of the post-war period than an approbation of the fantastic schemes of the Negro leader. Its significance lies in the fact that it was the first and only real mass movement among Negroes in the history of the United States and that it indicates the extent to which Negroes entertained doubts concerning the hope for first-class citizenship in the only fatherland of which they knew.[23]

Garvey's larger significance as a leader lies in the fact that he made the established American Negro leadership class painfully aware of its distance from the rank and file of blacks. After Garvey's deportation, and particularly during the period of the Second World War, civil rights organizations tried more strenuously than before to close the gap between themselves and the majority of American Negroes.

The less attractive face of Garveyism was its authoritarianism, paramilitarism and failure to confront directly the problems facing those Negroes (the overwhelming majority) who wished to remain both physically and psychologically within the United States. Garvey himself has been typified as a charismatic leader and a shameless demagogue, a revolutionary and a reactionary, a racial realist and a racial fantasist, the father of recent black nationalist ideologies, and the purveyor of a falsified version of the African past and the Afro-American experience. Two of his biographers, while disagreeing as to the nature of Garveyism, are in substantial agreement as to Garvey's major accomplishment as a race leader in America. David Cronon, a severe critic of Garvey's failure to devise a meaningful programme for the 'redemption' of black Americans in their own country, suggests that: 'The creation of a powerful feeling of race pride is perhaps Garvey's greatest and most lasting contribution to the American race scene.'[24] Similarly, Theodore Vincent asserts that in the twentieth century, 'Garvey did more than anyone else to stimulate race pride and confidence among the black masses.'[25]

MALCOLM X

An admirer of Garvey, and the pre-eminent black separatist spokesman of the 1960s, Malcolm X was a more complex and ambiguous figure than his West Indian predecessor.

> He was feared and hated by both blacks and whites, and often the same individuals who shared these sentiments admired him for his intellectual ability and candor. During his lifetime his appeal among Afro-Americans, especially the youth, was widespread, but he was constantly maligned by black integrationists and whites in general. After his assassination he finally achieved a position of respect from all segments of the black community and from younger white radicals.[26]

As a Black Muslim minister and as an independent leader of his own movement after his break with Elijah Muhammad, Malcolm X was dedicated to the spiritual regeneration of black Americans, and employed the rhetoric of racial separatism to affirm the determination of blacks to exist on their own terms within (but apart from) the surrounding white society. An accomplished and artful public speaker, Malcolm analysed the plight and dilemma of the Afro-American with remarkable clarity and vividness. His speeches were filled with visual images, slogans, and allusions to black history, music and folklore. 'To the end of his life, his speeches were delivered in the cadence and style of Bible-thumping Baptist and Pentecostal preachers and prophetic leaders of millenaristic sects.'[27] Unable to establish a sound institutional base for his post-Nation of Islam activities, Malcolm X, through his exposure by the media, reached an American and an international audience. In this respect, Malcolm, like Booker T. Washington, owed his elevation to race leadership partly to white publicists.

The most remarkable feature of Malcolm's remarkable life, was his capacity for intellectual growth. 'From the relatively simplistic racist and separatist outlook of his Black Muslim period, he moved toward a somewhat socialist world view at the time of his death. Far from being Machiavellian or calculating, as many of his admirers and enemies have contended, Malcolm's inconsistencies and reversals may better be comprehended in terms of his augmented understanding.'[28] As an independent (or aspiring) leader, Malcolm made few actual converts, yet he voiced the feelings of ghetto youths who were either hostile or indifferent to Martin Luther King's philosophy of non-violence and the power of redemptive suffering. As a Black Muslim minister, Malcolm energized and greatly increased the membership and visibility of what had been a relatively obscure and largely elderly sect. But from 1963, he became increasingly impatient with the political disengagement enforced on the Nation of Islam by Elijah Muhammad, and attempted to raise the struggle for civil and human rights to include all the coloured peoples of the world. In particular, Malcolm pointed up the weaknesses in the objectives of a civil rights coalition which, after some successes in the South, had come to regard racial integration as a panacea.

Before his contemporary rival and ideological opponent, Martin Luther King, Malcolm X highlighted the economic and educational condition (and needs) of Negroes, and the failure of non-violent resistance to effect meaningful change in the lives of the lower classes. Moreover, Malcolm espoused (and personified) black leadership from the grass roots, free from the domination of the established black and white middle classes. This aspect of Malcolm's thought appealed to the younger elements in the civil rights movement – the members of CORE and SNCC – who, after Malcolm's death, were even more estranged from the strategies and pronouncements of Martin Luther King.

Like Garvey, Malcolm X has been claimed as a revolutionary, a black nationalist and a latter-day (but unwitting) follower of Booker T. Washington. Like Garvey also, Malcolm X had more followers than those who formally belonged to the OAAU. Where Garvey spoke to the mood of the 1920s, Malcolm X was receptive to the despair of the enduring black ghettos of the 1960s, which he sought to transform into centres of black consciousness, enterprise and liberation. Two differing estimates of Malcolm X, both delivered after his death, illustrate his strengths and limitations as perceived by black contemporaries. Asked why he 'eulogized' Malcolm X, Ossie Davis, the actor, director and playwright, replied:

> We used to think that protocol and common sense required that Negroes stand back and let the white man speak up for us, defend us, and lead us from behind the scenes in our fight. This was the essence of Negro politics. But Malcolm said to hell with that! Get up off your knees and fight your own battles. ... That's the way to make the white man respect you. ... Malcolm, as you can see, was refreshing excitement. ... Once Malcolm fastened on you, you could not escape. ... He would make you as angry as hell, but he would also make you proud. It was impossible to remain defensive and apologetic about being a Negro in his presence. ... I knew the man personally, and however much I might have disagreed with him personally from time to time, I never doubted that Malcolm X, even when he was wrong, was always that rarest thing in the world among us Negroes: a true man.[29]

Bayard Rustin, who had earlier expressed the view that Malcolm was a lost leader in search of followers, conceded after his death that: 'Malcolm strove to retrieve the Negro's shattered manhood from the wreckage of slavery, from the debris of family instability, from poverty and narcotics, from conditioned aimlessness, self-hatred and chaos.' Yet his efforts were doomed to failure 'because these are not problems that can be exorcized by religious mysticism or denunciatory rhetoric. ... If only he had cast his lot with the civil rights revolution! We could have profited mightily from his talents, now so wastefully silenced.'[30]

MARTIN LUTHER KING, JR

From the time of the Montgomery bus boycott, Martin Luther King was the great proponent of passive resistance as the strategy for achieving racial equality in America. To his admirers, white and black, King was the outstanding black leader of the twentieth century, whose contributions to the civil rights cause were uniquely Christian and Southern. King's confrontations with the forces of Southern racism resembled (as they were intended) a medieval passion play, in which the forces of good engaged (and eventually overcame) the forces of evil. To his critics, King was the exponent of an unrealistic, if not pathological doctrine, which enjoined its adherents to love their oppressors, and to resort to prayer rather than decisive action against injustice. Yet, as his critics also recognized, King's appeal rested on his profound religious faith. August Meier, writing three years before King's murder, suggested that:

> Publicity alone does not explain the durability of King's image, or why
> he remains ... the symbol of the direct action movement, the nearest
> thing to a charismatic leader that the civil rights movement has ever had.
> At the heart of King's continuing influence and popularity are two facts.
> First, better than anyone else, he articulates the aspirations of Negroes
> who respond to the cadences of his addresses, his religious phraseology
> and manner of speaking, and the vision of his dream for them and
> America. King has intuitively adopted the style of the old-fashioned
> Negro Baptist preacher and transformed it into a new art
> form. ... Second, he communicates Negro aspirations to white America
> more effectively than anyone else. His religious terminology and
> manipulation of the Christian symbols of love and nonresistance are
> partly responsible for his appeal among whites. To talk in terms of
> Christianity, love, nonviolence is reassuring to the mentality of white
> America. At the same time, the very superficialities of his
> philosophy – that rich and eclectic amalgam of Jesus, Hegel, Gandhi and
> others ... make him appear intellectually profound to the superficially
> educated middle-class white American .... by uttering moral cliches, the
> Christian pieties, in a magnificent display of oratory, King becomes
> enormously effective.[31]

Until the emergence of the Black Power slogan, King managed to hold together an obviously fragmenting civil rights coalition through the force of his own personality and prestige among white and black Americans. In this respect, he served as the vital centre of the movement, standing between the 'conservatism' of the NAACP and Urban League, and the 'radicalism' of SNCC and CORE. The Vietnam War, a growing awareness that the black protest movement needed to include economic rights, and a realization that the structure of American society itself needed drastic alteration, moved King, in his final years, towards a more radical and less sanguine assessment of the racial/class situation in America. Like Malcolm X, at the time of his death King was also a figure in transition. But if he is judged only by his contribution to the civil rights revolution in the American South, his shaming of Congress into passing the 1964 Civil Rights Act, his courage in the face of physical danger, and his inspired and visionary address during the 1963 March on Washington, King will be remembered as the greatest black leader of the twentieth century.

From Booker T. Washington's Atlanta Address of 1895, to Martin Luther King's last (and prophetic) speech in Memphis in 1968, five outstanding (although not the only) black American leaders attempted to realize for themselves and their followers the fundamental aspiration of the Afro-American as expressed by W. E. B. Du Bois:

> He simply wishes to make it possible for a man to be both a Negro and an American, without being cursed and spit upon by his fellows, without having the doors of Opportunity closed roughly in his face. ... Merely a concrete test of the underlying principles of the great republic is the Negro Problem, and the spiritual striving of the freedmen's sons is the travail of souls whose burden is almost beyond the measure of their strength, but who bear it in the name of an historic race, in the name of this the land of their fathers' fathers, and in the name of human opportunity.[32]

REFERENCES

1. Myrdal, G., *An American Dilemma* (New York, 1944), p. 1133.
2. Randall, D., 'Booker T. and W.E.B.', in A. Chapman (ed.) *Black Voices* (Mentor Books, New York, 1968), p. 470.
3. Meier, A., *Negro Thought in America, 1880–1915* (Ann Arbor, Michigan, 1963), p. 196.
4. Cruse, H., *Rebellion or Revolution* (New York, 1968), p. 157.
5. Dollard, J., *Caste and Class in a Southern Town* (3rd edn, New York, 1957), p. 305.
6. Myrdal, op. cit., p. 61.
7. Barbrook, A. and Bolt, C., *Power and Protest in American Life* (Oxford, 1980), p. 145.
8. Moses, W. J., *Black Messiahs and Uncle Toms: social and literary manipulations of a religious myth* (London, 1982), p. 86.
9. Ellison, R., *Invisible Man* (Penguin, Harmondsworth, 1952), p. 119.
10. Myrdal, op. cit., p. 741.
11. Hercules, F., *American Society and Black Revolution* (New York, 1972), pp. 197–8.

12. Thornbrough, E. L., 'Booker T. Washington as seen by his white contemporaries', *JNH* 53 (1968), 180.

13. Harlan, L., *Booker T. Washington: the making of a black leader, 1865–1901* (Oxford U.P.; New York, 1972), p. vii.

14. Pole, J. R., 'Of Mr Booker T. Washington and others', *Paths to the American Past* (Oxford U.P., 1979), pp. 184–5.

15. Meier, op. cit., (1963), pp. 205–6.

16. Hercules, op. cit., pp. 190–1.

17. Rampersad, A., *The Art and Imagination of W. E. B. Du Bois* (London, 1976), p. 168.

18. Broderick, F. L., *W. E. B. Du Bois: Negro leader in a time of crisis* (Stanford, California, 1959), pp. 230–1.

19. Du Bois, W. E. B., *The Autobiography of W. E. B. Du Bois: a soliloquy on viewing my life from the last decade of its first century* (1968), pp. 422–3.

20. Hercules, op. cit., pp. 214, 286.

21. Draper, T., *The Rediscovery of Black Nationalism* (New York, 1969), p. 52.

22. Myrdal, op. cit., p. 749.

23. Franklin, J. H., *From Slavery to Freedom: a history of Negro Americans* (New York, 1967), p. 492.

24. Cronon, E. D., *Black Moses: the story of Marcus Garvey and the UNIA* (Madison, Wisconsin, 1955), p. 201.

25. Vincent, T., *Black Power and the Garvey Movement* (San Francisco, 1972), p. 245.

26. Pinkney, A., *Red, Black, and Green: black nationalism in the United States* (Cambridge U.P., 1976), p. 64.

27. Blair, T. L., *Retreat to the Ghetto: the end of a dream?* (London, 1977), p. 49.

28. Margolies, E., *Native Sons: a critical study of twentieth century black American authors* (New York, 1968), p. 151.

29. Davis, O., 'Why I eulogized Malcolm X', in J. H. Clarke (ed.) *Malcolm X: the man and his times* (New York, 1969), pp. 128–31.

30. Kahn, T. and Rustin, B., 'The ambiguous legacy of Malcolm X', *Dissent,* 12(1965), 189.

31. Meier, A., 'The conservative militant', in C. E. Lincoln (ed.) *Martin Luther King Jr: a profile* (New York, 1970), p. 147.

32. Du Bois, W. E. B., 'Of our spiritual strivings', in *The Souls of Black Folk* (1961), pp. 17, 22.

BIBLIOGRAPHICAL ESSAY

ABBREVIATIONS FOR JOURNALS:

AAS	*Afro-American Studies*
AHR	*American Historical Review*
AJS	*American Journal of Sociology*
AL	*American Literature*
AQ	*American Quarterly*
BAAS	*British Association for American Studies*
JAH	*Journal of American History*
JAS	*Journal of American Studies*
JHI	*Journal of the History of Ideas*
JNH	*Journal of Negro History*
JSH	*Journal of Southern History*
MassR	*Massachusetts Review*
SAQ	*South Atlantic Quarterly*

INTRODUCTORY AND GENERAL STUDIES

The following texts contain useful and pertinent information on the period covered by this study: John Hope Franklin, *From Slavery to Freedom: a history of Negro Americans* (3rd edn, New York, 1968); August Meier and Elliott Rudwick, *Along the Colour Line* (Urbana, Illinois, 1976); Robert H. Brisbane, *The Black Vanguard: origins of the Negro social revolution, 1900–1960* (Valley Forge, Pennsylvania, 1970); Mary Ellison, *The Black Experience: American blacks since 1865* (London, 1974); Mary F. Berry and John W. Blassingame, *Long Memory: the black experience in America* (New York, 1982).

They should be supplemented by an appropriate collection of documentary materials. Two of the best are: August Meier, Elliott Rudwick and Francis L. Broderick, *Black Protest Thought in the Twentieth Century* (2nd edn, New York, 1971), and John H. Bracey, August Meier and Elliott Rudwick, *Black Nationalism in America* (New York, 1970).

168

The classic work on the black experience to the New Deal remains Gunnar Myrdal's *An American Dilemma* (New York, 1944 and 1962), the most influential study of American race relations ever published. It contains some penetrating insights into the problems faced by black leaders.

Three excellent articles which treat black leadership in historical perspective are: Guy B. Johnson, 'Negro racial movements and leadership in the United States', *AJS,* 43 (1937–38), 55–71, and more recently, Wilson Record, 'Negro intellectuals and Negro movements in historical perspective', *AQ,* 8 (1956), 3–20; Leslie H. Fishel, Jr., 'Repercussions of Reconstruction: The Northern Negro, 1870–1883', *Civil War History,* 14 (1968), 325–45.

On black leadership see also: D. C. Thompson, *The Negro Leadership Class* (Englewood Cliffs, New Jersey, 1963); M. Elaine Burgess, *Negro Leadership in a Southern City* (New Orleans) (University of North Carolina Press, 1960); and Raymond Gavins, *The Perils and Prospects of Black Leadership: Gordon Blaine Hancock, 1874–1970* (Duke U.P., 1977).

For a summary of black protest within the wider context of minority group activities, see Alec Barbrook and Christine Bolt, *Power and Protest in American Life* (Oxford, 1980), and John Higham (ed.), *Ethnic Leadership in America* (The Johns Hopkins U.P., 1978). John Dollard's famous study, *Caste and Class in a Southern Town* (3rd edn, New York, 1957) originally appeared in 1937. It is a novel appraisal by a social psychologist of the relations between blacks and whites in a Southern community. The responses of Southern white businessmen to the civil rights movement in the 1950s and 1960s are treated in a valuable collection of essays edited by Elizabeth Jacoway and David R. Colburn, *Southern Businessmen and Desegregation* (Louisiana State U.P., 1982). Collectively, as the editors observe, these essays 'suggest that the response of the southern leadership to the desegregation challenge was an accommodation to what was perceived as inevitable change ... although they did not moderate their racial attitudes, they did allow racial considerations to slip from the dominant position in their hierarchy of values'.

Black protest movements from 1895 to 1968 are covered chronologically by the following books and articles: E. L. Thornbrough, 'The National Afro-American League, 1887–1908', *JSH,* 27 (1961), 494–512. A. Meier and E. Rudwick, 'The boycott movement against Jim Crow street cars in the South, 1900–1916', *JAH,* 55 (1969), 756–75. E. M. Rudwick, 'The Niagara Movement', *JNH,* 42 (1957), 177–200. Charles F. Kellogg, *NAACP: a history of the National Association for the Advancement of Coloured People,* vol. 1, *1909–1920* (Baltimore, Maryland, 1967). The National Urban League's first three decades are given comprehensive and analytical treatment in Nancy J. Weiss, *The National Urban League: 1910–1940* (Oxford U.P., New York, 1974).

On black Americans during the Progressive era see: D. W. Grantham, 'The Progressive Movement and the Negro', *SAQ,* 54 (1955), 461–77; Gilbert Osofsky, 'Progressivism and the Negro', *AQ,* 16 (1964), 153–68; Thomas G. Dyer, *Theodore Roosevelt and the Idea of Race* (Louisiana State U.P., London, 1980); N. J. Weiss, 'The New Negro and the new freedom: fighting Wilsonian segregation', *Political Science Quarterly,* LXXXIV (1968), 61–79; K. L. Wolgemuth, 'Woodrow Wilson's appointment policy and the Negro', *JSH,* 24 (1958), 450–71; Raymond Wolters, *The New Negro on Campus: black college rebellions of the 1920s* (Princeton U.P., 1975); H. Blumenthal, 'Woodrow Wilson and the race question', *JNH,* 48 (1963), 1–21.

Black attitudes to the First World War are discussed in T. Kornweibel, Jr, 'Apathy and dissent: black America's negative responses to World War I', *SAQ,* 80 (1981), 322–38. Negro responses to the Depression and New Deal are included in the Du Bois bibliography (below), but see also J. A. Harrell, 'Negro leadership in the election year 1936', *JSH,* 34 (1968), 546–65.

Black responses to the Second World War have been extensively treated. See especially Neil A. Wynn, *The Afro-American and the Second World War* (London, 1976); A. Russell Buchanan, *Black Americans in World War II* (Oxford, 1977) and Phillip McGuire, *Taps for a Jim Crow Army: letters from black soldiers in World War II* (Oxford, 1983). Four distinctive interpretations of Afro-American protest activities during the war are to be found in: Richard M. Dalfiume, 'The forgotten years of the Negro revolution', *JAH,* 55 (1968), 90–106; N. A. Wynn, 'Black attitudes towards participation in the American war effort, 1941–1945', *AAS,* 3 (1972), 13–19; H. Sitkoff, 'Racial militancy and interracial violence in the Second World War', *JAH,* 58 (1971), 661–8; Lee Finkle, 'The conservative aims of militant rhetoric: black protest during World War II', *JAH,* 60 (1973), 692–713. See also K. T. Anderson, 'Last hired, first fired: black women workers during World War II', *JAH,* 69 (1982), 82–97.

The civil rights movement after 1945 is treated in August Meier and Elliott Rudwick, *CORE: a study in the civil rights movement, 1952–1968* (New York, 1973); Clayborne Carson, *In Struggle: SNCC and the black awakening of the 1960s* (London, 1981); Benjamin Muse, *The American Negro Revolution: from nonviolence to black power* (Bloomington, Indiana, 1968); Harvard Sitkoff, *The Struggle for Black Equality, 1954–1980* (New York, 1981); and in Robert Penn Warren's collection of taped interviews, *Who Speaks for the Negro?* (New York, 1965). A. Meier and E. Rudwick have collected an informative series of articles from the *New York Times* on the civil rights movement: *Black Protest in the 60s* (Chicago, 1970). See also: Monroe Billington, 'Civil rights, President Truman and the South', *JNH,* 58 (1973) 127–39.

Three articles which cover developments to recent years are: W. H. Chafe, 'The civil rights revolution, 1945–60', in R. H. Bremner and G. W. Reichard (eds), *Reshaping America: society and institutions, 1945–60* (Columbus, Ohio, 1982); John White, 'American minorities: the non-melting pot', in H. S. Commager and Marcus Cunliffe (eds), *The American Destiny: an illustrated bicentennial history of the United States,* Vol. 19, *The Unquiet Years* (New York, 1976), pp. 50–64; Faustine C. Jones, 'External crosscurrents and internal diversity: an assessment of black progress, 1960–1980', *Daedalus* (Spring 1981), 71–101.

There have been several notable interpretive studies of American Negro thought. Particularly recommended are: August Meier, *Negro Thought in America, 1880–1915* (Ann Arbor, Michigan, 1963, 1966); Harold Cruse, *The Crisis of the Negro Intellectual: from its origins to the present* (New York, 1967); Frank Hercules, *American Society and Black Revolution* (New York, 1972); Alfred A. Moss, *The American Negro Academy: voice of the Talented Tenth* (London, 1981); David G. Nielson, *Black Ethos: Northern urban Negro life and thought, 1890–1930* (London, 1977); William Toll, *The Resurgence of Race: black social theory from Reconstruction to the Pan-African Conferences* (University of Pennsylvania Press, 1979), and two provocative and stimulating books by Wilson J. Moses: *The Golden Age of Black Nationalism, 1850–1925* (Connecticut, 1978) and *Black Messiahs and Uncle Toms: social and literary manipulations of a religious myth* (London, 1982).

The writings of Booker T. Washington, W. E. B. Du Bois and Malcolm X are analysed in Stephen J. Butterfield, *Black Autobiography in America* (University of Massachusetts Press, 1975), and Addison Gayle, Jr, *The Way of the New World: the black novel in America* (New York, 1976). Du Bois and Malcolm X are discussed sympathetically in Edward Margolies, *Native Sons: a critical study of twentieth century black American authors* (New York, 1968).

Ralph Ellison's towering reputation as a black novelist derives from one book, *Invisible Man* (New York, 1952). It is recommended here as a fictionalized account of the black experience in the South and the North. Readers will discover both oblique and direct references to Frederick Douglass, Booker T. Washington, Marcus Garvey and Du Bois.

The concerns and content of recent black American writing are admirably summarized in A. Robert Lee's essay: 'Black American fiction since Richard Wright' (*BAAS Pamphlet in American Studies,* 11, 1983).

BLACK PROTEST AND ACCOMMODATION: 1800–1877

There is an enormous literature on slave life, culture and 'resistance'. For a sampling of this work, see: E. D. Genovese, *Roll, Jordan, Roll: the world the slaves made* (New York, 1974); John W. Blassingame, *The Slave Community: plantation life in the antebellum South* (New York, 1972); Leslie H. Owens, *This Species of Property: slave life and culture in the Old South* (New York, 1976); Nathan Huggins, *Black Odyssey: the Afro-American ordeal in slavery* (New York, 1977). See also three articles by the author: John White, 'The novelist as historian: William Styron and American Negro slavery', *JAS,* 4 (1971), 233–45; 'Whatever happened to the slave family in the Old South?', *JAS,* 8 (1974), 383–90; 'Veiled testimony: Negro spirituals and the slave experience', *JAS,* 17 (1983), 251–63.

The standard work on free blacks in the slave South is Ira Berlin, *Slaves Without Masters: the free Negro in the antebellum South* (New York, 1974). For the Southern black experience immediately after the Civil War, see L. F. Litwack's excellent study, *Been in the Storm So Long: the aftermath of slavery* (New York, 1980); C. Vann Woodward, *The Strange Career of Jim Crow* (3rd revised edn, New York, 1974); Howard N. Rabinowitz, *Race Relations in the Urban South, 1865–1890* (Oxford U.P., New York, 1978).

The activities of Northern free blacks before the Civil War are surveyed in L. F. Litwack, *North of Slavery: the Negro in the free states, 1790–1860* (Chicago, 1961); Robert C. Dick, *Black Protest: issues and tactics* (Westport, Connecticut, 1974); F. J. Miller, *The Search for a Black Nationality: black emigration and colonization, 1787–1863* (Urbana, Illinois, 1975); J. H. and W. H. Pease, *They Who Would Be Free: blacks' search for freedom, 1830–1861* (New York, 1974); Benjamin Quarles, *Black Abolitionists* (New York, 1964). Quarles has also written an excellent brief biography: *Frederick Douglass* (Washington, DC, 1948). See also, Philip Foner (ed.), *The Life and Writings of Frederick Douglass,* 4 vols (New York, 1950–55). John W. Blassingame has begun to edit the collected speeches, writings and interviews of Douglass in what promises to be a major addition to Afro-American historiography. Two volumes have appeared to date. J. W. Blassingame (ed.), *The Frederick Douglass Papers, Series One: speeches, debates and interviews,* Vol. 1, *1841–46;* Vol. 2, *1847–54* (Yale U.P., New Haven and London, 1979 and 1982). Howard N. Rabinowitz has edited a valuable collection of essays: *Southern Black Leaders of the Reconstruction Era* (University of Illinois Press, 1982).

BOOKER T. WASHINGTON

The leading authority on Washington's life is Louis R. Harlan. His two-volume biography, *Booker T. Washington: the making of a black leader, 1865–1901* (Oxford U.P., New York, 1972), and *Booker T. Washington: the wizard of Tuskegee, 1901–1915* (Oxford U.P., New York, 1983), is a massively researched and well-written account of Washington as race leader and educator, but tends to judge him by the standards of present-day white liberalism. Harlan is also one of the editors of *The Booker T. Washington Papers* (15 vols), (University of Illinois Press, 1972–83). Fully indexed, with cross-references and informative notes, these volumes can be mined to extract material on every aspect of Washington's activities and interests. Volume I contains Washington's autobiographical writings – *Up From Slavery, The Story of My Life and Work,* and extracts from *The Story of the Negro* (1909), and *My Larger Education,* together with shorter autobiographical pieces. Professor Harlan has also produced several informative articles on Washington: 'Booker T. Washington and the white man's burden', *AHR,* 71 (1965–66), 441–67; 'Booker T. Washington in biographical perspective', *AHR,* 75 (1970), 1581–99; 'The secret life of Booker T. Washington', *JSH,* 37 (1971), 393–416; 'Booker T. Washington and the "Voice of the Negro" ', *JSH,* 45 (1979), 45–62.

Earlier but valuable biographies of Washington are: Samuel J. Spencer, *Booker T. Washington and the Negro's Place in American Life* (Boston, 1955); Basil Mathews, *Booker T. Washington: educator and inter-racial interpreter* (London, 1949); Bernard A. Weisberger, *Booker T. Washington* (New York, 1972). Hugh Hawkins has edited a valuable collection of essays on Washington by his contemporaries and later commentators: *Booker T. Washington and His Critics* (2nd edn, Boston, 1974). On Washington and Roosevelt, see Seth M. Scheiner's article 'President Theodore Roosevelt and the Negro', *JNH,* 47 (1962), 169–82. Other recommended articles are: August Meier, 'Booker T. Washington and the Negro press', *JNH,* 38 (1953), 67–90; Donald J. Calista, 'Booker T. Washington: another look', *JNH,* 49 (1964), 240–55; John P. Flynn, 'Booker T. Washington: Uncle Tom or wooden horse?', *JNH,* 54 (1969), 262–74; Emma Lou Thornbrough, 'Booker T. Washington as seen by his white contemporaries', *JNH,* 53 (1968), 161–82; Lawrence J. Friedman, 'Life in the lion's mouth: another look at Booker T. Washington', *JNH,* 59 (1974), 337–51; Daniel Walden, 'The contemporary opposition to the political and educational ideas of Booker T. Washington', *JNH,* 45 (1960), 103–15. (See also the reply by Philip S. Foner, 'Document: is Booker T. Washington's idea correct?', *JNH,* 55 (1970), 343–7.) J. R. Pole's review essay 'Of Mr Booker T. Washington and others', in his *Paths to the American Past* (Oxford U.P., 1979), offers some refreshing comments on Washingtonian historiography. Judith Stein's essay, 'Of Mr Booker T. Washington and others: the political economy of racism in the US', *Science and Society*, 38 (1974–75), 422–63, surveys race relations and politics in the South from 1877 to 1910, with particular reference to Washington, Populism and black disfranchisement.

On one of Washington's fiercest black critics, see Yvonne Williams, 'William Monroe Trotter: race man, 1872–1934', *AAS*, 1 (1971), 243–51 and C. W. Puttkammer and R. Worthy, 'William Monroe Trotter, 1872–1934', *JNH*, 43 (1958), 298–316. Emma Lou Thornbrough's *T. Thomas Fortune: militant journalist* (London, 1972), includes a careful account of his ambivalent relationship with Washington, and later association with Garvey as an editor of *The Negro World*. Charles F. Kellogg's *NAACP*, already cited, contains a detailed discussion of Washington's dealings with that organization up to his death in 1915. August Meier's *Negro Thought in America, 1880–1915* (cited above), has three judicious assessments of Washington: 'Booker T. Washington: an interpretation', 'Booker T. Washington and the Talented Tenth', 'Booker T. Washington and the politicians'. In *The Resurgence of Race,* cited above, William Toll presents Washington as an outstanding educator, racial realist and black separatist. Harold Cruse in *Rebellion or Revolution* (New York, 1968), also offers a 'radical' assessment of Washington. Tuskegee's most famous black teacher is given succinct and balanced evaluation in Linda O. McMurry, *George Washington Carver: scientist and symbol* (Oxford U.P., New York, 1981). It can be supplemented with A. W. Jones' article, 'The role of Tuskegee Institute in the education of black farmers', *JNH,* 60 (1975), 252–67. That Washington's empire collapsed with his death is made clear in C. S. Matthews, 'The decline of the Tuskegee Machine, 1915–1925: the abdication of political power', *SAQ,* 75 (1976), 460–9.

W. E. B. DU BOIS

Du Bois has been well served by biographers. The best three studies are: Elliott Rudwick, *W. E. B. Du Bois: propagandist of the Negro protest* (New York, 1969); Francis L. Broderick, *W. E. B. Du Bois: Negro leader in a time of crisis* (Stanford, California, 1959, 1966); and Arnold Rampersad, *The Art and Imagination of W. E. B. Du Bois* (London, 1976). Rudwick's book is primarily concerned with Du Bois' conflicts with his contemporaries, from his opposition to Washington down to his resignation from the NAACP in 1934. Broderick covers much of the same ground, but takes Du Bois' career to 1952, when he had become increasingly involved in peace and socialist movements. Rampersad's biography stresses Du Bois' 'essentially poetic vision of human experience', and examines in detail his major writings, including his novels and poetry. Du Bois, Rampersad concludes, 'lived at least a double life, continually compelled to respond to the challenge of reconciling opposites'.

Rayford W. Logan has edited an uneven collection of essays which treat Du Bois' careers as propagandist, historian, race leader and Pan-Africanist: *W. E. B. Du Bois: a profile* (New York, 1971), and includes extracts from the Rudwick and

Broderick biographies. Julius Lester has collected and edited a representative selection of Du Bois' work: *The Seventh Son: the thought and writings of W. E. B. Du Bois,* 2 vols (New York, 1971). See also John Henrik Clarke *et al., Black Titan: W. E. B. Du Bois, an anthology by the editors of Freedomways* (Boston, 1970).

The following articles offer good introductions to significant aspects of Du Bois' life and preoccupations: E. M. Rudwick, 'W. E. B. Du Bois in the role of *Crisis* editor', *JNH,* 43 (1958), 214–40; Mary Law Chafee, 'W. E. B. Du Bois' concept of the racial problem in the United States', *JNH,* 41 (1956), 241–58; Ben F. Rodgers, 'W. E. B. Du Bois, Marcus Garvey and Pan-Africa', *JNH,* 40 (1955), 154–65; Wilson J. Moses, 'The politics of Ethiopianism: W. E. B. Du Bois and literary black nationalism', *AL,* XLVII (1975), 411–26; Clarence G. Contee, 'W. E. B. Du Bois, the NAACP and the Pan-African Congress of 1919', *JNH,* 57 (1972), 13–28, and 'The emergence of W. E. B. Du Bois as an African nationalist', *JNH,* 54 (1969), 48–60; Jean Fagan Yellin, 'Du Bois *Crisis* and womans' suffrage', *MassR,* 14 (1973), 365–75; K. M. Glazier, 'W. E. B. Du Bois' impressions of Woodrow Wilson', *JNH,* 58 (1973), 452–9. C. H. Wesley, 'W. E. B. Du Bois: historian'. *JNH,* 50 (1965), 147–62.

For Du Bois' responses to the Depression and New Deal, see in addition to the biographies cited: Raymond Wolters, *Negroes and the Great Depression: the problem of economic recovery* (Westport, Connecticut, 1970), Ch. 10; John B. Kirby, *Black Americans in the Roosevelt Era* (Knoxville, Tennessee, 1980); Harvard Sitkoff, *A New Deal For Blacks: the emergence of civil rights as a national issue,* Vol. 1, *The Depression Decade* (Oxford U.P., New York, 1978).

Du Bois' major works, available in several editions, include: *Dusk of Dawn* (1940), which he described as 'not so much my autobiography as the autobiography of a concept of race', and *The Autobiography of W. E. B. Du Bois: a soliloquy on viewing my life from the last decade of its first century* (1968). His major historical and sociological writings (all of which are currently in print) include: *The Suppression of the African Slave Trade to the USA, 1638–1870* (1896); *The Philadelphia Negro* (1899); *The Souls of Black Folk* (1903); *The Negro* (1915); *Black Reconstruction in America* (1935); *Colour and Democracy* (1945).

MARCUS GARVEY

Garvey's biographers have reached very differing conclusions about their subject and the movement he led. Edmund David Cronon's *Black Moses: the story of Marcus Garvey and the Universal Negro Improvement Association* (Madison, Wisconsin, 1955), offers a mixed verdict. On the one hand, Cronon found Garvey to have been an inept leader with such serious deficiencies that they 'overbalanced the sounder aspects of his programme'. But on the other, Cronon conceded that Garvey was essentially honest, was harassed by his black and white critics, and yet managed to make a permanent contribution to the concept of black nationalism in America. Theodore G. Vincent's *Black Power and the Garvey Movement* (San Francisco, California, 1972), depicts Garvey as the inspiration of the later leaders of independent African states, and the UNIA as a heterogeneous body, some of whose members were concerned with racial equality in America. Vincent argues that Cronon displayed a 'negative attitude' towards the UNIA, since he 'could not visualise a black nationalism that was neither reactionary nor demagogic'. Vincent sees Garvey as the ideological forerunner of the black separatist theorists of the 1960s. In *Race First: the ideological and organizational struggles of Marcus Garvey and the UNIA,* (Westport, Connecticut, 1976), Tony Martin claims that Garvey was 'the greatest black figure in the twentieth century'. Martin's study ignores factionalism within the UNIA, and unconvincingly claims that Garvey was a 'revolutionary' nationalist. But the Du Bois–Garvey feud receives the fullest documentation in Martin's book.

Briefer and generally sound assessments of Garvey can be found in: Robert G. Weisbord, *Ebony Kinship: Africa, Africans, and the Afro-American* (Westport, Connecticut, 1973); Leonard E. Barrett, *Soul Force: African heritage in Afro-American religion* (New York, 1974); Alphonso Pinkney, *Red, Black, and Green: black nationalism in the United States* (Cambridge U.P., 1976); Theodore Draper, *The Rediscovery of Black Nationalism* (New York, 1969). For a succinct estimate, see K. L. Kusmer, *A Ghetto Takes Shape: black Cleveland, 1870–1930* (University of Illinois Press, 1978), pp. 228–32.

The opposition of black socialists to Garvey is covered in Theodore Kornweibel, Jr, *No Crystal Stair: black life and the Messenger, 1917–1928* (Westport, Connecticut, 1975). For a brief account of Randolph's career see William H. Harris, 'A. Philip Randolph as a charismatic leader, 1925–1941', *JNH,* XLIV (1979), 301–15. On relations between black Americans and West Indians in Harlem, see D. J. Hellwig, 'Black Meets black: Afro-American reactions to West Indian immigrants in the 1920s', *SAQ,* 77 (1978), 206–24. Two important studies of Harlem are: Gilbert Osofsky, *Harlem: the making of a ghetto, 1880–1930* (New York, 1963), and Nathan I. Huggins, *Harlem Renaissance* (New York, 1971). Also recommended is Jervis Anderson, *Harlem: the great black way, 1900–1950* (London, 1982), a vivid account by a journalist of the culture and politics of the most famous black ghetto.

Of the 'eyewitness' descriptions of Garvey in Harlem, the most graphic are Claude McKay, *Harlem: Negro metropolis* (New York, 1940, 1968); Roi Ottley, *'New World A-Coming'* (New York, 1943, 1968); James Weldon Johnson, *Black Manhattan* (New York, 1930, 1968). Richard Wright, the black novelist, describes his meeting with Garveyites in Chicago during the Depression in *American Hunger* (New York, 1944, 1977).

R. H. Brisbane, Jr, has provided a brief account and assessment of Garvey's American activities in 'Some new light on the Garvey Movement', *JNH,* 36 (1951), 53–62. Garvey's widow edited the valuable *Philosophy and Opinions of Marcus Garvey* (New York, 1969), the sayings and writings of Garvey before 1925. See also Amy Jacques-Garvey, *Garvey and Garveyism* (Kingston, Jamaica, 1963), a partisan but fascinating description of the man and the movement, and a previously unpublished Garvey letter included in C. S. Matthews' article, 'Marcus Garvey writes from Jamaica on the mulatto escape hatch', *JNH,* 59 (1974), 170–6.

A recent study which examines Garvey's wider American influence is Emory J. Tolbert, *The UNIA and Black Los Angeles: ideology and community in the Garvey Movement* (Los Angeles: UCLA's Centre for Afro-American Studies, 1980). Tolbert demonstrates that a large percentage of Garveyites in Los

Angeles were homeowners and experienced activists, but unlike New York Garveyites, they did not 'engage in the open ideological warfare' that characterized relations between the UNIA and the NAACP in Harlem.

The religious component of Garveyism is fully explored in Randall K. Burkett, *Garveyism as a Religious Movement: the institutionalization of a black religion* (London, 1978). After this book was completed, the first two volumes in *The Marcus Garvey and UNIA Papers* (ten volumes are projected) appeared. See Robert A. Hill (ed.), *The Marcus Garvey and UNIA Papers* (University of California Press, 1983).

MALCOLM X

The Autobiography of Malcolm X (New York, 1965), is available in several paperback editions; the British Penguin edition (1980) contains a useful index. Written with 'the assistance of Alex Haley' (later the author of the phenomenal best seller and TV series, *Roots*), the *Autobiography* is, on every count, a remarkable document. Haley's 'Foreword' is also essential for an understanding of the genesis of the book, and for the insights it gives into Malcolm's personality, style and development. Peter Goldman, a senior editor of *Newsweek* magazine, in *The Death and Life of Malcolm X* (London, 1975), offers a sympathetic but overblown biography. More succinct, but equally favourable assessments of Malcolm are to be found in: Thomas L. Blair, *Retreat to the Ghetto: the end of a dream?* (London, 1977), and Alphonso Pinkney, *Red, Black, and Green: black nationalism in the United States* (cited above). Archie Epps, editor of *The Speeches of Malcolm X at Harvard* (New York, 1969), includes an informative analytical and descriptive essay, 'The paradoxes of Malcolm X'. John Henrik Clarke (ed.), *Malcolm X: the man and his times* (New York, 1969), is a collection of black estimates (all of them eulogistic) of Malcolm, together with a selection of his speeches and interviews. George Breitman has also collected statements by Malcolm in *By Any Means Necessary: speeches, interviews, and a letter by Malcolm X* (New York, 1970). In *The Last Year of Malcolm X* (New York, 1970), Breitman claims that Malcolm was 'one of the most slandered and misunderstood Americans of our time', and offers 'what is missing or muted in the *Autobiography*' as a corrective to the view that it contains a full record of Malcolm's intellectual development.

The Autobiography of Malcolm X has been subjected to rigorous scholarly interpretation and exegesis. See especially: Barrett J. Mandell, 'The didactic achievement of Malcolm X's autobiography', *AAS*, 2 (1972), 269–74; Frederick D. Harper, 'A reconstruction of Malcolm X's personality', *AAS*, 3 (1972), 1–6; Cedric J. Robinson, 'Malcolm Little as a charismatic leader', *AAS*, 4 (1972), 81–96; Samuel A. Weiss, 'The ordeal of Malcolm X', *SAQ*, 67 (1968), 53–63; Carol Ohmann, 'The autobiography of Malcolm X: a revolutionary use of the Franklin tradition', *AQ*, 22 (1970), 131–49.

On the origins and growth of the Nation of Islam, see: C. Eric Lincoln, *The Black Muslims in America* (revised ed, Boston, 1973), and his article 'The Black Muslims revisited or the state of the black Nation of Islam', *AAS*, 3 (1972), 175–86; E. U. Essien-Udom, *Black Nationalism: the rise of the Black Muslims in the USA* (Penguin Books, Harmondsworth, 1966); Louis E. Lomax, *When the Word is Given: a report on Elijah Muhammad, and the Black Muslim world* (New York, 1964).

A critical assessment of Malcolm X is provided by Tom Kahn and Bayard Rustin, 'The ambiguous legacy of Malcolm X', *Dissent,* 12 (1965), 188–92. For more favourable verdicts see: Le Roi Jones, 'The legacy of Malcolm X and the coming of the black nation', in his collected pieces *Home: social essays* (New York, 1966), and the white journalist, I. F. Stone's thoughtful essay, 'The pilgrimage of Malcolm X', in his collected reviews *In a Time of Torment* (New York, 1967), pp. 110–21.

Wilson J. Moses in *Black Messiahs and Uncle Toms* (cited above), suggests that Malcolm X might 'expediently be characterised as a sort of "apostle to the gentiles"', because he expended an appreciable amount of energy during his last years addressing predominantly white audiences'.

In *One Day When I Was Lost* (London, 1974), James Baldwin created an intriguing 'scenario based on *The Autobiography of Malcolm X'*, dictated in part by 'the legal complexities created by Malcolm's rupture with the Nation of Islam Movement'. It is a sensitive evocation of the 'much-maligned, groping and very moving character of a man known as Malcolm X'. See also Eldridge Cleaver's tribute, 'Initial reactions on the assassination of Malcolm X', in *Soul on Ice* (London, 1969).

On President Kennedy and civil rights, see John Hart's article, 'Kennedy, Congress and civil rights', *JAS,* 13 (1979), 165–78.

MARTIN LUTHER KING, JR

There is no satisfactory full-length biography of King. David L. Lewis, *King: a critical biography* (London, 1970), contains some valuable insights into King's personality, and charts the major stages of his career. It is, however, marked by a sloppy prose style and a patronizing tone. Stephen B. Oates, *Let the Trumpet Sound: the life of Martin Luther King, Jr,* (London, 1982), covers much the same ground, but is also poorly written and avoids any serious or sustained assessment of King's stature as a black leader. On King's surveillance by the FBI, see David J. Garrow's excellent *The FBI and Martin Luther King, Jr: from 'Solo' to Memphis* (London, 1981). Garrow argues convincingly that King was a real rather than an imagined threat to the established order in America, in that he had become, by the last years of his life, a revolutionary figure. For King's relationship with SNCC and black militants, see Clayborne Carson, *In Struggle: SNCC and the Black Awakening of the 1960s* (cited above). Adam Fairclough provides a detailed picture of King and the Southern Christian Leadership Conference in his article 'The SCLC and the Second Reconstruction, 1957–1973', *SAQ,* 80 (1981), 177–94. Fairclough treats King's growing radicalism in 'Was Martin Luther King a Marxist?', *History Workshop Journal,* 15 (Spring 1983), 117–25.

King's intellectual and spiritual development receives considered attention in Hanes Walton, Jr, *The Political Philosophy of Martin Luther King, Jr* (Westport, Connecticut, 1971), and in three important articles: John W. Rathbun, 'Martin

Luther King: The theology of social action', *AQ,* 20 (1968), 38–53; Warren E. Steinkraus, 'Martin Luther King's personalism and non-violence', *JHI,* 34 (1973), 97–111; and Mohan Lal Sharma, 'Martin Luther King: modern America's greatest theologian of social action', *JNH,* 53 (1968), 257–63.

For more critical assessments of King's leadership, see especially: Frank Hercules, *American Society and Black Revolution,* cited above, and August Meier's influential essay of 1965, 'On the role of Martin Luther King', which is reprinted in John Bracey, August Meier and Elliott Rudwick's collection *Conflict and Competition: studies in the recent black protest movement* (Belmont, California, 1971). For a contemporary black radical evaluation, see Eldridge Cleaver, 'The death of Martin Luther King: requiem for non-violence', in Cleaver, *Post-Prison Writings and Speeches* (New York, 1969).

C. Eric Lincoln has edited an excellent collection of essays, *Martin Luther King Jr: a profile* (New York, 1970), with contributions from James Baldwin, Ralph Abernathy and August Meier's essay, retitled 'The conservative militant'. Lerone Bennett, Jr, has written a brief but balanced biography, *What Manner of Man: a biography of Martin Luther King, Jr* (New York, 1964, 1968). For a loving account of King's life and work see Coretta Scott King, *My Life With Martin Luther King, Jr* (New York, 1970).

On the Memphis strike, see David M. Tucker, 'Rev. James M. Lawson, Jr, and the garbage strike', in his study *Black Pastors and Leaders: Memphis, 1819–1972* (Memphis State U.P., 1975).

King's major books were: *Stride Toward Freedom: the Montgomery Story* (London, 1959); *Why We Can't Wait* (New York, 1964); *Where Do We Go From Here: Chaos or Community?* (London, 1967); *The Triumph of Conscience* (New York, 1968).

For an analysis of the Montgomery bus boycott within the context of earlier black protests against segregated transportation, see Catherine A. Barnes' excellent study, *Journey From Jim Crow: the desegregation of Southern transit* (New York, 1983).

Lyndon Johnson's sympathetic attitudes towards blacks and civil rights are discussed in Monroe Billington, 'Lyndon B. Johnson and blacks: the early years', *JNH,* 61 (1977), 26–42, and in Eric F. Goldman's biography, *The Tragedy of Lyndon Johnson* (Macdonald, London, 1969).

For a persuasive statement of the thesis that 'many important features of black and white relations in America are not captured when the issue is defined as majority versus minority and that a preoccupation with race and racial conflict obscures fundamental problems that derive from the intersection of race and class', see William Julius Wilson, *The Declining Significance of Race: blacks and changing American institutions* (2nd edn, University of Chicago Press, 1980).

INDEX

Adams, Lewis, 30
Addams, Jane, 47
African Methodist Episcopal Church, 15, 25
Afro-American Realty Company, 69
Afro-American Steamship Company, 25
Alabama Christian Movement for Human
    Rights, 135, 136
Alabama State Teachers Association, 31
Albany, Georgia, 134-5
Ali, Duse Mohammed, 73
Ali, Noble Drew, 99
Allen, Richard, 15
Amendments to the Constitution, 19, 23, 26
Amenia Conference, 54
American Colonization Society, 16, 85
American Communist Party, 65, 99, 133
American Negro Academy, 51
American Revolution, 10, 13, 14
Amsterdam News, 130
Anderson, Charles W., 69
Armstrong, Samuel Chapman, 28-30
Atlanta University, 51, 58
Autobiography of Malcolm X, 114-18, 146

Bagnall, Robert W., 88
Baker, Ella, 131, 132
Baker, Ray Stannard, 47
Baldwin, James, 1, 146
Barnett, Ida Wells, 47
Barnett, Ross, 140
Berlin, Ira, 10
Bilbo, Theodore G., 79, 100
Birmingham, Alabama, 135-7
Birth of a Nation, 36
Black Codes, 24
Black Panther party, 102
Black Power, 101-2, 140-1, 145
Black Reconstruction in America, 62
Black Star Steamship Line, 77-9

*Booker T. Washington and the Negro's Place
    in American Life*, 65
Boston Guardian, 39
Boutwell, Albert, 135
Brazier, Arthur, 139
Broderick, F.L., 62
Brooke, Edward, 150
Brotherhood of Sleeping Car Porters, 123
Brown, John, 19
Brown v. Board of Education, 125
Brownsville, Texas, 36
Burroughs, James, 27

Carmichael, Stokely, 101, 140, 143
Carnegie, Andrew, 1, 32, 39, 41
Carter, Jimmy, 151
Carver, George Washington, 31
Chaney, James, 124
Charles, Ray, 121
Chicago, 139-40
Chisholm, Shirley, 149
Christian Examiner, 38
Civil Rights Act
    of 1875, 19
    of 1964, 101, 137
Clark, Edward Young, 79
Clark, Kenneth, 108
Clay, William, 149-50
Cleaver, Eldridge, 102, 143
Coleman, Milton, 151
Colour and Democracy, 66
Committee of Twelve for the Advancement
    of the Negro Race, 41
Compromise of 1877, 19
Congress of Industrial Organizations
    (CIO), 122
Congress of Racial Equality
    (CORE), 101-2, 124
Congressional Reconstruction, 24

Connor, Eugene, 135-6
Coolidge, Calvin, 80
Cornish, Samuel, 15
Crisis, 5, 41, 52-61, 93
Cronon, E. David, 162
Crummell, Alexander, 17

Daley, Richard J., 139-40
Davidson, Olivia, 30
Davis, Ossie, 164
De Valera, Eamon, 78
Delany, Martin R., 17
Democratic party, 24, 30, 122, 133, 149, 152
Dennis, Willie, 8
Dewey, Thomas, 125
Diwaker, Ranganath, 128
Dixon, Thomas, Jr., 158
Dollard, John, 155
Douglass, Frederick, 1, 3-4, 18-21
Du Bois, W.E.B., 1, 5, 23, 33, 48-46, 159-60, 166
    and Garvey, 89-95
    and Pan-Africanism, 59-61
    and Washington, 6, 37, 40-2, 45, 63-5
    and World War I, 55-6
Dusk of Dawn, 62-3

Eastman, George, 32
Eisenhower, Dwight D., 125, 133
Ellison, Ralph, 156
Emancipation Proclamation (1863), 11, 17
Encyclopedia Africana, 65
Executive Order
    8802 (1941), 123
    9981 (1948), 124
'Exodusters', 68

Fard, W.D., 100, 104-5
Farmer, James, 119, 124
Farrakhan, Louis, 151
Father Divine, 100
Faubus, Orville, 125
Fellowship of Reconciliation (FOR), 124-5, 129
Fisk University, 50
Fortune, T.Thomas, 45, 69, 85
Foster, Wilbur F., 30
Frazier, E.Franklin, 81, 83-5
Free People of Colour, 13-14
Freedmen's Bureau, 17, 28
Freedmen's conventions, 25-6
Freedom's Journal, 15

Gandhi, Mahatma, 123-4, 127, 129
Garnet, Henry Highland, 3, 16-17
Garrison, William Lloyd, 3, 15, 19

Garvey, Amy Jacques, 68, 77
Garvey, Marcus, 2, 6, 72-95, 161-2
    and Africa, 82-3
    and Du Bois, 89-95
    and Malcolm X, 103, 111-12
    and Washington, 74-5
Ghana, 62, 65, 132
Goldwater, Barry, 109
Goodman, Andrew, 124
Gordon, Mittie, 100
Grant, Ulysses S., 19, 26
Great Depression, 56, 62
Great Migration, 68-9
Grimke, Francis, 58

Haiti, 19
Haley, Alex, 14
Hampton, Lionel, 103
Hampton Normal and Agricultural
    Institute, 27-9
Harding, Warren G., 79
Harlem, 69-70
Harlem Renaissance, 72, 81
Hayes, Rutherford B., 24
Hercules, Frank, 121, 157, 159
Hodges, Johnny, 104
Hoover, J.Edgar, 133
Hope, John, 39
Hughes, Langston, 158

'I Have a Dream', 137-8
International League of Darker Peoples, 87
International Migration Society (IMS), 25
Invisible Man, 156-7
Isaacs, Harold R., 44, 68

Jackson, Jesse, 8, 149, 151-2
James, C.L.R., 76
James, William, 50
Johnson, Andrew, 24, 48
Johnson, Charles S., 86-7
Johnson, James Weldon, 34, 40, 58, 69, 85
Johnson, Lyndon Baines, 101, 137, 138, 141, 142
Jordan, Vernon, 8

Kennedy, John F., 110, 133-5, 137
Kennedy, Robert, 133
Kenyatta, Jomo, 61, 76
King, Coretta Scott, 119, 128, 141, 152
King, Martin Luther, Jr., 2, 6-7, 65, 81, 126-46, 165-6
    and Du Bois, 144-5
    and Garvey, 145
    and Malcolm X, 146
    and Washington, 143-4
Ku-Klux-Klan, 24, 79, 88

Lawson, James, 142
League of Nations, 60
'Letter From a Birmingham Jail', 136
Levison, Stanley, 133
Lewis, John L., 122
Liberia, 25, 80
Lincoln, Abraham, 19, 46
Lincoln, C.Eric, 98
Little Rock, Arkansas, 125, 133
Lomax, Louis, 109
London Anti-Slavery Society, 37

Mackie, Mary F., 29
Malcolm X, 2, 7, 103-18, 163-4
     and Garvey, 103, 111-2
     and King, 108-9, 136
March on Washington (1963), 7, 137-8
March on Washington Movement
     (MOWM), 6, 99, 123
Marshall, James, 30
Massachusetts Anti-Slavery Society, 18
Mays, Benjamin E., 81, 127
McGuire, George Alexander, 81
McKay, Claude, 72, 85-6
McKissick, Floyd, 101, 140, 143
Mecca, 117
Meier, August, 165
Memphis Commercial Appeal, 142
Memphis, Tennessee, 142-3
Meredith, James, 140
Milholland, John E., 37
Miller, Kelly, 21
Montgomery, Alabama bus boycott, 6,
     66, 126-30
Montgomery Improvement Association
     (MIA), 126-8
Morgan, Juliette, 129
Moskowitz, Henry, 47
Moton, Robert R., 75
Muhammad, Elijah, 105-7, 163
Muhammad, Wallace D., 150
Murray, Anna, 18
Muslim Mosque,Inc., 110-11
Myrdal, Gunnar, 1-3, 4-5, 44, 153, 157

*Narrative of the Life of Frederick
     Douglass*, 18
Nation of Islam, 7, 104-7, 150-1
     and Washington, 106
National Afro-American League, 45, 47
National Association for the Advancement
     of Coloured People (NAACP), 1,
     37, 40, 46-8, 98-9, 154-5
National Negro Business League, 35, 58, 69
National Negro Committee, 47
National Urban League, 70-1, 84, 86-7

Negro Convention Movement, 15-17, 18
Negro Factories Corporation, 77
Negro World, 76-7, 85
New Deal, 57, 62, 122-3
New York *Post*, 47
Newton, Huey P., 102
Niagara Movement, 40, 45-6, 60
Niebuhr, Reinhold, 127-8
Nixon, E.D., 126
Nixon, Richard M., 133, 143
Nkrumah, Kwame, 60, 65
North Star, 18

Operation Breadbasket, 151-2
Opportunity, 78, 84, 86
Organization of Afro-American Unity
     (OAAU), 112
Ottley, Roi, 78
Ovington, Mary White, 47, 92
Owen, Chandler, 87-9

Pace, Harry H., 88
Pan-African Congresses, 59-60
Parks, Rosa L., 126
Penn Warren, Robert, 119
Peyton, Philip A., 69
Pickens, William, 79, 88
Pitts, Helen, 19
Plessy v. Ferguson, 36, 125
Pole, J.R., 158
Poor People's March on Washington, 141-2
Populism, 26
Powell, Adam Clayton, Snr., 85-6
Pritchett, Laurie, 133
Prosser, Gabriel, 12

Randall, Dudley, 153
Randolph, A.Philip, 6, 55, 87-9, 123, 130
Rauschenbusch, Walter, 127
Redeemer governments, 24, 68
Reeb, James J., 138
Republican party, 26, 30, 36, 122
Róbeson, Paul, 45
Rockefeller, John D., 32
Rogers, Henry C., 32
Roosevelt, Franklin D., 56-7, 122-3
Roosevelt, Theodore, 1, 35-6
Rosengarten, Theodore, 23
Royce, Josiah, 50
Ruffner, Viola, 28
Russwurm, John, 15
Rustin, Bayard, 118, 129, 139, 164

Santayana, George, 50
Saudi Arabia, 117
Schwerner, Michael, 124

Scott, Emmett J., 35
Seale, Bobby, 103
Selma, Alabama, 138-9
Share-cropping, 24
Shuttlesworth, Fred, 135
Slavery in the United States, 11-13
Souls of Black Folk, 40, 49, 51-2, 153
Southern Christian Leadership Conference
    (SCLC), 8, 131-2, 134-40
Spencer, Samuel R., 65
Spingarn, Joel, 54
Spock, Benjamin, 141
Steffens, Lincoln, 47
Stockholm Peace Appeal, 64
Stokes, Carl, 149
Storey, Moorfield, 48
Stowe, Harriet Beecher, 19
Student Non-Violent Coordinating
    Committee (SNCC), 101-2, 132,
    138, 140
Styron, William, 13
Supreme Court, 26, 36, 48, 71, 129

Taft, William Howard, 35-6
Talented Tenth, 49, 51, 57, 62
Taylor, Julius F., 39
Thoreau, Henry David, 127
Thurmond, Strom, 124
Tilden, Samuel J., 24
Tocqueville, Alexis de, 14
Travis, Joseph, 12
Trotter, William Monroe, 39-40, 48
Truman, Harry S., 101, 124-5
Turner, Henry McNeal, 25, 28, 36
Turner, Nat, 12-13
Tuskegee Institute, 29-32
'Tuskegee Machine', 32, 48, 63, 65

Uncle Tom's Cabin, 85
United Nations, 64
Universal Negro Improvement Association
    in America, 75-83
    in Jamaica, 73-5
Up From Slavery, 34-5, 73

Vesey, Denmark, 12
Vietnam war, 139, 141
Villard, Oswald Garrison, 47, 63, 92
Vincent, Theodore, 162

Waco, Texas, 53-4
Walker, David, 3, 10, 16
Wallace, George, 137
Walling, William E., 47
Walters, Alexander, 47
Ward, Samuel Ringgold, 17
Washington, Booker T., 1, 5, 27-42, 69, 81,
    156-8
    Atlanta Compromise address, 32-4
    and Douglass, 20-1
    and Du Bois, 40-2, 63-5
    and Garvey, 74-5
    and King, 143-4

Washington, Jesse, 53
Watson, Tom, 26
Wells, H.G., 37
West Indians, 71, 161
White, Walter, 58
Wilberforce University, 51
Wilkins, Roy, 7, 118, 130
Wilson, Woodrow, 36, 55
Wise, Stephen S., 47
Woodson, Carter G., 81
Wright, Richard, 83

Young, Andrew, 151-2
Young, Whitney M., 118